The Last Testament of Bill Bonanno

ALSO BY BILL BONANNO

Bound by Honor: A Mafioso's Story

The Last Testament of Bill Bonanno

The Final Secrets of a Life in the Mafia

Bill Bonanno with

Gary B. Abromovitz

HARPER

NEW YORK ● LONDON ● TORONTO ● SYDNEY

HARPER

THE LAST TESTAMENT OF BILL BONANNO. Copyright © 2011 by
One-Hour Books, L.L.C. All rights reserved. Printed in the United
States of America. No part of this book may be used or reproduced
in any manner whatsoever without written permission except in the
case of brief quotations embodied in critical articles and reviews. For
information address HarperCollins Publishers, 10 East 53rd Street,
New York, NY 10022.

HarperCollins books may be purchased for educational, business, or
sales promotional use. For information please write: Special Markets
Department, HarperCollins Publishers, 10 East 53rd Street, New
York, NY 10022.

Designed by Michael P. Correy
Maps by Tamara Eve Jerardo

Library of Congress Cataloging-in-Publication Data is available
upon request.

ISBN 978-0-06-199202-5

11 12 13 14 15   OV/RRD   10 9 8 7 6 5 4 3 2 1

*This book is dedicated to Bill Bonanno,
who could have been anything he wanted to be in life,
if he had been free to choose a different path.*

Qui aliquid statuerit,
parte inaudita allera, aequum licet dixerit,
haud aequum facerit.

He who determines any matter, without hearing both sides,
though he may decide correctly,
has not done justice.

Contents

Contents

Prologue

My name is Salvatore "Bill" Bonanno. My father, Joseph Bonanno Sr., was *rappresentante* of the Bonanno Family of New York during some of the most turbulent and exciting years in the history of "our world," from the 1930s through the early 1960s. I became a made member of the Family in 1954, a *capodecina* (group captain) in 1959, and *consigliere* in 1964. My wife, Rosalie, is the niece of Joseph Profaci, the leader of the Profaci Family—like the Bonanno Family, one of the original five New York Mafia Families whose leaders formed what became known as "The Commission" in 1931. My firsthand involvement in the life of Mafia Families affords me the unique position of being able to share with you the secrets within this volume. What I am about to share with you has never been told by anyone who actually attended the Commission meetings. It is a story that I authorized to be published only after my death.

The material presented here is organized into three Books, each covering a part of the epic story of the Mafia from its secret sects in Sicily to its establishment of a powerful organized crime base in the United States through the 1960s. Much of what is included here has never been revealed before. It was shared with me by my father, Joseph Bonanno Sr., or by others familiar with the history and practices of our world. We have included a glossary translating Italian, Sicilian, and Yiddish words and other words not commonly used; it can be found on p. 327 for easy reference.

Book I, "The Birth of the Mafia," offers a survey of the historical background of the Mafia—a survey that is necessary for anyone who wishes to understand the nature of our world. It explains how and why the Mafia evolved, the beliefs and orientations of the Sicilian people who founded it, and why we did certain things the way we did.

Book II, "The Commission," offers an accurate, and formerly untold, story of the highly confidential, and highly misunderstood, body of selected men in our world who were responsible for decisions at the highest level to ensure peace among the Families—a group that lasted from its inception in 1931 into the 1960s. The Commission has been portrayed in all manner of novels, works of dubious "nonfiction," equally dubious "documentaries," and fictionalized feature films—and the result has been to leave the American public with the belief that the Commission was the supreme bureaucracy that controlled organized crime, an organization patterned after the hierarchical structure of most modern-day corporations. The sources of these stories are inevitably outsiders; no one who ever actually attended a meeting of the Commission would have described the group in any such terms. Yet this perception persists—a tribute to the power of the imagination of the novelists, screenwriters, and others who have promulgated it.

In this second Book, I will take you into each of the formal Commission meetings attended by my father, beginning in 1931, including the meetings after 1954 that I attended myself.

You will learn where these meetings were held, who attended, what security was required, how business was conducted, and what issues were discussed—from the decision to eliminate Benjamin "Bugsy" Siegel, to the near assassination of special prosecutor and New York governor Thomas E. Dewey, to aiding the United States and its Allies in the invasion of Sicily during World War II.

Book III, "The Family," offers a more intimate history of the Mafia as I knew it in my time, drawing on personal anecdotes and true experiences that I witnessed, or that were recounted to me by those in the highest positions of power in our world. I will give you insight into specific topics of this elusive and mysterious world. I will dispel myths and reveal a lifestyle, based on centuries of tradition, that faded during the 1960s and has never been the same since.

My father's book *A Man of Honor*, published in 1983, and my book *Bound by Honor*, published in 1999, described some of the events told here. But many important details were purposely left out of our accounts in those books, or were described ambiguously. This was because, in both instances, there were men in our world still alive who might be a danger to our Family or to others, if the full story were told. This book is intended to fill in the blanks, eliminate those ambiguities, and relate incidents that occurred but have long been untold, because I want history to record the truth. There are many well-written books about what most people think of as "organized crime." But most of them sensationalize our world, making the text more like a circus sideshow designed to appeal to prurient interests looking for violence without purpose. Even the more purely historical books and articles about our world were largely penned by authors who were outsiders. Such books tend to rely on secondary research—which means that they simply repurpose stories and incorrect "facts" found in other accounts. Every new entry in this category only supports the theory that, if you tell enough untruths over and over again, people will believe you.

I should also add that books written or cowritten after 1968 by Americanized leaders or enforcers in our world have little or nothing to do with the world I lived in prior to that time—as you'll understand after reading this book.

And one final word of clarification: I have no desire to sugarcoat the Bonanno Family. I make no claims that my father, Joe Bonanno, was an innocent, noncombative, even-tempered man. He wasn't. He did consider himself a fair man in running his Family, and those of us who observed his behavior tended to agree. However, if you crossed him, it was *Goodbye, Jack*.

That's the way it was.

Bill Bonanno

Introduction

You must be willing to put your whole life at our disposal.

John Tartamella (1892–1966),
consigliere of the Bonanno Family

People have asked me how I can defend the lifestyle of "this thing of ours." I've been confronted, though gingerly, by news reporters asking questions such as, "How do you justify that most of your life you made your living from criminal activities?" It's funny, but when I look in the mirror every morning while shaving, I don't see the bad person I'm supposed to be. I see someone who lived in a world where ethics and loyalty meant something.

I do not intend to defend or justify the actions of the Bonanno Family during the 1930s through the 1960s. But I will explain the lifestyle so you can try to understand why I have no regrets about the way I lived and would not change most of what occurred—if the circumstances were the same today as they were back then.

To begin, let's address a question that is beyond logical comprehension in your world: How was I able to put the interests of a group of men ahead of the interests of my wife and my children? The answer isn't easy—because I did and

I didn't. The idea that a member of our world, if summoned, would leave the bedside of a dying relative instantly if called to do so by his Family, defies natural instinct—unless you live in our world.

This bond of brotherhood has been with me my entire life. As a result, the rules of conduct I lived by superseded the rules, or laws, that society placed upon me. The strengths of this pact, among men whose beliefs and actions were woven from the same cloth, protected this small world of ours. This is the world we knew and had to survive within on a daily basis. The laws that society imposed upon those of us who chose to live in America were secondary to our way of thinking. Our people lived in a much smaller world, where we spoke a more familiar language and lived according to centuries-old traditions that our people brought to this country.

The Family came first. It had to, in order to ensure its survival.

You may look upon some of the things I have done as unacceptable—even if many of you may have done similar things yourselves. Our definitions of *faithfulness* and *fidelity* may have very different meanings than yours.

In our world, faithfulness and fidelity are two different things. Throughout my life, I was always faithful to my wife and family. Straying from this obligation would have meant disavowing the tradition that was the foundation upon which the concept of the Family was built—a tradition that valued security to ensure survival. No matter what I may have done in other areas of my life—be it lack of fidelity or something else—my wife and children always knew they would be secure as long as I was alive. This faithfulness is the same bond that brought the "band of men" in Sicily together to form a secret society.

When these men arrived in America, more than one hundred years ago, the laws of American society were confusing to them. When they first arrived, they came into a world where they could traffic in liquor legally. Then came Prohibition, which changed the rules by imposing criminal liability for doing what they used to do under protection of the law. Then, after Prohibition was repealed, they were once again allowed to do what they had since grown accustomed to doing under the radar, on their own terms.

Prohibition provided a means of making a lot of money for many, including such esteemed citizens as Joseph P. Kennedy Sr., the U.S. ambassador to the United Kingdom from 1937 to 1940 and father of a future president. We were opportunists, along with Kennedy and many others seeking prosperity in those turbulent times. The liquor trade was what we knew, and during Prohibition the income it created gave us a basis to expand into other areas. Some of these areas would be criminal activities at the time, but were later sanctioned as legal for others to pursue. For example, the numbers rackets would develop into the government lotteries, which today provide huge revenue sources for many states. Gambling and off-track betting would eventually expand outside Nevada to New Jersey and Indian casinos all over the country. Even narcotics trafficking would be used on a large scale by government officials, to finance coups or wars in other countries. It was a triumph of double standards. Doesn't it seem that in many respects the government took over our rackets and put us out of business?

When you choose a job in an automobile factory as your life's work and the factory closes, chances are that you can switch to another industry, even if it requires moving to another state. This is not so easy if your monetary survival depends on activities that society has deemed illegal—at least for the moment— and your skills are "street skills." The breakdown in our world began when we found ourselves too slow to change, to adapt to the shifting landscapes of twentieth-century America. By the

1950s, the concept of banding together to protect the Family had started to weaken; it was this erosion that, in many cases, destroyed the so-called Mafia Families.

In some ways, I suppose, our way of life was bound to disappear—because after a while its original reason for being no longer existed. In our first several decades on these shores, Sicilian and Italian immigrants had gradually assimilated into American society, eliminating the need for protection from aggressors that our Sicilian fathers had experienced.

I lived my entire life in two worlds: our world and yours. My instincts, and the concepts of ethics and morality of our world, were so ingrained from childhood that I could never quite cross the bridge into your world. But I did make it a good part of the way. There is a basic rule of nature: *Adapt or perish.* That rule is somewhat less absolute when you account for the important element of time. As a *mafioso,* but one who was born in America, I adapted the best I could, balancing the principles of both worlds, while adding another element: *accommodation.*

It has been said that a man is never really a man as long as his father is alive. In 2002, when my father passed away at the age of ninety-seven, I was also relieved of a pressure I had lived under all my life: the burden of trying to please him and gain his respect. Powerful men in our world often instill a strong sense of obligation in their children, making it difficult for us to live up to the standards they expect. But the obligations, loyalty, and fearlessness he taught me, and the oath I subscribed to—that all *mafiosi* must act in a manly way—did not pass with him. It is in that tradition that this book is written, and you will see how and why it all started as you read the history of our world presented in Book I, "The Birth of the Mafia."

Book I

The Birth of the Mafia:
A Historical Perspective

We declare our own destiny. Destiny speaks to us through the choices we make, so either choose to be a victim and remain stuck in the past or . . . live for now. Don't let the past dictate who you are, but let the past be part of who you are.

Joe Bonanno

1

Sicily: A History of Oppression

Society, when ruled by a regime bent on oppressing the people for the benefit of those in power, is ripe for revolution. Oppression spawns revenge, the need for protection, and a group of men willing to fight.

Joe Bonanno, quoting Giuseppe Garibaldi,
leader of the unification of Italy

In Italian, the word *paisano*, or *paesano*, means countryman. Our story begins in the home of my *paesani*: Sicily, the largest island in the Mediterranean Sea.

The island's political history left its mark on Sicily's language and customs as surely as it has on its familiar cuisine. This choice piece of real estate, lying in the middle of the Mediterranean, has lured every kind of invader to its shores since the mythical Cyclops. With each invasion, another layer of hatred and mistrust of outsiders was etched into the consciousness of its people. The centuries of political turmoil and foreign rule created a free-floating Sicilian distrust of governments and had the unintended effect of strengthening the bonds within Sicilian families, binding them together for protection against aggressors.

This explains why, historically, Sicilians have been ungovernable: because they long ago learned to distrust and neutralize written laws and govern themselves instead through their own natural laws. Sicily is confusing and exasperating to anyone but a Sicilian. The Greeks, Romans, Arabs, French, Normans, Spanish, even the United States Army have all tried to understand and govern Sicilians—to cater to their needs and solve their fundamental problems. Yet each of these powers has failed.

It is an art to be Sicilian. It is the art of building up power to overcome competitors, rivals, or enemies by defending your honor and maintaining your welfare, and that of your friends at all times. If this concept sounds familiar to you, perhaps that's because the same principles are used to govern countries, institutions, and other organizations of "respectable" people.

Most Sicilians are bilingual, speaking both Italian and the Sicilian language, known as *Sicilianu*. *Sicilianu* is no mere derivative of Italian, but a distinct Romance language with Greek, Latin, Arabic, Catalan, and Spanish influences. Dialects of the language are also spoken in the southern and central regions of Calabria and Puglia.

Sicilian is no longer the first language of present-day Sicilians, especially among the young. With the advent of television and the predominance of Italian in the schools, Sicilian has become a second language. In its time, however, it had an important influence on the Maltese language of the island of Malta, which was originally a part of the Kingdom of Sicily until a residence on the island was granted to the Knights of Malta by the Holy Roman Emperor Charles V (as King of Sicily) and sanctioned by Pope Clement VII.

The Sovereign Military Order of Saint John of Jerusalem of Rhodes and of Malta, known as the Sovereign Military Order of Malta, or the Knights of Malta for short, traces its beginnings to about 1040 A.D. It is a humanitarian order that dates back to the Crusades. The Knights were originally recruited to protect commerce from robbers who preyed on merchants doing business between the Italian city of Amalfi and the Holy Land. In 1565, the Knights of Malta heroically defended Malta against Turkish attacks. Without their steadfast

Joe Bonanno being inducted into the Order of the Knights of Malta of Saint John of Jerusalem on January 21, 2000. From left to right: me, Dr. Jim Laws, Supreme Commander of the Knights of Malta of Saint John of Jerusalem, my father (seated), and a priest.

courage and bravery, all of Europe would have been engulfed in the Turkish Empire. Today, the Order exchanges ambassadors with sixty governments. It has more than a thousand Knights in thirty-nine national associations throughout the world, continuing to espouse charity, reverence for God, and high principles of life. On January 21, 2000, during the week celebrating my father's ninety-fifth birthday, he and I had the honor of being inducted into the Order.

Secret Sects

The story of the *mafiosi* is really about people—about the people of Sicily, about the threats they faced, what they did to counter them, and why. To understand this story, one must study their motives, their conduct, and the effect of that conduct on people both within and outside our world.

For centuries, the island of Sicily faced almost constant threat from foreign peoples looking to overrun and rule their country. To counter this threat, Sicilian men gathered to form nonorganized, secret alliances—the groups that would eventually evolve into what is commonly known today as the Mafia.

Among these first *mafiosi* was a group of men who banded together in 1185 to form a secret society called the Vendicatori ("the Avengers"), formed to avenge popular wrongs and abuses of power in Sicily.

About a hundred years later, in 1282, when the people of Palermo rebelled against French rule one evening just after the beginning of Vespers, a secret society known as the Vespri Siciliani (Sicilian Vespers) emerged—a group whose existence, some believe, would give birth to the very word *Mafia*.

I should point out that, in our world, the word *Mafia* was never used. We understood the concept of *mafiosi* to refer to men with a shared ideology and lifestyle based on tradition, not a criminal organization. In twentieth-century America, novelists, crime writers, filmmakers, and U.S. law enforcement officials found it useful to promote the idea that the group they called the Mafia was a dedicated, active criminal organization. In truth, the Sicilian *mafiosi* were men who shared a philosophy of life that we call *cosa nostra* ("our thing") bound by certain core beliefs: that we must aid one another, be true to our friends against all enemies, defend our dignity and that of our friends against all threats, and never let trespasses go unavenged.

This perspective has its roots in a series of stories that can be traced back to ancient Sicily.

In 1282, while the island was under French rule, legend has it that a French soldier attacked and raped a young Sicilian girl walking with her mother on their way to Easter

Sunday Vespers. The mother, unable to defend her daughter, ran through the streets of Palermo screaming *Ma fia! Ma fia!* ("My daughter! My daughter!") until she reached the nearest *chiazza* (piazza), where some young men of Palermo had gathered, including her daughter's fiancée. The men rushed to the young girl's aid. The fiancée pulled out his dagger, stuck it in the heart of the soldier, and then slit the soldier's throat from ear to ear. The people of Palermo, fighting mad, rebelled; they slaughtered every Frenchman in the city they could find, including civilians, and expelled the French from the island. As the legend goes, the Sicilians identified Frenchmen by their inability to pronounce the Sicilian word *ceci* (chickpeas). This uprising became known as the Sicilian Vespers, and was later celebrated in an opera by Giuseppe Verdi, first performed under the French title *Les Vêpres Siciliennes* in Paris in 1855 and the following year under the Italian title *Giovanna di Guzman* at La Scala opera house in Milan, attaining its final name, *I Vespri Siciliani*, in 1861.

Another tradition maintains that the motto of the Sicilian Vespers insurrection was *Morte Alla Francia, Italia Anela,* or "Death to France, Italy Cries!" when the French were thrown out of Sicily, thus liberating the island from occupation of the French soldiers bent on raping Sicilian women and their daughters. According to this legend, the first letter of each word in that phrase later gave rise to the acronym M.A.F.I.A. Either way, it's ironic that the government and the American public have come to see the word *Mafia* as synonymous with a despicable criminal organization—when its origins, in the story of the Sicilian Vespers, have a historically honorable meaning.

Yet a third story insists that the name was derived from a common word used in the Borgo section of Palermo by street peddlers advertising their brooms for sale. *Scupi da mafia!* the vendors would cry out. *Haju chiddi mafiusi veruu!* ("Brooms that can't be beat! I have the real stuff!") The phrase came to connote beauty, charm, or excellence, and also to evoke a sense of superiority, bravery, or the feeling of boldness associated with being a man—though never with arrogance or braggadocio.

The first organized group of men known as Mafia is believed to have been the Beati Paoli (Blessed Pauls), a secret confraternity whose lair was hidden under the Piazza Beati Paoli in the capital city of Palermo. It is located in a dingy square within a few minutes' stroll of the Biblioteca Regionale and the magnificent opera house Teatro Massimo (the location of the famous opera scene in the movie *The Godfather, Part III*), bookended by the Baroque church of Santa Maria di Gesù and a four-hundred-year-old convent. The site still exists today, although a visit there may not be what it seems: On arrival, one expects to be enlightened, but in keeping with secretive Sicily, all one finds there is more antiquity. Beneath the stones, most Sicilians believe, lies a citadel—the hidden stronghold of Sicily's avenging monks. The piazza's real focal point is not what one sees, but what one does not see.

The Beati Paoli, a lay fraternity, is believed to have been composed of men of all walks of life belonging to the congregation of San Francisco di Paola. There has been some speculation that the Beati Paoli were dedicated to protesting the excesses of the inquisition in Sicily as early as the 1600s, but Sicilian folklore dates its impact on Sicilian society and culture only back to around 1861, the time of the unification of Italy. They opposed blatant abuse of authority and saw themselves as agents of both political and social justice. They were the alternative to what they considered the lack of justice and fairness and the corruption in Sicilian society—and took it as their mission to correct the wrongs brought about by oppressive rulers.

The Beati Paoli avenged women who were wronged, and chastised and punished corrupt officials. According to legend, the group would meet in the labyrinth of rooms beneath the

Piazza Beati Paoli, hear the evidence of wrongdoing, and render their verdicts. Then, at the stroke of midnight, they would venture forth, dressed as monks in black-hooded Franciscan cloaks, to administer their sentences.

Although direct links between the Beati Paoli and what's known today as the Mafia have been suggested in books, stage plays, and sociological studies, too little is known to establish a definite historical connection. But there are interesting parallels between the two.

Later, when our way of life emerged in Palermo, it was focused on a secret society we called La Mano Fraterna (the Brotherly Hand). This group adopted elaborate secrecy requirements and embraced mysterious rites inherited from the Beati Paoli.

A prospective member of the Brotherly Hand would have to pass through a "novitiate" period of instruction before being qualified for "baptism." When the right to baptism was achieved, the candidate was taken to a secret meeting place, seated in a room surrounded by the other members of the group, and asked to take the Oath of Loyalty before the other members in front of a wooden image of a saint. A senior member of the group would take the extended hand of the inductee, prick his finger with a needle, and drip some of the flowing blood on the image of the saint, while reciting a time-honored oath that committed the initiate to an "inviolable" mandate for the rest of his life.

In a similar vein, southern Italy fostered such groups as the Camorra and the Mano Negro (Black Hand) during the nineteenth century. These non-Sicilian groups were formed to accommodate local situations. The Camorra, at its inception, consisted of a loose confederation of local clans or gangs that practiced theft and extortion and sold "protection," but it evolved into a more organized syndicate to fight the injustices of the reigning government.

The Black Hand is among the most famous groups commonly associated with the Mafia in the public imagination—but that is another myth. The Black Hand actually had its origins in ancient Spain and reappeared at the beginning of the twentieth century in the Balkans. History clearly shows it developed exclusively into a band of extortionists who adopted the Black Hand symbol and name. An early FBI report claims that the Black Hand symbol was invented by an Italian newspaperman covering a bomb extortion case in Italy. Apparently, a threatening note was found with the identifying mark of a black-inked handprint. But the Camorra and the Black Hand never existed in Sicily; they had nothing to do with what Americans call the Mafia. In the Mario Puzo novel *The Godfather* and in the film *The Godfather, Part II*, you may recall, the man in white called Fanucci, in the scenes set in 1900, was feared as the local purveyor of the Black Hand. Fanucci was nothing more than an extortionist preying on his own Italian people.

2

The Unification of Italy

Historically, the Sicilian has grown suspicious, intolerant of injustice, with a thirst for freedom and little faith in the officers of the law and the governments they served.

Joe Bonanno

The modern history of our way of life has its roots not in legend or myth, but in a time of very real political upheaval: the struggle for political power in mid-nineteenth-century Italy. While the unification of Italy in 1861—recent history compared even to that of the United States—was a catalyst to the growth of the *mafiosi*, the beginnings of our way of life expand much deeper into European history.

The period from the twelfth to the seventeenth centuries contributed two very important structural changes in the social and economic environment in Sicily. Over this time, the infrastructure of Sicilian life changed from a region of small rural independent farms and communities to an era of large land ownership by absentee barons. This changed the dynamics of traditional feudal agrarian communities, depleting the countryside of its inhabitants. Ownership and markets were established in the big cities. Hierarchy and interdependence between neighboring towns disappeared. The regions were now subservient to the economies of the big cities and coastal collection depots. At the same time, the dominant powers established physical force to control and safeguard their "possessions." Absentee landlords hired local men to act as guards, enforce performance, and protect property. With time, land was "retrieved" by the same guards who were hired by the barons to protect their local interests.

Although most average Americans have heard of the glories of Rome, many outsiders fail to understand that, from the beginning of the Middle Ages until 1861, what we think of as "Italy" was not a single political entity, but a land composed of many small, independent city-states—much like the thirteen colonies before they became the United States. For the most part, Italy had a single religion and common language. But these different regions were politically separate, driven by local politics, and often hostile toward one another. The popes supported these city-states, especially in northern Italy, keeping them distinct and mediating their disputes—all so that no single city-state would ever grow powerful enough to overshadow the papacy.

One of these states was Sicily, an island whose sovereignty has been eclipsed countless times through the centuries, from the time of the Sicilian Vespers in 1282 until the mid-1800s. In 1816, King Ferdinand IV of Naples (and simultaneously Ferdinand III of Sicily), member of a tyrannical and far-reaching branch of the Spanish Bourbon dynasty, declared himself King Ferdinand I, ruler of the Kingdom of the Two Sicilies (referring to northern Italy and the joint dominion of southern Italy and Sicily). Ferdinand would rule Sicily and nearly half the Italian peninsula for decades.

By the 1840s, however, revolution was in the air—in Sicily and throughout Italy. In 1848, the people of Sicily revolted against Ferdinand II, a grandson of Ferdinand I; their popular revolt, inspired by democratic principles, freed the Sicilian people from Bourbon rule for sixteen months until the island was retaken by force, restoring Ferdinand to power. During the revolt, he ordered the bombing of Messina, earning himself the nickname "King Bomba." The Sicilian revolt sparked several similar revolutions across Europe in the months that followed—and presaged a much larger revolution that would sweep the Italian peninsula just over a decade later.

In the wake of the 1848 revolutions, a secret organization known as La Giovine Italia ("Young Italy") emerged. Its mission was to overthrow the Bourbon dynasty, to force reform, and to secure an Italy for all Italians, controlled by the people and not by sovereigns. The three leaders of this movement were Giuseppe Mazzini, a dedicated visionary for revolution; Giuseppe Garibaldi, a soldier and man of action; and Camillo Benso di Cavour, founder of *Il Risorgimento,* a newspaper that became the official voice for the Italian national movement. These men all had different perspectives on what Italy needed, but the underlying principles that motivated them—unity, independence, and liberty—were the same that had prompted the American Revolution, and that would soon animate the Civil War in the United States. In fact, Garibaldi, who had spent time in the United States, living in Staten Island as a political refugee in exile, even offered his military services to President Abraham Lincoln at the outbreak of the War Between the States.

Mazzini, the visionary, stirred and inspired the rebellious youth. Although his own repeated attempts at insurrection were continually defeated, he made the people aware of their strength and power. After King Bomba died in 1859—believed to be as a result of an infection from a bayonet wound in an assassination attempt three years earlier—Mazzini instigated a new revolt against the Bourbon rulers, who were now led by Bomba's son, King Francis II. The Neapolitan forces of the Bourbon dynasty quickly suppressed the insurrection. But the revolt demonstrated that the Sicilians, who wanted freedom, could overcome their longstanding divisions of ideology and class and unite against a common opponent, even against overwhelming odds.

Garibaldi, the soldier, was a man of honest character who won the hearts of the people, the loyalty of his men, and the favor of public opinion. He was able to recruit men from all walks of life, including professional adventurers, social outcasts, citizens, and bands of *mafiosi*, to crush the Bourbons at their stronghold in Naples.

Cavour, the newspaper founder, was born to the feudal aristocracy of Piedmont, the only Italian state free of foreign or papal rule. While Garibaldi and Mazzini had visions of a united republic controlled by the people, Cavour had another form of government in mind. Convinced that the historical monarchy was compatible with liberal principles, he envisioned a constitutional monarchy as opposed to either absolute monarchy or republicanism, and publicly advocated a constitution for Piedmont early in 1848. King Charles Albert of Sardinia-Piedmont reluctantly granted the people a limited constitution in February 1848 and a month later declared war on Austria, an unwelcome holder of power in the Italian peninsula. The war with Austria was unsuccessful, causing the king to abdicate in 1849 in favor of his son, Victor Emmanuel II.

The series of insurrections led by these three revolutionaries became known as the Risorgimento (or "uprising"). At first they were unsuccessful, but in 1860 they finally became victorious. That year, Garibaldi led a volunteer army of a thousand men in an expedition by sea from Genoa to Sicily in May, and, after taking control of most of that island by July, marched on Naples, freeing the regions south of Rome from two hundred years of Bourbon tyranny and paving the way for a union of southern Italy and Sicily with the northern Italian cities. A political upheaval, centuries in the making, had been accomplished in just over three months.

The Kingdom of the Two Sicilies prior to 1861.

In 1850, Cavour became Sardinia-Piedmont's minister of agriculture and commerce, then finance minister in 1851; and in 1852 he became prime minister of Sardinia-Piedmont, promoting economic development (such as railway expansion) and mounting a series of reforms frowned upon by the pope, continuing the policies of his predecessor, D'Azeglio, in limiting the privileges of the Catholic church. However, Cavour also relegated Sicily and southern Italy to colonial status, which only intensified existing animosities: as the new government issued edict after edict affecting the south adversely, it was brought into the Italian nation dragging its feet.

In March 1861, an Italian Parliament session in Turin completed the unification, recognizing Victor Emmanuel II as king of Italy "by the grace of God and the will of the people." The southern regions were then amalgamated into the recently formed northern Kingdom of Italy. The purpose of this movement was to oust all foreign rulers and the papal authority and to establish a fully united Italian Republic.

In 1870, with none or little fanfare and with only token resistance of the papal guards (said to have been ordered by the pope), Rome became part of the Kingdom of Italy. Finally, the unification of Italy was complete. In southern Italy and Sicily, the Vatican's halfhearted resistance was seen as another indication that the Church, indifferent to the plight of the poor in the south, had abandoned its time-honored commitments to its people—and therefore that it lacked true legitimacy.

As great an improvement as it was, the newly "unified" Italy was by no means a perfect solution to the problems of the Italian people. For one thing, it was missing an important piece of geography: the great expanse in the center, sea to sea, that still belonged to the Catholic Church. Garibaldi blamed the Church for the generally passive attitude of the poor during the campaign for unification. "This stalwart and laborious class," he wrote of the peasantry, "belongs to the priests, who make it their business to keep it in ignorance."

Worse yet, the people of Sicily remained neglected by the central government, and the island's economic and social problems remained unattended. Garibaldi was reluctant to order the breakup of secular landed estates, and trouble between Naples and Sicily began almost as soon as unification was formalized in 1861. The south, when voting for annexation, fully expected to be granted some form of local autonomy; political promises had been made to ensure that it would happen. Instead, once the voting was over, the new government began to issue decrees and imposed new taxes and new rules for military conscription. While the taxes were imposed on both the north and the south, it was the north that received the bulk of the tax proceeds. Taxes paid by the people of Sicily were used to fuel the industrial enterprises in the north.

The government's unfair treatment of Sicilians was profound. Peasants who had been considered too poor to be taxed in Bourbon times were now required to pay taxes for the first time, throwing their very economic survival into question. Mules, for example—an indispensable working staple for untold numbers of farm workers and their families—were subject to taxation; cows, almost always the property of the affluent landowners, were not. Farm implements, usually the property of the individual farmer, were taxed; larger farm equipment, which only wealthy landowners could afford, was not. However, of all the edicts imposed by the government in Turin, none antagonized the Sicilians and other Southerners more than the new conscription law, which mandated seven years of military service.

Still smarting from the realization that the autonomy they had expected when voting for annexation had been denied them, Sicilians reacted by fomenting dissent against the new government in Turin, and by disregarding the edicts it imposed on them. Corruption flourished as never before. The same bands of *mafiosi* that had supported Garibaldi's campaign now became involved in a wide variety of activities that were prohibited by law, often with the collaboration of administrative officials from the North.

This is when our tradition took hold. After the excitement surrounding unification died down, the peasants waited in vain for the dazzling promises of dignity and social justice to materialize. They were sorely disappointed. Sicily was soon being overrun with corruption by a new breed of conqueror:

the northern Italians, whose promises of independence had proven hollow. Having given themselves over to the new nation of Italy, the Sicilians had been forgotten. The people of the middle class saw their livelihoods eroded by the free-market policy that shifted industry to the North, while exacerbating rural poverty in Sicily.

Although the North and South were politically united, the economic disparity between the two parts of the country grew. Within a few months, intense rebel activity blossomed in the Naples region. Determined to demonstrate its ability to exert control over any region within its borders, the new government dispatched an army unit to Naples, with orders to shoot every person bearing a weapon. When a similar rebellion broke out in Sicily, the general sent to put down the rebels reported that "soldiers had been crucified, policemen burnt alive, and the flesh of *carabiniere* [federal police] was sold in the marketplace." Such rumors later proved unfounded, but not before the government troops who heard them determined to take their vengeance. Whole villages were burned to the ground on the mere suspicion that they were providing food and shelter for rebels. Any insult to the national flag, or to King Victor Emmanuel, was considered reason enough to shoot the perpetrator. In a two-month period, more than two thousand people, including women and children, were arrested in Palermo alone. Summary execution took place in other towns and villages. The military commander gave orders that anyone of military age, or with the "face of an assassin," should be arrested and shot.

Rebellion raged throughout the South for the next five years, resulting in a historic divide between the *veddani*, the Sicilian peasant population, and the Italian officials in Palermo. By 1865, thousands of these *veddani* had been expelled from their lands. These were the same men who had fought with Garibaldi against the Bourbons. The only place left for them to go was the hills along the northern coast to Castellammare del Golfo, west of Palermo. In this region, they would continue the same fight they had waged when the hero Garibaldi came to free Sicily of the Bourbons—the fight for self-determination.

In 1866, a group of young boys known as *picciotti*—natural leaders within the peasant population, who had learned the lessons of life at the knees of the ancients—gathered in a fierce insurrection against King Victor Emmanuel's political appointees in Palermo. With few losses, the *picciotti* withdrew into the Madonie mountains to the southeast and the hillside towns surrounding Castellammare del Golfo to the west, where their supremacy would remain unchallenged for generations.

In 1870, a number of young men in the cathedral mountain town of Monreale, overlooking Palermo, formed the first new group dedicated to *il sistema del potere*—the first full expression of the power structure of the system embracing our philosophy of life. On the surface, *il sistema* was nothing more than an association of businessmen endorsed by both the Church and the politicians. The name adopted by this new group was Stoppaglier, or saboteurs, in the vocabulary of the *picciotti*. Before long, these groups—or sects, as the authorities called them—began to spread throughout western Sicily. These groups could consist of as little as four men in smaller villages and up to twenty or more in larger cities such as Palermo or Trapani. Size was not important. What mattered were local influence, respect, wealth, charisma, and unbending loyalty.

As the term Mafia developed over the years, it became a catchphrase for rebellious, illegal, or criminal activity. But the ideology of *il sistema* or *cosa nostra* that was born in those Sicilian hills was intended not as a vehicle to break the law for its own sake, but as a way for an oppressed people to band together, to favor personal connections over exploitation by a foreign power, and to ignore oppressive laws when they conflict with local moral traditions. It was this same set of shared principles that carried through to my day: Whether it was called *il sistema*, *cosa nostra*, or *Unione Siciliano* (as Charlie "Lucky" Luciano referred to it), the ideology was the same.

In the days when foreigners trampled over the Sicilian countryside taking what was not theirs—including their women—Sicilian men were forced to take action in order to survive. Survival required secret societies of loyal and trusted friends. The bonds built during that time among this Family of men had to be so strong and so secretive that it could not be penetrated. Even spouses and children could not be privy to the workings of the group, lest they be tortured into revealing the names of the very men who were protecting them.

Sicilian Criminal Activity and Protection Rackets

From the 1870s onward, bandit raids on cattle and sheep, as well as extortion, kidnappings, and nighttime assaults, were rampant throughout Sicily. Smuggling was everywhere, most of it with the connivance of corrupt custom officials. To preserve order in the south, politicians in the Republic came to depend on the region's big landowners, most of whom were foreigners living in other countries, and who depended in turn on the local *gabelloti* (overseers) to administer their property. These estate managers hired *campieri* (private armed guards) to protect the large agricultural estates owned by these absentee landlords. Land was a good investment, and the peasant caretakers were sometimes rewarded with sections to cultivate for themselves. Predictably, over time these sections were "cultivated" by the same guards hired by the barons to protect their interests.

The *campieri* could offer protection from these bandit raids—a guarantee made possible because these "agents of the law" were themselves recruited from the bandit kingdom. The *campieri*, who had the benefit of an unlimited labor force, pioneered the concept of private security patrols.

In a parliamentary report of the time, it was noted that law enforcement was "offered only to those who agreed to pay." In another report on public corruption in one town, twenty-two of the police department's thirty-nine members were found to be involved in criminal activities including blackmail, theft, and paid assassination. The *campieri* can also be credited with creating the "protection rackets" that followed the immigrants to the United States in the early 1900s, although human nature would suggest they were not the first in history to use this method of "commerce."

The tax system, as it was administered throughout Italy, was a breeding ground for graft, corruption, and even terrorism. During the Bourbon reign, the police had held a monopoly on crime. Under the new unified government, crime became the monopoly of criminal groups, especially the *mafiosi* from every segment of society. With assistance from *mafiosi*, the Sicilian *veddani* were quick to adjust to the challenge of being governed by the *forestieri* (foreigners) from the North.

It soon became clear that these northern officials were easier to manipulate than their Bourbon predecessors—and even more susceptible to corruption. This period of southern Italian history left the masses with a profound sense of disenchantment over the character of the "new Italy." The disillusionment only deepened when the Turin government, alarmed by the island's continued disregard for legitimate authority, finally sent an army of occupation into Sicily, where it would remain for the next ten years. It was a bitter reminder that the Sicilians were expected to behave as subserviently as they had been forced to for centuries. The presence of the northern army may have prevented rebellions, gatherings, and strikes, but it was powerless to quell the Sicilians' growing dissatisfaction with the regime—or their habit of disregarding and disobeying government edicts they considered unfair.

In these years, *il sistema* offered Sicilian peasants a vehicle to live by their own principles. Under the philosophy of *il sistema*, the people themselves decided who should lose and who should gain according to a strict division of labor and a firm adherence to loyalty. *Il sistema* also decided who qualified as a "friend" to be advanced, and who was a "problem" to be eliminated. It made no difference if the problem was a troublesome judge or a recalcitrant outlaw: those who followed our way of life trusted *il sistema* to put an end to the chaos that had infected Sicily.

The Emergence of "the Mafia" as a Government Scapegoat

In this atmosphere of heightened tensions and illegitimate authority, Sicilians in need of assistance began relying on friends, relatives, or friends of friends, rather than government, to solve their problems. This reliance became an instilled habit. Self-help and mutual-aid societies sprang up everywhere, until eventually they dominated the island. The *mafiosi* used the power of social revolt to combat the laws used by the government to control society—revolt not through outright confrontation, but through integration into the political and social systems of the time. The *mafiosi* placed themselves in the middle, subduing outright revolt for the interests of the central authority, while protecting those less capable of protecting themselves from that central authority.

In reaction, government agents imposed a broad definition of "crimes against the state," criminalizing "any form of
behavior that threatened or diminished the authority of the
state." In one move, Sicily's mutual-aid societies had been re-
classified as criminal agencies. In their paranoia, these agents
from northern Italy began using the term *Mafia* for the first
time—using the word in their reports to Turin to character-
ize any group activity that appeared to defy the State's monopoly on authority.

This misguided use of the term had an amusing side. The
government, having coined a name for this criminal group as
Mafia, concluded that members of this new criminal group
were called *mafiosi*, not understanding that the prefects understood the word *mafiosi* to be a thought process, not members
of a criminal group. In 1874, the government was preparing a
"war" against a number of rebellious factions that it had erro-
neously identified as the Mafia. In preparation, the prefects of
each Sicilian province were ordered to submit a list of *mafiosi*
in their province. The prefect of the province of Girgenti (the
Sicilian name for Agrigento) responded that to comply with
the order would mean listing all Girgenti's male population
between the ages of seventeen and seventy. When other provinces responded similarly, the government canceled its plans
for "war."

By the 1890s, a group of ambitious young southern Italians rebelled in one of the first Socialist movements in Europe,
called the Fasci Siciliani. When they were put down with the
usual ferocity by northern troops, none could return to their
old life. Fortunately, they had someplace else to go, but it was
not easy to leave a place, a home, a culture as old as memory, a
deeply rooted language, and legends and proverbs that served
as guides to life.

The Sicilians faced a constant parade of new challenges
to their lifestyle in these years. For the first time in the long

history of the island, they had to contend with elections. They soon found that this presented no problem at all. The deputies in the Turin parliament were quite willing to entrust management of local affairs to influential members of the various areas in Sicily, in exchange for their electoral support. Some Turin deputies, up for election, never set foot on Sicilian soil at all. However, with a little more than 1 percent of the population eligible to vote, predicting the outcome of the elections was easy.

There are many stories that can be told about this state of affairs. Norman Lewis, in his 1964 book *The Honored Society: A Searching Look at the Mafia*, relates a famous story concerning communal elections in 1881. It appears that the marquis of Villalba was an influential *mafioso*. He took the precaution of locking up all 218 eligible voters in his sector in a large granary several days before the election, releasing them a few at a time to be escorted to the polls to vote under armed guard; obviously, he was elected.

The real code of the *mafiosi* was to serve as "protector of the people." There was a time in Palermo when the government approved of the real, traditional *mafiosi*, even enacting a law allowing them to take the law into their own hands to protect themselves and their country. They called this *il braccio della giustizia* (the arm of justice), which was the code conferring this power upon them.

Immigration of Italians and Sicilians to the United States

From the time of Christopher Columbus to the beginning of the twentieth century, some five and a half million Italians followed in the explorer's footsteps and crossed the Atlantic to the New World. The years between 1880 and 1924 saw a virtual hemorrhaging of people from Italy to the United States. Roughly 60 to 80 percent of them were from the impoverished southern half of the Italian peninsula and the island of Sicily.

A whole culture was leaving its ancient roots to move to a new land. Of the many ironies in Italian history, none can be greater than the phenomenon of Italians leaving Italy so soon after it became a unified nation. Only by realizing that a united Italy meant substituting oppressive northern Italians for their Bourbon predecessors can one truly understand why that mass exodus began when it did.

After unification, the social, political, and religious hierarchy existed to promote and enforce their own interests. Individual ambition and competitive warfare allowed for a new upward mobility, as falling nobility and upwardly advancing peasantry passed each other on the social ladder—and a new class of men developed that lived outside the social structure altogether, men governed by their own rules and traditions.

In the nineteenth century, Italians came to the United States as men of learning, as connoisseurs of art and founders of conservatories, as musicians, painters, and sculptors from the land of the mother of the arts. Most of their names are long forgotten, although much of the work of their craft remains—from Columbus Circle in New York to the Capitol Rotunda in Washington, D.C. Along with these men of learning came the organ grinders, the cobblers, the fishermen, the farm workers, and the persecuted. By the early 1900s, Italian immigrants swarming to the United States were bringing the *mafiosi* rules and traditions with them. As the new century dawned, tens of thousands of unskilled immigrants from southern and eastern Europe were flooding into America. Ellis Island was the principal debarkation point through which they were processed and left to fend for themselves in a new country. After processing, they boarded a ferry for the twenty-minute boat ride to the Battery, the area

Getty

The Battery and the skyscrapers of lower
Manhattan from the air, circa 1900.

at the southern tip of Manhattan named for the artillery battery stationed there to protect New York Harbor.

Like their fellow immigrants from Russia, Poland, Ireland, and other countries, most Sicilians and other Italians arriving in America could not even read the words of the sonnet "The New Colossus," written by the American Jewish poet Emma Lazarus in 1883 engraved on the bronze plaque mounted on the pedestal of the Statue of Liberty: "Give me your tired, your poor, your huddled masses yearning to breathe free." These immigrants formed small enclaves in New York and other cities, especially in the Northeast, gathering with others who spoke the same language and hailed from the same regions of their turbulent homeland.

The Italian family played a complex role in the lives of its members. It gave its members a sense of security in a very hostile land, but Italian traditions also kept the second generation set firmly in the working-class ways of the parents. Remember the old proverb they all absorbed: "The little satisfies me, abundance overwhelms me."

All of these groups were easy prey for exploitation—even by their own kind. Uneducated for the most part, they were easily taken advantage of by unscrupulous rivals or enterprising tough guys. As in most societies, jobs for the uneducated were the most menial; it would take at least a generation for them to advance to some kind of social status. The contributions of the children of these immigrants have been varied and indelible. In music, the influence of the Italian players in the earliest recorded New Orleans jazz bands; the modern crooning of Russ Columbo, and the singing style of Frank Sinatra, which incorporated the lyricism of both Columbo and the Italian street singers of the mother country. The singing of Frankie Laine gave us echoes of peasant coarseness. In sports, Joe DiMaggio reflected the ideal to be *civili* (civilized); Yogi Berra continued the tradition of peasant humor; and Vince Lombardi exemplified the peasant obstinacy to succeed. In his memorable words, "Winning isn't everything, it's the only thing."

In the years that followed, enterprising young men of Sicilian heritage moved westward from New York, finding work as section hands on the railroads under construction along the way as they made their way to California to pursue the American dream. Some settled in small farming and ranching towns of east Texas, and along the Brazos River. Others went to Galveston to work the oil fields. By the time of World War I, Texas and Louisiana had large Sicilian populations from Corleone, Poggioreale, Salaparuta, and other small Sicilian villages mainly in the provinces of Palermo and Trapani in western Sicily. Many Sicilians from Palermo settled in Alabama. Life was rough, the work hard, the pay meager. Sicilian wives and daughters even joined their men working in the fields—something almost unheard-of in their homeland.

Our people generally fared better in the West, where what mattered was how well one integrated into life on the frontier. What mattered was how quickly you could build a house or how well you could farm. Nationality was not as much of a concern—with one notable exception: Sicilians and Italians arrived in Colorado to work in the mining camps alongside other foreigners. At first they were looked upon with suspicion by the English-speaking workers, but they all soon learned that the real adversaries were their employers. When the workers' grievances were ignored, they decided to form a union to defend themselves against the abuses of the mine owners. For most Italians, this was their first experience with organized labor. The Italians comprised about 40 percent of the union membership. The foreign-speaking members decided to strike, but the English-speaking workers refused to join them. That refusal prompted the strikers to arm themselves and force their colleagues out of the mines. The governor sent in the state militia, and an agreement was reached between the workers and the owners at the expense of the Sicilians, who were required to leave. Things changed around the time of World War I, when the Sicilians, undeterred, numbered some forty thousand, with most of them settling in the area around Denver, Colorado.

Except in California, Italians remained a minority in the states west of the Mississippi. One Italian interviewed in Brooklyn observed, "If California had not been so far away from Italy, all the Italian immigrants would have gone there in search of heaven. I got the idea that California would be like the best parts of Italy . . . but without the poverty." Four railways connected the Mississippi River area with all the western states, but Italians congregated mostly in California, Washington, and Colorado.

Utah did attract some Italian converts to the Mormon faith, who settled in the Salt Lake City area. Mormon mine owners sought out the Italians; recognizing that they would likely work better in the company of their own kind, the owners encouraged immigration and arranged for Italian families to receive special allotments and treatment.

With the discovery of gold in the Klondike region east of Alaska, Seattle, as the gateway to Alaska, attracted many Italian immigrants; many stayed on in the city, some to become fishermen, others because Seattle was burgeoning into a metropolis that required strong backs and arms to clear forested land and to load and unload cargo at the seaport. Seattle gave Italians work for the next fifty years—music to the ears of work-hungry immigrants.

In Arizona, Italians worked in the copper mines and the gold mines of the southern part of the state and in the farming communities of central Arizona. The most notable Italian-American (at that time) to come out of Arizona was an Army brat who went on to national prominence: Fiorello LaGuardia, who grew up in Prescott, Arizona, but went on to become a U.S. congressman and mayor of New York City.

3

The Beginning of
the American Mafia

*Human nature tends to trust one's own kind for protection
against uncertain or mistrustful authority in a hostile land.*

Joe Bonanno

The real origins of the American Mafia occurred in New Orleans, from around 1877 to 1879. It was during these years that our way of life slowly began taking shape as a social and political power to be reckoned with, especially as it took immigrants from Tampa, Florida, under its wing. The Sicilian immigrants of the time could be easy targets for blame when things went wrong. When an outbreak of yellow fever reached epidemic proportions in New Orleans in 1897, in the Little Palermo district (the lower French Quarter, populated mostly by immigrants from Sicily after about 1880), Sicilians were blamed for the outbreak when, in fact, contaminated water was the culprit. The new Mafia coalesced in the United States at this time as a way of protecting Italian immigrants from this kind of prejudice.

Slowly, the American Mafia paddled up the Mississippi and Missouri rivers, stopping at St. Louis and then Kansas

City; moving eastward to meet up with groups of southern Italian immigrants that, by the turn of the century, had formed at around the same time in New York, Philadelphia, Chicago, Boston, and Pittsburgh. Outposts in Buffalo, Detroit, and Cleveland were added later; then came Newark, New Jersey (later moving to Elizabeth); Providence, Rhode Island; Scranton, Pennsylvania.; Birmingham, Alabama; Rockford, Illinois; and Milwaukee and Madison, Wisconsin. Out West, Sicilian groups had gathered in San Diego as early as 1920; by the 1930s they had branched into Los Angeles, where they had their eyes set not on bootlegging, but on a new industry in its infancy called "talking pictures." A chapter also formed in the San Francisco/San Jose area around 1931, with Denver, Colorado, and Dallas, Texas, rounding out the Families.

There has always been tremendous confusion within the government as to who belongs to what Families and in what cities. This problem for the authorities was due basically to the horizontal mobility of American society prior to, during, and after World War II. Young men who had never strayed more than a few miles away from the safety and familiarity of their neighborhoods were now finding that there was more to the world than what they had known.

Before World War I, New York was a melting pot of peoples from all over the world, particularly from Eastern Europe. Italians were not the dominant immigrant group in New York; they were next in line after the Irish and Jews. After the Irish ascended the socioeconomic ladder, the void was quickly filled by Jews, and right behind them the Italians.

During this period, thousands of Italians congregated into small groups in various sections of the five boroughs that make up New York City. There was Little Italy in Manhattan, Greenpoint and Williamsburg in Brooklyn, and a few smaller groups in the far reaches of eastern Brooklyn and in the Bronx. They saw themselves first as Christians, then as men or women

The five boroughs of New York City.

from a particular region, town, or village; a man from Naples was *napolitano*, a man from Bari was *baresi*. Because of the long-held tradition that natives of Sicily considered themselves distinct from mainland Italians, most referred to themselves first as Sicilians; only if pressed would they reveal their town or village. Not until they had spent some time in America did the immigrants find their identity as Italians and begin answering simply "Italy" when asked where they were from.

Early immigrants from Sicily found themselves in a strange and foreign culture where ancient habits such as strolling in the piazza did not exist. They clustered together for comfort, security from other foreigners, and for the social interaction of being with those who spoke their language, cooked the same foods, and understood the same fears, following the same pattern as the Irish and the Jews. To outsiders, their language meant nothing more than the noises of animals. Just as they had under northern rule at home, these *paesani* (fellow countrymen and women) looked to their own, rather than outsiders, for protection.

The tradition of providing protection from oppressors had traveled with the men from their native land. The secret societies they formed in the United States, like those formed in the old country, were societies of honor following the concepts of *il sistema*. And they were regenerated on these shores in the form of Families, with familiar names such as Bonanno, Profaci, and Mangano—each of which had positioned itself to protect its own.

The Evolution of the Families

In the large cities of New York, Boston, and Philadelphia, the ethnic enclave was the starting point for most immigrants. These enclaves, populated by recently arrived immigrants, brought back to life familiar sights, sounds, and smells that reminded neighbors of the old country. Fellow *paesani* slowly rekindled their spirits, making life in a strange land a little more bearable.

The vulnerability of newly arrived immigrants led to the establishment of a number of societies aimed at making life tolerable. These societies would offer advice and assistance in complying with the strange laws and customs of this new land. They also interceded to help prevent the maltreatment of the new immigrants and to sponsor legislation that would protect them. Immigrants from Castellammare del Golfo had the Concordia Society. Immigrants from Corleone, Marsala, Cinisi, Palermo, and Lercara Friddi created similar benevolent and protective societies. In later years, some of these societies became powerful political arms of national political parties, wooed by politicians and promoted loyally by their adherents.

The various enclaves were also home to elite opportunists known as *prominenti*, who worked to enable immigrants to become masters of their own destiny. Among them were lawyers trained in Italian law, but unable to qualify to practice law in this new land; former teachers from the upper levels of universities; and sons of well-bred southern Italian gentlemen. Most established themselves as "notaries," a position that commanded respect in the homeland, because one required substantial training to achieve it.

The typical notary was a middle-class southern Italian male sufficiently educated to set him apart from his illiterate *paesani*. Thousands of saloonkeepers, boarding-house owners, bankers, steamship agents, and others with education also became notaries. Many of these exploited the immigrants' faith in their professional status, taking money from illiterate local Italians who entrusted them to help send funds home to their families, or who needed help with real-estate transactions involving family land back home. One noted Italian journalist described them as "leeches of the Italian immigrants." Nevertheless, notaries often fostered close-knit networks of local entrepreneurs, and they flourished wherever Italian immigrants settled.

Other groups of immigrants intermingled with the impoverished and uneducated immigrants arriving from the *Mezzorgiorno*, who were generally maligned and despised. Some were fleeing from what would become known as *la parentesi fascista*, the period when Italy was ruled by the oppressive Fascist regime of Benito Mussolini. Still others, neither oppressed nor poor and even somewhat educated, came to these shores simply looking for a better life.

Some new arrivals attended night school or tried to learn English from their children. But their use of the language seldom developed beyond a blend of fractured English with a distinct dialect. New words crept into the language of those in the enclaves, creating a jargon that reflected their first contacts with the new land: boss became *bosso*, ticket became *ticchetto*, job became *gioba*, factory became *fattoria*. Later, as the world of the immigrant expanded beyond the boundaries of the enclaves, so did their language. Soon the women went to the *marachetta* (market) to shop, *a fari la spisa* (to buy groceries), while the men took relaxing strolls on *lu strittu* (the street) in the evening after dinner.

These enclaves were the strength and refuge of the immigrant world, a place to band together and stave off the basic fear of failing to survive in an environment that was often unfriendly, even antagonistic. Within their own neighborhoods, the immigrants felt almost as if they were back in their villages. Here they were able to criticize and complain about this American world without worrying about insulting their neighbors. What they experienced and learned about this strange country often repelled and frightened them. As historian Rudolph Vecoli observed, "*Mericani* appeared a foolish people, without a sense of humor, respect, or proper behavior. Ideas of youthful freedom, women's rights, and the efforts on the part of teachers or social workers to Americanize [immigrants] and their children were resented as intrusions on the sovereignty of family."

It wasn't long before some immigrants reacted to the hostility by forming neighborhood groups to protect themselves and other families. Men familiar with *il sistema* were experienced at combating oppressors in the old country, and they empowered themselves to settle problems as they arose within the neighborhoods. Soon their influence extended outside the enclaves following the immigrants to where they worked or shopped.

This is how the group of men known as *amici nostri* ("friends of ours") took hold on American shores. For the Sicilians, who had long since learned not to trust outside authority, these *amici nostri* were quickly entrusted with guiding newly arrived immigrants through the unfamiliar culture—as well as dispensing justice. It was the beginning in America of *il sistema del potere*, the system of power followed by Sicilians at home.

In America, *il sistema* soon came to govern daily life for many Sicilian immigrants. The links between the Italian villages and America, extending back to the beginning of the new century, were strong. Men of the old tradition were mainly in the people business. They derived satisfaction from being responsible to a Family of men, who in turn were beholden to them. This cooperation usually led to the mutual monetary satisfaction of all concerned. The making of money, however, was not their highest consideration. The main purpose of banding together into a Family was to establish a network of relationships that would give its members an advantage in dealing with outsiders.

Men of the tradition of *il sistema* were always reluctant to deal with or associate with non-Sicilians. This was not bigotry, but rather common sense. In the Old World, exposure to the ideals and beliefs of the *mafiosi* philosophy started in the cradle. It is impossible, with rare exception, to instill those beliefs in someone not born into our culture. Tradition is not something one learns overnight; it is the work of a lifetime. Even southern Italians—such as Albert Anastasia, from Calabria, or Frank Costello, also from Calabria, or Charlie "Lucky" Luciano, who was born in Lercara Friddi, twenty-eight miles southeast of

Palermo, but who came to the States as a young boy—could not fully appreciate the old tradition of Sicily.

The banking profession deserves the harshest criticism during this era. *Banchistas* (bankers) who were devoid of capital or major resources, used immigrants' money for personal gain; much like the Catholic Church, they used their position to keep the immigrant population subjugated to their whims while enriching themselves. During the first twenty years of the new century, nearly $1.5 million was deposited with these men with only $500 repaid. The bankers paid no interest on the money. In the minds of the immigrants, it was enough that a *persona d'onore* (a person of honor) was safeguarding their money. Not until the end of World War I did the immigrant depositors in these neighborhood banks begin to realize that their faith and trust in *banchistas* had been seriously misplaced.

By the midpoint of the twentieth century, changes in our world developed that would dominate both the core principles of our Tradition and its effectiveness as a way of life.

In the cities where the larger Families had taken root, Sicilian tradition had been the major influence because all of the leaders were from Sicily. By the early 1950s, however, that generation of leadership was slowly giving way to younger leaders— mostly first-generation American-born men who had never "lived" the tradition. Many, in fact, paid nothing more than lip service to it. The Americanization of our world had begun.

To these new leaders and their followers, our ways were antiquated. They considered the old talk about "honor" and "respect" just rant and banter. Although these new leaders would never say so when face-to-face with the old-style Sicilians, they harbored a certain contempt for their forefathers' old-world ways. And, since they never lived the tradition, they never truly understood it instinctively; it was never really a part of their nature.

In many respects, the men of this new breed were true Americans, free from ties to the past and from the responsibilities of tradition. Having grown up in America, they developed a marketplace mentality, focused primarily on the bottom line—on making money. The old Sicilians had never considered it evil to make money; men of honor have always considered wealth a by-product of power. But these new figures placed money above the old-world values we relied upon for survival. They were iconoclasts, who had no qualms about brushing aside, even destroying, the widely accepted ideals or beliefs that had guided our tradition for almost eight hundred years.

The Post–World War I Era and the Rise of the Families

Most recorders of history tend to judge yesterday's events by today's standards, or by their own notions of how things were at a given time. My account of the evolution of the Families in America, early in this century, is just as it was told to me by my father, Joseph Bonanno Sr., a percipient witness of some of these events and a participant in most.

By the end of World War I, in 1918, immigrants of every nationality had begun branching out from their tightest, most insular enclaves, until their presence could be felt throughout many northeastern cities. The Italians who landed at the Battery at the southern end of Manhattan moved to points further up the island, into the southern Bronx, Brooklyn, and for some hardier souls, into the outlying areas of Queens. Others, who just couldn't get the dirt out of their veins, found acreage and established small farms on Long Island, bringing them, at least emotionally, back to their roots. My grandfather was among these.

For those who remained in the cities, their ethnic neighborhoods had become centers of security and familiarity for the Irish, Italians, and Jews. The social structures they had developed were both sound and stable. Many Anglos looked upon these enclaves with fear, associating them with what happened in Russia when the Bolsheviks banded together and mounted a successful overthrow of the autocratic rule of Czar Nicholas II in the 1917 Russian Revolution. The Bolsheviks then took over the labor unions of the industrialized north in Italy and the economic battle against the new Fascist Party of Mussolini for control began. The fear of anarchism and potential economic loss now found its way to the United States.

The spread of criminal activity in America perpetuated these fears. Anarchism and criminality there were not different from what happened in Sicily when the new Italian government began its oppression of the peasants after Italian unification. When Italy's unskilled workers arrived in the United States, they faced appalling working conditions—slaving away in textile mills and other manufacturing trades for fifty-six hours a week, earning less than nine dollars per week, working alongside children. Crowded into overcrowded tenements with other families, they soon recognized that the only way to improve their lot in life was to assimilate into the mainstream of society—despite the cultural, economic, and language barriers in their way.

One way they did this was by joining labor unions. One mission of labor unions in the United States was to secure social justice, including fairness and equality for working immigrants. But their efforts were often curtailed. Leaders of industry collaborated with the government to discourage the formation of unions—for instance, by holding union leaders legally responsible for any violence committed during demonstrations or strikes, even if the leaders were not present.

It was in this atmosphere that Italians and Sicilians recognized their need to escape the subservient and docile mass that was American society, whose only interest appeared to be making money by exploiting the unskilled working class. By 1925, when President Calvin Coolidge declared that "The chief business of the American people is business," the "bottom line" was replacing most, if not all, our old-world values.

The garment factory run by my uncle,
Jim DePasquale, 1928.

Book II

The Commission

What I am about to share with you has never been told by anyone with firsthand knowledge. From the time I was made in 1954, I personally witnessed formal and informal meetings of the group known as the Commission, attended by the leaders of the Families, their *sotto capos*, *consiglieri*, and the other high-ranking members.

My father, Joe Bonanno, had helped to make those meetings possible, more than two decades earlier, when he helped pave the way for the creation of the Commission. As the worst of the power struggle known as the Castellammarese War died down in the early 1930s, my father had worked in consultation with Lucky Luciano to persuade the leaders of the other Families that none of us would prosper until a peace was established, and a structure put in place to mediate disputes among the Families.

It's been said that every man is the master of his fate. But often he meets his destiny by taking a road to avoid it. In 1926, Joe Bonanno had been faced with just such a choice. Should he learn to be a barber, or should he join the crowd that was preparing to take advantage of the gift that America's politicians had bestowed upon the country in the form of Prohibition? For good or bad, he chose to join his immigrant *paesani* to take advantage of this gift. Just five years later, he would play a key role in the formation of the Commission and the realignment of the Five Families of New York.

4

The Kennedy Connection
Before the Commission

She was riding low in the water just outside the three-mile limit, pushing the waves at a speed of no more than eight knots. The boat owned by Joseph P. Kennedy Sr., father of the future president, was heavy with her cargo of bootleg whiskey and illegal aliens. She was transporting her contraband from Canada, bound for the U.S. to be unloaded at Sag Harbor, New York. It was a perfect night for such a mission, with heavy clouds blocking most of the light from the moon and stars. Pursuing her at a distance—but gaining on her—was a 75-foot U.S. Coast Guard patrol boat, sirens blaring, searchlights bouncing as the vessel plowed through the waves. Once Kennedy's boat was inside the three-mile limit, the Coast Guard officers were on deck, ready to cut off her escape route and board the smaller boat.

Suddenly, the Kennedy boat picked up speed and began to plane, rising higher in the water until it was skimming the surface, leaving the Coast Guard patrol boat in its wake and disappearing into the night—evidently carrying a lighter load.

Commission Members or

FAMILIES	TERRITORIES	Early 1931 5 Members	Late 1931 7 Members	1936 7 Members	1941 7 Members
GAGLIANO(1)	Bronx	Gaetano Gagliano	Gaetano Gagliano	Gaetano Gagliano	Gaetano Gagliano
MANGANO(2)	Brooklyn & Manhattan	Vincent Mangano	Vincent Mangano	Vincent Mangano	Vincent Mangano
BONANNO	Brooklyn	Joseph Bonanno	Joseph Bonanno	Joseph Bonanno	Joseph Bonanno
LUCIANO(3)(4)	Manhattan & New Jersey	Charlie Luciano	Charlie Luciano	*Vito Genovese	*Frank Costello
PROFACI	Brooklyn	Joseph Profaci	Joseph Profaci	Joseph Profaci	Joseph Profaci
MAGADDINO	Buffalo		Stefano Magaddino	Stefano Magaddino	Stefano Magaddino
RICCA(5)	Chicago		Paul Ricca	Paul Ricca	Paul Ricca
ZERILLI	Detroit				
LAROCCA	Pittsburgh				
BRUNO	Philadelphia				

(1) 1953 renamed LUCCHESE FAMILY
(2) 1951 renamed ANASTASIA FAMILY
(3) 1953 renamed COSTELLO FAMILY
(4) 1957 renamed GENOVESE FAMILY
(5) 1957 renamed GIANCANA FAMILY

Acting Family Representatives

1946 7 Members	1951 7 Members	1956 9 Members	1957-1960 9 Members	TERRITORIES	FAMILIES
Gaetano Gagliano	Gaetano Gagliano	Tommy Lucchese	Tommy Lucchese	Bronx	GAGLIANO
Vincent Mangano	Albert Anastasia	Albert Anastasia	*Carlo Gambino	Brooklyn & Manhattan	MANGANO
Joseph Bonanno	Joseph Bonanno	Joseph Bonanno	Joseph Bonanno	Brooklyn	BONANNO
Frank Costello	Frank Costello	Frank Costello	Vito Genovese	Manhattan & New Jersey	LUCIANO
Joseph Profaci	Joseph Profaci	Joseph Profaci	Joseph Profaci	Brooklyn	PROFACI
Stefano Magaddino	Stefano Magaddino	Stefano Magaddino	Stefano Magaddino	Buffalo	MAGADDINO
Paul Ricca	Paul Ricca	Anthony Accardo	Sam Giancana	Chicago	RICCA
		Joseph Zerilli	Joseph Zerilli	Detroit	ZERILLI
		John LaRocca		Pittsburgh	LAROCCA
			Angelo Bruno	Philadelphia	BRUNO

* Acting Family Representatives

Kennedy's business partner, a Sicilian named Montecchia, had been watching for the Coast Guard. As soon as he was sure they had spotted the Kennedy boat, Montecchia later told my father, he was under orders to make the boat lighter to gain speed. And he did—not by throwing the whiskey overboard, but by throwing people.

For that, my father considered Kennedy "no good."

In that summer of 1925, my father was delivering whiskey to make some money before he got his own still. Montecchia told him Joe Kennedy was shrewd and good to make money with—but to be careful because Kennedy was also a liar.

My father had no qualms about Kennedy thwarting Prohibition by bringing in whiskey, along with boatloads of aliens, from Canada. "Kennedy was no different from the rest of us, except his whiskey went mainly to society people capable of paying the higher price for quality goods," he told me. What he didn't like was Kennedy's indifference to the Sicilians and other immigrants who were being smuggled into the country at the same time, whom Kennedy treated as mere second-rate cargo.

Smuggling whiskey, rum, and other alcoholic beverages was the main source of income for gangs along the eastern seaboard during Prohibition. Immigration to Canada was easy for Sicilians and other foreigners, and a cottage industry developed smuggling these illegal aliens, who had little choice but to take second place to the cases of whiskey. They were just human commodities and additional sources of illegal revenue for Kennedy, his partners, and others competing for the business.

Kennedy did his bootlegging business hand in glove with many members of our world during this period—including such leaders as Joe Masseria, Salvatore Maranzano, and Lucky Luciano. They were all in competition with one another, some friendly, some deadly. For the Sicilians, the day of reckoning would come in the form of the Castellammarese War. The

Sicilian groups were like the arms of an octopus flailing all about. They would chaotically strike everything in their path. Unless the arms were given direction by a head joining them together in some fashion, there was little chance any of them would survive. Formation of the Commission would be the first step.

In years to come, my father, and others in positions of power, would explain the purpose of the Commission to me in great detail, divulging the contents of earlier discussions among the members, and recounting issues addressed and actions sanctioned at meetings that occurred before I was made. I later realized that this tutoring was carefully planned in case my destiny should someday elevate me to a leadership position, possibly even the *rappresentante* of the Bonanno Family.

Today, most of the American public probably imagines the Commission as a kind of supreme bureaucracy that controlled organized crime. But that's not how it worked. The Commission had little in common with the hierarchical structure of most modern corporations. Rather, it served a unique purpose for this thing of ours—as a means of stabilizing relations among all the Families across the country whose agendas, left unchecked, could have been mutually destructive.

The Castellammarese War (1928–30) Before the Formation of the Commission

In New York, the struggle within Italian immigrant factions gave rise to a violent period, from 1928 to 1930, that has come to be known as the Castellammarese War. Some writers, historians, and law enforcement officials have described it as a bloody power struggle between two factions for control of the Italian-American Mafia. They are only partially correct. The true history of this period, based on actual information available, has long since been mixed in with the fantasies of writers of the era. In fact, this war represented not just a conflict between two specific groups, but a larger internal struggle that was taking place during this time in American history—one that involved rivalries between Italians and Sicilians, and was also influenced by Anglo resentment toward Italian immigrants due to events taking place in Europe at the time.

The northwest coast of Sicily stretches from Cefalù west through Palermo to Trapani and then south through Marsala, looping around to Agrigento and returning north again to Cefalù. This coastline takes in most or all of the roughly thirty-five major Sicilian cities within the world of the Mafia—including the homes of two of the three principal rivals in the Castellammarese War.

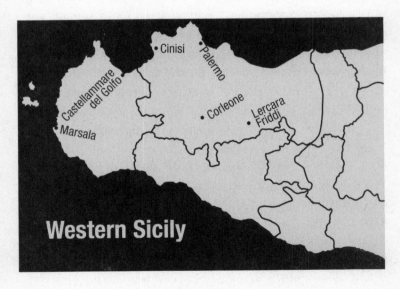

Map of Sicily.

These rival groups emerged from what were really bands of disorganized opportunists hoping to take advantage of others on the gold-paved streets of New York in the early twentieth century. These groups engaged in illegal activities, acting independently in what might be considered the heyday of "disorganized crime," from the early 1900s through 1930.

The first group, which I'll call the Masseria Group, consisted of southern Italians and Sicilians with roots in the area of Italy south of Rome called the Mezzogiorno. Hailing from Palermo, Naples, and other parts of the region, these men had never really ended their war with the oppressive governments that had been foisted on them for centuries, and their worldview was shaped by their resentment of the tyrannical new Italian government. The leaders of this group included Giuseppe "Joe the Boss" Masseria (the top Mafia don in New York City), Ciro Terranova, Giuseppe "Peter the Clutch Hand" Morello, Frank Scalice, Salvatore D'Aquila, Giacomo "Big Jim" Colosimo of Chicago, Johnny Torrio, and Alphonse "Al" Capone. They began as neighborhood leaders, with absolute power over the Lower East Side, but extended their influence in wider concentric circles as time went on. Masseria, a Sicilian Mafia enforcer, came to New York in 1903 at the age of seventeen. In the mid-1920s he became leader of the group, which had already become the dominant bootleggers in the Sicilian world. Through intimidation, strong-arm tactics, bullying, and tenacity, Masseria rose through the ranks to rule the most powerful New York Family of his time.

A second, Brooklyn-based group, the Maranzano Group, was first led by Nicola "Cola" Schiro, a wealthy, genteel businessman who, along with the other members, was from the Castellammare del Golfo region of Sicily. These were mostly die-hard Sicilians fighting the good fight against the forces of Mussolini and his new Fascist government, which came to power in the 1920s. This group came to the United States after

World War I and settled mostly along the eastern seaboard in New England, New York, and Pennsylvania, with some going west as far as Illinois and Missouri, and south to Louisiana. Although these Brooklyn Castellammarese always retained old-country ties to the Castellammarese who had settled in Buffalo and elsewhere, there was no organized central power uniting them.

This second group had come to these shores as nearly grown men, indoctrinated from birth in the ways of the Sicilian culture, and they never really lost their identities as Sicilians banding together against a new outsider—even when the outsiders were Americans, to whose land they had only recently relocated. To outsiders, these men appeared clannish and odd; with their big mustaches, old-fashioned clothes, and broken English, they were referred to by many as Mustache Petes. For decades, they remained shadowy figures in American culture—and that's the way they liked it. Their understated presence and manner (which some found almost buffoonish) allowed them to stay under the radar, able to accomplish more because their abilities and intelligence weren't taken seriously by others.

The third group was the Luciano/Lansky Combine, made up mostly of Americanized Calabrians and Sicilians, including Charlie "Lucky" Luciano, Umberto "Albert" Anastasia, and Frank Costello, and Neapolitans Vito Genovese and Joe Adonis; as well as a number of powerful Russian and Polish Jews, including Arnold Rothstein, Meyer Lansky, and Benjamin "Bugsy" Siegel. All the Italians were born in Italy, but came to this country as youngsters, and grew up on the streets of New York. The familiar sights and smells of the old country brought to these neighborhoods a sense of unity and togetherness, but the boys who grew up here were never indoctrinated with the old-world philosophy, and operated without specific loyalty to any established group.

Masseria wanted to take control over all the Castellammarese, whether in Brooklyn, Detroit, Chicago, or elsewhere. He needed an alliance with the Luciano/Lansky Combine in order to carry out his plan. Masseria had been courting Luciano since the early 1920s, recognizing the rising power of the Americanized Italians (Luciano's *paesani*) and the Jewish contingent—Luciano's childhood street pals Meyer Lansky, Bugsy Siegel, Louis "Lepke" Buchalter (Lepke is a shortened form of the Yiddish for "Little Louis"), and others, all of whom grew up on Manhattan's Lower East Side. They later teamed up with the Brownsville Boys (led by Abe Reles and Martin Goldstein) as members of what came to be known as Murder, Inc., a much-feared group of enforcers. It was known that Lansky had a friendship connection with the ruthless Purple Gang, another group of Jewish and Italian gangsters, which monopolized the liquor business in Detroit.

Masseria suggested a merger, but Luciano turned him down. The Combine, together with its friends and allies, had taken bootlegging, influence peddling, the numbers game (i.e., the lottery), and even early narcotics trafficking to new heights.

A number of other, less prominent groups also emerged around this time, including three headed by Alfredo "Al Mineo" Manfredi, Gaetano "Tommy" Reina, and Salvatore DiBella, respectively. Each of these groups had take-charge members who eventually became leaders, but the groups themselves were disorganized, just as the original Sicilian sects had been. Mineo's group, which operated in Manhattan and parts of Brooklyn, included men who would rise to powerful positions in the Families in the 1930s and 1940s, including Albert Anastasia, Salvatore "Tata" Chiricho, Giuseppe "Joe" Traina, Vincent Mangano, and Frank Scalice. Mineo was an avowed ally of Masseria.

In the Bronx, Reina was the dominant group. This group, which controlled the monopoly on ice distribution—a good business in those days, when everyone used iceboxes—included such men as Tommaso "Tom" Gagliano, Gaetano "Tommy" Lucchese, and Stefano "Steve" Rondelli. Reina had a relationship of convenience with Masseria; he was never a committed ally, but went along to keep things peaceful.

In Brooklyn, another group came on the scene headed by Salvatore DiBella, which included such men as Joseph Profaci and Joe Magliocco. Profaci and Vincent Mangano had recently arrived in New York from Chicago. Immigrants arriving in the new world tended to gravitate toward neighborhoods where relatives or others from their hometowns had relocated; hence Mangano remained in Manhattan, while Profaci went to Brooklyn.

Luciano's importance was growing, and the bad blood between Masseria and the Castellammarese worsened. On September 14, 1923, eighty-two thousand people gathered at New York's Polo Grounds arena to watch heavyweight champion Jack Dempsey defeat challenger Luis Firpo. Yet just as many people were there to see Luciano; for many, he was the real star of the evening. Tickets had been harder to get than an invitation to the White House, but Lansky made arrangements through the sportswriter Bill Corum; that night, more than two hundred people were Luciano's guests. Masseria met Luciano at the fight that night, and once again invited him to a meeting. A few days later, Luciano and Frank Costello met with Masseria in Little Italy. This time, Masseria offered Luciano the number-two position in his group, asking him to join forces in exchange for an equal say in Masseria's business. It was a rather disingenuous offer, considering that Masseria's real intent was to control everything himself. But Luciano made it clear (and Masseria agreed) that he would not demand any interest in the Combine's liquor business, and this piqued Luciano's interest. He told Masseria he would talk to his people and get back to him. Frank Costello advised him to "go for the deal," but Luciano's Jewish associates were suspicious of the Sicilians: Siegel came down against the proposed merger, and Lansky was cautious. Luciano turned down the offer a second time.

However polite his refusal may have been, in our world a second turndown is still an affront, and Luciano's decision soon became the talk of the town. It did, however, win Luciano some admirers among his peers—including the Mangano brothers (Vincent and Philip), Enoch "Nucky" Johnson of Atlantic City, and Moe Dalitz and John Scalise of Cleveland. More important, his decision was noted by two important liquor manufacturers, Sam Bronfman in Canada—a successful bootlegger who would found the Distillers Corporation in 1924 (just after Prohibition was repealed in Ontario) and acquire Joseph E. Seagram & Sons in 1928—and Lewis Rosensteil, the head of Schenley Products Company (predecessor of Schenley Industries, Inc.). It sent the message that Luciano was his own man and had no fear of Masseria.

In the New York area—which stretched south through New Jersey as far as Philadelphia and north as far as Boston—the bootlegging industry quickly grew from a handful of small independent operators trying to take advantage of one another, and became a profitable business and principal source of income for these groups. By the late 1920s, a trend toward consolidation had begun, as larger operators took over smaller ones and the intense competition brought about mergers.

If Prohibition proved an irresistible opportunity for these groups, it also gave rise to unbridled greed, which led to the Castellammarese War. The seven deadly sins of lust, gluttony, greed, sloth, wrath, envy, and pride were taught by the early Christians to educate followers concerning man's tendency to sin. The Catholic Church later grouped the sins into two categories: venial (relatively minor) sins, which could be forgiven through any sacrament of the Church, and capital or mortal

Police prohibition enforcement officers pouring out barrels of corn mash, 1921.

sins, which could be forgiven only through the sacrament of confession or through perfect contrition on the part of the penitent.

In addition to this array of sins large and small, Joe Masseria was guilty of a ravenous, insatiable, and unquenchable thirst for everything, with no thought of confession or contrition—only vengeance. Have you ever wondered why, when Sicilians emigrated all over the world, the only place where the Mafia developed was in the United States? The answer lies in the behavior of Masseria and others like him.

One of those men was Al Capone. The story of the Castellammarese War starts with an understanding of Capone's appetite for power.

Capone, a youngster in Brooklyn of Neapolitan ancestry, got his start working as a bartender for Francesco "Frankie" Ioele (a.k.a. Frankie Yale) in one of Yale's saloons in Coney Island. Yale was in the Masseria Family, with Brooklyn as his area of responsibility. Johnny Torrio, who had come to New York at the turn of the century from the Italian province of Basilicata, had gotten Yale involved in New York's famous Five Points Gang; he eventually became close to Masseria, and met Capone through them.

By the 1920s, however, Torrio was looking for some peace and quiet, so he moved to the more "relaxed" city of Chicago. Almost immediately, he began to disturb the status quo, elbowing his way into the lucrative liquor trade in Illinois. That business was mostly controlled by the Castellammarese Joe Aiello and the Irishman George "Bugs" Moran. It wasn't long before Torrio called for help from his old friends, Yale and Masseria. Masseria, seeing an opportunity to bolster his money, prestige, and power, ordered Yale to send Capone to Chicago to help Torrio.

In 1925, after surviving a near-fatal assassination attempt and spending a year in jail on a Prohibition rap, Torrio decided to retire and headed back to Italy. In his place, Capone took over his Chicago territory. Soon, Capone was expanding further into Castellammarese territory, encroaching on Aiello's business.

Capone's aggressive behavior couldn't go on indefinitely, and in 1929 a meeting was held in Chicago to talk about the "business encroachment" problem. The principal players present were Aiello of Chicago, Masseria of New York, and Gaspar Milazzo of Detroit.

Milazzo had immigrated to Brooklyn in 1911 from Castellammare del Golfo, becoming a respected senior member of the Castellammarese clan. Moving to Detroit in 1921, he established himself as a powerful Castellammarese *mafioso* in that city. When Capone began infiltrating his territory, Milazzo told Masseria to make Capone back down, or problems would erupt. But Masseria refused; instead, he warned Milazzo and Aiello to reconsider. On the surface, it might seem that Masseria's motivation was a desire to expand his liquor business from New York to Chicago. But his real intent was to consolidate power. His plan was to subjugate the Castellammarese, bringing them and other challengers under his control, while reaping the economic rewards that followed.

Masseria, only months earlier, had consolidated his power base in New York. Recognizing that Frankie Yale had too much territory and was becoming an uncomfortable threat, he dispatched (ordered the death of) Yale—who was gunned down on July 1, 1928—and divided up his territory: gambling and bootlegging went to Anthony "Augie" Carfano, and Al Mineo got the Brooklyn waterfront. A few months later, Masseria also dispatched Salvatore D'Aquila, Newark's local leader, who sided with Brooklyn's Castellammarese. The Newark group was then placed under the control of Al Mineo and absorbed into the Masseria group.

Masseria's goal wasn't just control over the Castellammarese in Chicago; he wanted control over all the Castellammarese. His strategy was to cut off the arms first, saving the head—the Maranzano group, the most powerful of the Castellammarese, operating out of New York—for last, when it would be most vulnerable.

After Masseria returned to New York, he ordered Milazzo and Stefano "Steve" Magaddino, leader of the Buffalo, New York, group, to a meeting in New York City. Magaddino, a fellow Castellammarese (and my father's cousin), refused even to consider the order. Milazzo told Masseria, "We already had our meeting in Chicago." This sent Masseria into a rage. In his grandiose, pompous, bombastic style, Masseria convened his group leaders and declared war on all Castellammarese Sicilians, lashing out at them as "people who are disrespectful and unruly."

In February 1930, in what is generally accepted as the first blow in the Castellammarese War, Joe Masseria ordered the killing of Bronx *mafioso* Gaetano Reina, a former ally he now suspected (rightly) of siding with Maranzano. Masseria continued the bloodshed by eliminating Milazzo along with Rosario "Sasa" Parrino, who had been with the Brooklyn Castellammarese Family and left to join the Milazzo Family in Detroit. Masseria dispatched Aiello later that year in Chicago, and also ordered the killing of my father's second cousin Vito Bonventre of the Brooklyn Castellammarese clan, one of Maranzano's men. He then sent word to Magaddino in Buffalo, threatening him with a similar fate if he didn't come to New York immediately.

Shortly thereafter, the Castellammarese held a meeting, calling in the leaders of five other Castellammarese Families, those in the Bronx, Buffalo, Chicago, Brooklyn, and Detroit. Salvatore Maranzano, a soldier in the Family, declared Masseria's words were "a dirty spot on the honor of Castellammare," and that was enough to rally the Families to action.

Masseria was aware that Colo Schiro did not have the stomach for war and would be ineffective as the leader of Brooklyn's Castellammarese, if challenged. Schiro was considered a weak link among the Castellammarese Families. He was really no more than a puppet fronting for Stefano Magaddino of the Buffalo Family. Masseria flaunted his power by ordering Schiro to bring him ten thousand dollars. Schiro, afraid of war, paid the money. Shortly thereafter he disappeared, probably on his own accord, out of shame for not standing up to Masseria.

But Masseria's attempted takeover was short-lived; after Schiro's disappearance in 1930, a stronger successor to Schiro emerged. Salvatore Maranzano, who had emigrated from Castellammare del Golfo in 1925, was selected as leader of the

Castellammarese. A respected *mafioso* in Sicily, Maranzano used his skills to unite the Castellammare clan in the United States as a closely knit group of men that followed the *mafioso* traditions from the old country. Although the Castellammarese were the smaller of the two prominent groups, its members were fiercely loyal, and with Maranzano at the helm it soon became an organized and formidable foe to other clans. It was a tight-lipped and an almost impenetrable group; anyone who was not an insider, and not Sicilian, was excluded on principle. Over time, this group would include a number of prominent names: Joe Parrino (Sasa's brother), Vito Bonventre (my father's uncle), Angelo Caruso, Frank Garofalo, John Tartamella; later on, Gaspar DiGregorio, Steve Cannone, Philip Rastelli, Carmine Galante, and Joseph Massimo, as well as my father, Joe Bonanno, and myself.

As early as 1928, Luciano and Lansky had concluded that the dizzying days of a booming economy and prosperity spurred by profits mainly from the illegal sale and distribution of liquor wouldn't last forever. Problems in the liquor business were looming: pricing; importation from Europe, Canada, and the Caribbean; and the real possibility of repeal of the Volstead Act.

There was also growing concern that the fierce competition with the Masseria and Maranzano groups would soon lead to a showdown. Luciano had made a big impression, especially in New York, and plenty of people were anxious to claim some affiliation with this rising star who controlled the liquor business during Prohibition. The Luciano/Lansky Combine would be the fly in the ointment, a pivotal factor in the outcome of the war.

Masseria wasn't the only leader trying to join forces with Luciano. Maranzano had been wooing Luciano since about 1926, when they first met. Maranzano wanted Luciano to join him, but in return he wanted complete loyalty, including requiring Luciano to abandon his friendships with his Jewish brethren and do business only with Italians preferably from Sicily. Luciano found that hard to accept. He wasn't about to abandon his childhood friendships with Lansky and Siegel. Nor was he willing to look past Maranzano's longtime conflict with another of his close friends, Arnold Rothstein, a financier and mentor known for teaching these younger guys some style. (Rothstein was widely reputed to have been behind the 1919 World Series fix known as the Black Sox scandal.) Maranzano also wasn't on the best of terms with Luciano's Calabrian allies Costello and Anastasia, or with the Neapolitans Genovese and Adonis.

Some people in a higher social echelon were getting to know Luciano and showing him some respect—including influential families such as the Kennedys, the Whitneys, and the Gimbels (of department store fame), many of whom were either business associates or liquor customers. Even then, people were fascinated with our world: polo players and society girls enjoyed listening to Luciano's stories about hijacking trucks and shooting it out with the Feds. If Luciano were to join Maranzano, he would have to give up all that prestige and access.

The men in Maranzano's Castellammarese clan understood Luciano's concerns. They were increasingly wary of Masseria, who was growing crazier and crazier as they watched.

Food has always played an important part in Sicilian life. It was said you could tell a lot about a man by how he ate. Some people eat because they're happy or content; others stuff themselves because they're nervous. To us, Masseria seemed like the nervous type of eater; he seemed to eat because he was an incomplete person. While the food intake was feeding his belly, the glutton in him was feeding his bully nature and his ego. The Castellammarese were willing to look the other way and let Masseria take his fill, "as long as he didn't bother us." They never considered appeasing Masseria, because appeasement never brought concessions—Sicilian history had taught us that principle. If they could benefit from some type of "accommodation," that was a different story. Unlike the more violent Masseria, Maranzano and Luciano both believed in seeking peace rather than killing each other off. As my father, Joe Bonanno, told me many times, "The better path is to survive using accommodation rather than violence. If you use violence, remember, it can also be used against you."

Luciano was walking a tightrope anchored by Masseria at one end and Maranzano at the other. He really wanted nothing to do with either of these Sicilian groups, whom he saw as a bunch of old Mustache Petes who were either too greedy for power or more interested in the old traditions than in making money.

Always a thinker, Luciano played it smart. Convinced that war was imminent, he decided it was time to wheel and deal. He gave verbal assurances to Masseria that if he made a move against Maranzano, he would take Masseria up on his offer and become his number-two man. Masseria may have been a foreigner, he reasoned, but at least he was a known commodity. These others, while also foreigners, kept low profiles and did not telegraph their intentions. They were people to be wary of, and Luciano knew it. Luciano just couldn't get himself to trust Maranzano—and he really thought Masseria was the stronger of the two, in both wealth and power.

What Masseria never knew—which only the most intimate and highest echelons of the Maranzano group did—was that prior to Reina's death, Luciano had secretly sent word to Maranzano, via Reina, that he wasn't happy with Masseria's attitude, and would stand aside if hostilities developed between the two warriors.

Luciano was playing both ends against the middle.

On November 5, 1930, the Castellammarese retaliated by killing Al Mineo and Masseria's right-hand man, Stefano "Steve" Ferrigno; they just missed ambushing Masseria himself. The shootings raged on into 1931, with the M1928 Thompson submachine gun, invented in 1919, the new weapon of choice. There were literally hundreds of killings on both sides. Masseria's allies were either dead or about to be killed; Masseria himself had gone into hiding in an attempt to regroup.

Maranzano, in a strategic move, placed a call to Masseria's ally Al Capone in Chicago. "We broke Masseria's chain," he warned Capone—meaning that Masseria had lost his power and the end was near. Capone knew that Masseria's death would make him vulnerable because he did not yet have the official stamp as leader of Chicago. (The word *capone*, translated, is a capon, a castrated male chicken—ironic under the circumstances.) Maranzano's phone call was intended to alert Capone that he would be wise to change his allegiance—and that, if he did, Capone and other Masseria allies would be treated as "innocent" victims of Masseria and would not be harmed, in the interests of future peace.

Convinced that he would be on the losing side of a battle with the two Sicilian groups, Luciano was anxious to save his skin by switching to the now-obvious winning faction, and asked to meet with Maranzano, who agreed to see him. My father, Joe Bonanno, was second to Maranzano, and he attended that meeting. Luciano was accompanied by Vito Genovese— a Neapolitan, not a Sicilian—who shared Luciano's interest in making profits over honoring the old Sicilian traditions.

As my father recalled, Luciano told them that Masseria was crazy, that he was ruining things for everyone. Murdering Castellammarese demanded reprisals that would attract the attention of the police. That in turn affected our other businesses, which police had conveniently overlooked in the past. If the killings did not stop, soon we would kill each other off; the Castellammarese War had to end.

Luciano was desperate to keep the conversation secret, warning that Masseria would kill him if he found out about the meeting. Maranzano replied, "You are the son of a Siciliano, so I give priority to you. You have a week, two weeks at most to kill him. Otherwise, I will have Masseria killed." Maranzano assured Luciano and Genovese that they would not be held responsible for Masseria's death. "Joe the Boss got to go," he concluded. But if Masseria did not die within a week or two, there would be no clemency for Luciano or Genovese.

April 15, 1931, was warm and sunny, a beautiful New York spring day. After a morning of meetings, Luciano met Masseria at the Nuova Villa Tammaro restaurant in Coney Island, where he had invited the Sicilian boss and a couple of the boys to lunch. After everyone else had left, Luciano and Masseria stayed behind, idling the afternoon away playing cards in the empty restaurant. Gerardo Scarpato, the restaurant owner, was busy in the kitchen cleaning up from the luncheon crowd and preparing for dinner. Shortly before 3:30, Luciano excused himself to go to the men's room. He entered the restroom just as four men quietly entered the restaurant. Vito Genovese and Albert Anastasia came in by the side door, Joe Adonis and Ben Siegel by the front door. They walked over to where Joe Masseria was sitting and fired more than twenty bullets, six of which smashed solidly into Masseria and dispatched him to another place and time. Then the four—Genovese, Adonis, Anastasia, and Siegel—quietly but quickly turned and left as they entered. A car driven by Ciro Terranova carried them away from the scene.

Many stories have been written about that fateful day. Questions have been asked: How long was Luciano in the men's room? What was he doing inside? What did he tell the police once they arrived? How did the four shooters get into the waiting car? There were rumors that Terranova was too excited to drive and Siegel had to get behind the wheel. Exactly how the newspapermen of the time got these stories, and how much art reflected life, will never be known. The tradition of law enforcement, the media, and writers purporting to explain exactly how things happen—in a world they know little about—continues to this day.

One of the age-old criticisms of *cosa nostra* is the idea that everything cost more because of the activities of our world. But that relationship, like all things, is relative. In the early twentieth century, for instance, the garment industry and the stock market were core components of New York City's economy. And it was our world that kept the manufacturers going, by supplying certain services which, while condemned by some, were craved by others. In that respect, we were very creative. If manufacturers wanted their merchandise shipped without trouble or interruption, we were a reliable partner. We catered to one group, and the Stock Exchange catered to another. While we may have muscled some in the industry, what does a stockbroker do when his customer can't meet a margin call on a stock the brokerage firm pandered to him in the first place? He sells the client out and then the client ends up jumping off a building—which is just what happened in many cases after October 1929.

Needless to say, none of the activities in our world could have succeeded in the long term without the protection of the city's police and political structure. The politicians of the city kept New York rolling. Money bought protection, although the price grew from a free turkey at Christmas to thousands of dollars. Members of the city's law enforcement and political organizations already formed a brotherhood with those in our world, which was the price and condition of society's survival: politicians, law enforcement officials, and members of the press could be found each night in our illegal speakeasies, drinking our illegal liquor and supporting illegal payments to the highest echelons of this upper world.

The Castellammarese War was a struggle for who would control our half of that partnership—the Sicilian group leaders who had first brought our way of life to these shores, or the younger, more ambitious generation represented by Luciano and his associates. Lucky Luciano may have been born in Sicily, but he was never restricted by old-world traditions. At heart he was an American whose guiding principle was the bottom line. And his group, the Combine, had little tolerance for the old-world Sicilians who had preceded them to the United States. When the pressure between these competing factions reached the breaking point, the result was what many believe to be the bloodiest war the American underworld ever saw.

The Castellammarese War drew to a close in the spring of 1931. With the cessation of actual fighting after the death of Masseria, one job remained: a new order of affairs had to be established. In order for our world to regain a working relationship and live in peace, the various leaders of the Families had to realign themselves within the new reality.

In New York, the alignment was largely established by the outcome of the war. In a series of meetings among the leaders of our world, the new alignments were acknowledged and the birth of a new regime came into being. The Castellammarese group was now headed by Salvatore Maranzano; the Reina Family was now headed by Tom Gagliano; the old Mineo Family was taken over by Frank Scalice; Luciano took control of the Masseria Family; and Joe Profaci remained head of his Family. All the new leaders had either supported or had been allies of the Castellammarese, so Maranzano emerged clearly as the center of the new axis.

It was a good order, but it couldn't last. From the moment he established his conflicting alliances with Masseria and Maranzano, Luciano knew the day would come when only one would be left, and he would be facing one last battle. Now the leader of the Castellammarese group, Salvatore Maranzano, had emerged as his chief rival. Maranzano was a Mustache Pete, content with the status quo. In Luciano's view, he was no good for business. He had to go.

My father later recalled that after Masseria was dispatched in April 1931, Maranzano staked a claim to dominance among all the leaders. "Maranzano gives amnesty to everybody," he said of himself with typical grandiosity. "Everybody wants peace and everybody wants to see Maranzano. All the bosses in the United States bow to Maranzano."

The 1931 Meetings:
Wappingers Falls and Chicago

But it wasn't as simple as that. Although the new order was clear to the New York Families after the end of the Castellammarese War, there were other out-of-town Families that had participated directly in the war—some for the Castellammarese, some indirectly against them—and still others that had remained neutral. The leaders of all these regional Families had to be told how New York was aligned. And so, in May 1931, a month after Masseria's death, a meeting was arranged to clarify the situation.

The meeting would take place in the upstate New York village of Wappingers Falls, a small community in Dutchess County on the east side of the Hudson River south of Pough-keepsie. During the height of Prohibition, this area was a safe haven for the many stills producing bootleg alcohol for the Maranzano Family. The chosen location for the meeting was a large resort-style home owned by Gaspar DiGregorio, a trusted Maranzano group leader. One of the *capos* bragged that his son was an airplane pilot and offered Maranzano the use of an airplane for the meeting. Maranzano accepted brazenly, saying, "Yes, have your son fly around over the meeting with a bomb. If somebody don't follow my order, everybody will be bombed!" Maranzano would never have done any such thing, but his comment must have impressed the other Sicilians, as it was doubtless meant to do.

The two-day meeting in Wappingers Falls was a great success. By the time it was over, the Family alignments were in place, loyalties pledged, and a sense of future well-being filled the air. Now the only thing that remained was for all the Families nationwide to get together and establish a lasting peace.

Maranzano proposed the meeting to allow everyone to identify and place himself within the political structure, and to confirm Al Capone's position as the leader of the Chicago Family. At Wappingers Falls, my father later recalled, "Capone asked and offered Maranzano, 'If I may have the honor to host the grand meeting in Chicago, I will pay for everything.'" And so, a short time later, Al Capone went on to host a national meeting in Chicago at the Congress Hotel, which he is said to have owned and used as his headquarters. It would be the first—and, as it turned out, the last—national convention in our world.

Maranzano, along with John Montana, Steve Magaddino's second in command, and the men my father referred to as the "boys of the first day"—his supporters in the war with Masseria, including Vincent Danna, Magaddino, Sebastiano "Buster" Domingo, Natale Evola, Charles DiBenedetto, and my father—traveled to Chicago for the meeting. Their goal was to assure other Castellammarese across the country that the trouble among Capone, Milazzo, and Aiello was in the past and that a new day was dawning. After Maranzano was formally recognized as the new leader, his first act was to confirm Capone as the leader of Chicago. Many of the leaders of Families made speeches praising peace, and praising Maranzano. Then, my father recalled, Capone requested to address the conference. "Capone, he stands and he say, 'Can I have the honor to talk? Can I have the honor to nominate Mr. Maranzano as 'the boss of all the bosses'?"

A rare photo of Al Capone inscribed to my father:
"To my friend Joe Cool."

My father later told me, "Maranzano was the last boss of bosses, king of kings. The first one and the last one."

After returning to New York that May, everyone went about picking up the pieces from the preceding two years. My father was twenty-six, about to be married, somewhat affluent, his name now well-known throughout our world. Having distinguished himself with both the younger and the older elements in our world, he was optimistic, looking toward a future of peace and tranquillity—or so he hoped.

He was also looking forward to refocusing his attention on civilian life, on making a living for himself and his family. Most of the "boys of the first day" had no source of outside income per se. Maranzano, though, had real-estate holdings (income property, tenement buildings, acreage on Long Island leased out to farmers), and an import-export business, plus a fleet of fishing boats and a farm in upstate New York. Maranzano had been sent to the New World by the acknowledged leader of the Sicilian Mafia, Vito Cascio Ferro, to pave the way for Ferro to come to the United States in flight from Mussolini's oppressive regime. But Ferro was jailed in Italy before he could depart, leaving Maranzano to make his way on his own. In fact, Maranzano was well-equipped to carry on without Ferro: an educated man who had brought wealth with him from Sicily, he was no poor immigrant but a resourceful businessman.

During this period of adjustment, however, my father started seeing Maranzano less and less frequently. He had been with his mentor almost daily for nearly two years, but now days would go by without them seeing each other in person. As the old song goes, "Absence makes the heart grow fonder—for someone else." As the days went by, my father sensed a distancing between his mentor and the "boys of the first day." And they sensed that Maranzano's sense of obligation was drifting; Gaspar DiGregorio, a Maranzano group leader, grumbled about the tardiness of whatever rewards were to come their way.

By now, my father's wedding plans were beginning to take shape, and he was rarely going into the city. But he was hearing complaints from the others about how Maranzano was treating them. The leader was often late to appointments, and when he did arrive he acted increasingly aristocratic, imperious, and forbidding—behavior they had not seen in the past from him. The grumblings began to concern my father, but at first he dismissed them, thinking he was reading too much into them. My father later recalled one dinner when he had to sit through an entire evening's worth of complaints from his cousin Stefano Magaddino and DiGregorio about how Maranzano was slighting them.

On September 10, 1931, my father received an urgent phone call from Buster Domingo, telling him to leave his apartment at once. Salvatore Maranzano had been killed. Neither Domingo nor any of Maranzano's other lieutenants knew anything more. There was no time to wonder who had committed the act; their main concern was whether they were next. All six "boys of the first day" went into hiding.

My father told me his first thought was that Maggadino had finally settled his score with Maranzano. In subsequent talks with Maggadino, however, he learned that his fears were unfounded. Stefano may have been pleased to see Maranzano gone, but he wasn't the instigator of his departure. "Power went to his head" might have been an appropriate epitaph for Maranzano. My father told me that he might have agreed, at least in part, with that sentiment, but he was truly baffled by Maranzano's elimination. Just three months earlier, Maranzano had won a war; now he was a corpse. Obviously, something had gone wrong.

Over the years I had many occasions to discuss the history of our world with my father, a direct link to this bygone era. In all those discussions, the only time my father seemed reluctant to go into specifics was when the subject of Maranzano's death came up.

After Maranzano was killed, my father received a message delivered by Magaddino: Luciano had taken responsibility for the killing and wanted a meeting as soon as possible to discuss the situation. War was a real possibility.

Angelo Caruso, the leader of a strong non-Castellammarese group within Maranzano's predominantly Castellammarese

Family, stepped in as acting head of the Family. Caruso was not the type of leader needed in time of war. He wasn't sure if reprisals might follow, but he did know that if trouble was going to come, it would be from people like the "boys of the first day"— Danna, DiGregorio, Domingo, Evola, DiBenedetto, and my father, all of them group leaders who had stood beside Maranzano in the Castellammarese War.

Luciano asked to meet with Caruso and the Castellammarese. The nuances of protocol in our world would not permit Luciano to demand a meeting with specific individuals, so Caruso quickly called a Family meeting to decide whom to send, convinced that Luciano would be more comfortable discussing the situation with one of the group leaders most directly involved in the Castellammarese War.

Caruso knew that my father was not a bloodthirsty individual. But Joe Bonanno had a reputation for doing what he had to do, and he could be relied on to make the right decision for everyone. My father often used the expression *tagliare carne e osso*—as he explained, "When you make a decision, you have to use a knife that cuts meat and bone, and cut right down the middle. You do not go off to the side or try to go around it to avoid cutting the bone. If someone gets in the way, it's his fault, not yours." In other words, you have to cut right to the heart of the matter.

Later, when my father was elected to the position of *rappresentante* of the Bonanno Family, this attitude served him well. (After Maranzano's death, the group of men loyal to him elected Joe Bonanno as *rappresentante* when the Commission was formed in 1931. The Family was thereafter referred to as the Bonanno Family, a name which remains to this day. DiGregorio, who previously served Maranzano as a group leader, became a group leader in the Bonanno Family.) The fact that everyone knew he operated in this fashion kept them honest to the values of our tradition. There was no reason for anyone to worry about screwing up, as long as their errors weren't malicious. My father recognized that people made mistakes, and everyone knew it. He might pass on a verbal reprimand, maybe even some sort of sanction—along with an explanation to help you avoid making the same mistake again. If you made a wrong decision, you simply had to straighten it out. That was my father's way.

However, my father was not a man to be trifled with. Vincent Tarantola, a contemporary of my father and *capodecina* in the Bonanno Family, recalled that, at the height of his power, Joe Bonanno "was one of the most feared men in our world." He had a hot Sicilian temper that could be triggered instantly when provoked. Tarantola used the Sicilian slang word *ammazzalo* (meaning "Kill him!") whenever anyone had provoked Joe Bonanno after fair warning was given: "In English, Mr. B had a simpler phrase with the same meaning: 'Goodbye, Jack.'"

After Maranzano's death, the concept of *capo di tutti capi* (boss of all bosses) disappeared from our world. It would exist only in the minds of novelists, screenwriters, and law enforcement officials, nothing more than a myth.

The real world was far more complicated. In the summer of 1931, Lucky Luciano was desperate to keep the remaining members of both Sicilian groups from turning on the Combine and each other. He requested that meeting with the Castellammarese group to raise the prospect of reaching a shared understanding that would allow the Families to continue in peace.

Luciano's proximate agenda was to pacify the Castellammarese by explaining his involvement in the Maranzano killing. But he also intended his approach to set an example for how to resolve disputes among the Families. Luciano recognized that it made much more sense to sit and talk than to fight and spill blood. He seized the moment to step forward and advise the rival mob bosses that, in his memorable phrase,

"We can't make money with a gun in our hands." That single statement is at the core of Luciano's claim to have conceived what became known as the Commission.

In response to Luciano's request, the Castellammarese selected my father, Joe Bonanno, to meet with Luciano to consider the matter. Together, Luciano and my father formulated the blueprint and ground rules that would give shape to this new peace. And together they assumed the task of persuading the leaders of the other Families that a Commission to mediate disputes was the answer.

By the early 1930s, there were twenty-six Families in the United States. Each Family was autonomous and operated independently without consulting their counterparts. The first act of this new Commission was to declare that the day of the absolute leader—the boss of all bosses—was over. In its place would come a new era, one in which the sovereignty of each of the Families in New York and throughout the United States would be respected. The New York City Families would dominate the Commission; and, since those Families were now at peace, the rest of our world was at peace.

The Commission was an idea whose time had come. In the years that followed, there would be far fewer disturbances on the streets of New York, less friction among the Families, and less police involvement with members of our world (except for the weekly envelope collections to law enforcement officials and to the politicians). Politicians, police officers, newspapermen, ex-bootleggers, labor leaders, and the rest of society were all now involved in the monumental task of rebuilding, after hitting economic rock bottom during the Great Depression. The old ways, like yesterday, were gone—dead and buried.

By the mid-1930s, two of the twenty-six Families—Birmingham, Alabama, and Newark, New Jersey—were disbanded, reducing the total number of Families in the United

States to twenty-four. The Birmingham Family asked for disbandment when its youngest member turned eighty years old and the only prospect for membership was a youngster of seventy-four. The Commission, in its wisdom, granted the request for disbandment and assigned Gaetano Gagliano of the Bronx to look after the needs of the remaining surviving members. By 1938, there were no living members and the Alabama Family simply disappeared.

The Newark situation was another story. It is a story of violence and blood. Around 1928, just before the Castellammarese War, Joe Masseria had formed a Family of men loyal to him in Newark. After his death, however, the leaders of this Newark Family resisted the combined forces of Luciano and Maranzano. In response, the order was given for elimination of the Newark Family leadership. For the next few years, friction would continue between New York and the surviving members of the Newark Family. Finally, around 1934 or 1935, the Newark Family disbanded. The remaining members were given the option to join any of the New York Families. Some remained in the area, but others moved as far away as Buffalo and Pittsburgh.

The Commission was a purely American concept; no such idea would emerge in Sicily until after 1957. And it was a successful idea: As time went on, people in our world were able to interact with each other because now there was a stabilizing force to keep everyone honest.

The Families granted the Commission jurisdiction, power, and authority to determine certain issues. It was not a supreme power, as most outside our world believe. Rather, it simply administered diplomatic policy and ruled by consensus. It never told any Family what to do, beyond the limited powers it was granted by the Families themselves. The Commission's action or inaction, after diplomatic consensus, was final, but its policies could be reversed over time if the Families agreed to change them. As time went on, the Families empowered the Commission to take on other responsibilities aimed at maintaining peace among them.

Relationships, and the tradition of the *mafiosi* who emigrated from Sicily and became leaders of their Families, were the foundation for the Commission's success. Most of the twenty-six Family leaders had relationships with each other that had originated in Sicily. For example, Filippo "Phil" Bruccola (Boston), Stefano Magaddino (Buffalo), Gaspar Milazzo (Detroit), Giuseppe "Joseph" DiGiovanni (Kansas City, Missouri), Salvatore Sabella (Philadelphia), and my father, Joseph Bonanno (Brooklyn), were all from the same town of Castellammare del Golfo in Sicily. Many other Family leaders were from nearby towns and villages in western Sicily, and most of them had known each other in the old country. In similar fashion, the leaders of Tampa, Los Angeles, San Jose, Milwaukee, and Madison were interconnected through business and socially, with children intermarrying and forming such a tight circle that it was hard for outsiders—and even insiders—to penetrate.

5

The 1931 Initial Commission Meeting

We can't make money with a gun in our hands.

Charlie "Lucky" Luciano

The way to understand the role of the Commission is to picture it as the palm of your hand. The Families are like fingers extending from the palm, working independently of each other, but they are unified by their attachment to the palm.

The Original Five Commission Members

GAGLIANO FAMILY	• Gaetano Gagliano • Rappresentante
MANGANO FAMILY	• Vincent Mangano • Rappresentante
BONANNO FAMILY	• Joseph Bonanno Sr. • Rappresentante
LUCIANO FAMILY	• Charlie "Lucky" Luciano • Rappresentante
PROFACI FAMILY	• Joseph Profaci • Rappresentante

The tumultuous year of 1931 marked the beginning of a series of all-important Commission meetings, in which a series of conflicts and disputes were mediated and resolved, usually successfully.

The Half Moon Hotel, on the Boardwalk at West Twenty-ninth Street at Coney Island in Brooklyn, New York, was the site of the first meeting of the Commission, in October 1931. Its purpose was to discuss and ratify the concept of the Committee of Peace, changed to "the Commission," a shorter name that would be easier to refer to when speaking. The Half Moon Hotel would become better known for an event that occurred there ten years later: Abe "Kid Twist" Reles, a hitman for Murder, Inc., was being held in his sixth-floor room of the Half Moon under police protection (having turned government witness) when he "fell" to his death out the window, landing faceup on the roof of the hotel's kitchen. He was thereafter referred to, postmortem, as "the canary who sang but couldn't fly."

The Half Moon Hotel on the Boardwalk at West Twenty-ninth Street in Coney Island.

The first Commission consisted of the senior members of the five New York Families that lived through the Castellammarese War: Joseph Bonanno, Brooklyn; Joseph Profaci, Brooklyn; Gaetano "Tommy" Gagliano, Bronx; Vincent Mangano, Brooklyn and Manhattan; and Charlie "Lucky" Luciano, New Jersey and Manhattan. All five were Sicilian-born (although Luciano had emigrated to America around the age of ten).

Courtesy NYC Municipal Archives

*Abe Reles on the roof of the kitchen of
Half Moon Hotel.*

Luciano recognized that in order to make money, all of the Families—in New York and throughout the country—had to work together, to dismiss any thought of retaliation after the Castellammarese War. In particular, it was crucial to preserve our standing arrangement with politicians. If the Families continued to fight, and dead bodies kept showing up on the streets of New York City, public outrage would force the politicians to crack down and our political power would be lost.

The first principle of the Commission was that all Family leaders would be treated as equals and allies and each Family would have autonomy within its own jurisdiction. Some cities, including Chicago, remained aloof from Commission business except when it affected them directly, and enjoyed a somewhat quasi-independent status. By the time the Commission was empowered, the rival Chicago groups of the 1920s had merged into one Family controlled by Al Capone. There and elsewhere, most cities beyond New York were ruled by a single Family, an arrangement that created less tension and discord, giving each Family greater scope and flexibility to solve its problems without the burden of inter-Family conflicts in the same city.

Commission Members as of Late 1931

GAGLIANO FAMILY	• Gaetano Gagliano • Rappresentante
MANGANO FAMILY	• Vincent Mangano • Rappresentante
BONANNO FAMILY	• Joseph Bonanno Sr. • Rappresentante
LUCIANO FAMILY	• Charlie "Lucky" Luciano • Rappresentante
PROFACI FAMILY	• Joseph Profaci • Rappresentante
BUFFALO FAMILY	• Stefano Maggadino • Rappresentante
CHICAGO FAMILY	• Paul Ricca • Rappresentante

Before the year 1931 was over, there was one final Commission meeting, held in Chicago. By that time, the Commission had grown to include seven members. At this meeting, the Commission added another Sicilian, my father's cousin Stefano Magaddino, as the leader of the Buffalo family, and Al Capone, the first Neapolitan in the group, as leader of the Chicago Family. When Capone was indicted later that year for income-tax evasion, the Chicago Family replaced him with Paul Ricca, who took Capone's place on the Commission.

There was never an even number of members on the Commission. The original was five, then seven, and then nine. This was all for a very good reason. Since each member had an equal say in all matters, an odd number of votes would assure a decision.

At this 1931 meeting, the Commission resolved to meet roughly every five years, at which time the members would ratify its continuation for the next five years, if all agreed. Before adjournment, the Commission members would select a chairman, who would serve for the next five years and chair the next scheduled meeting, unless replaced in the interim. The chairman—in this case, Vincent Mangano—had no more formal authority than any other Commission member; however, his influence could change the outcome of a vote. Replacement could be for any number of reasons: death, natural or otherwise; retirement from active duty as a Family leader; sickness or other inability to continue—or for cause.

During the five years between meetings, the selected chairman would serve as the contact person whenever a problem surfaced that needed attention. It was the chairman's decision whether to discuss an interim problem with other Commission members. If a quorum of the Commission members agreed, it could hold an extraordinary, unscheduled Commission meeting. These extraordinary meetings usually pertained to local matters involving relationships that affected members of more than one Family. On a rare occasion, if requested by a Family, the Commission might aid in an intra-Family problem. If the Commission held an extraordinary meeting, the members most likely to be affected by the outcome would be responsible for gathering the facts and making a presentation to the full Commission.

The Commission, as Luciano and my father devised it, could remain in place for decades, provided all members ratified its continuation. But in those years, there were very few extraordinary Commission meetings. The matters discussed at those meetings were of such importance that they affected our world throughout the entire United States.

The Commission's Role in Death Sentences

The notion that the Commission was the ultimate authority for handing out death sentences is a myth—an unchallenged proposition perpetuated by authors, newspaper reporters, and other self-anointed experts writing about our world based on second- or thirdhand information from unreliable sources. Such ideas often came from informers such as Joe Valachi, who never rose above the rank of *soldato* (soldier, the initial level in the rank of made men) and never attended a Commission meeting. Through the years, such misconceptions have also resulted from eavesdropping on conversations between second-echelon Family members, or through faulty interpretations of events discussed in wiretapped conversations.

The purpose of the Commission was to maintain peace among the Families, not to promote war. The Commission never issued a death sentence requiring the elimination of a Family member. In a dispute between two Families, the Commission's role was to hear the facts, deliberate, and determine who was right and who was wrong. Once the Commission reached its finding, it would communicate its conclusion to both parties. The choice of punishment was left to the aggrieved party—up to and including the death penalty.

The method of communicating the Commission's findings had its own protocol. Each Commission member outside New York communicated with a specific New York liaison, chosen according to region. My father, Joe Bonanno, served as the contact for Families in Colorado and Dallas and for the three California Families.

The Commission member assigned to the Family involved in the dispute was delegated the responsibility to deliver the Commission's conclusion to the leader of that Family. Any decision that might involve a death sentence had to be delivered in person by two members. The second member was also required to be present at the meeting when the Commission reached its conclusion. This was a way of providing checks and balances within the system, to ensure that the communication was delivered correctly and without any potential misinterpretation. Then it was up to the aggrieved Family to carry out whatever sentence it deemed appropriate.

The offending Family lived by the consequences, knowing that the Commission would offer no reprieve or pardon. If the aggrieved Family decided that a death sentence was the appropriate remedy, it could act accordingly; the Commission leaders sitting in judgment on the matter would not interfere in the method of punishment selected, and would preserve the peace among the other Families.

If the Commission so chose, it could sanction the death of someone outside the Families—such as the death of a public figure, the head of a major corporation, or the leader of a foreign nation. If it did so, all the Families across the country took responsibility. If one or two Families decided to dispatch someone outside the Family, we considered it a local matter, unsanctioned by the Commission. Only the Families participating in an unsanctioned hit took responsibility for the outcome—whether good or bad.

In any group there are differences of opinion as to both interpretation and proper application of the rules in a given situation. Values instilled by Family members, experiences with others in our world, and outsiders all influenced these opinions. The job of the chairman of the Commission was to bring all these men into agreement. The goal was to reach a decision that reflected all points of view, in order to achieve a satisfactory resolution of a particular problem.

From the very onset of the Commission's creation, it was obvious that there were ideological differences between the liberal younger members and the older, more conservative members—between the men who grew up within the American business culture and those who remained faithful to the old Sicilian traditions. This division would plague our world for almost thirty years. Through most of that period, the conservative members generally prevailed. But the enticement of money from narcotics and the introduction of non-Sicilians into the Families—together with the aging of the conservative members and the younger members' ambition for power—ultimately tipped the balance toward the liberal faction.

But the real power base in the Commission was always the New York contingent.

Even after the Commission started including Families from other cities, the New York Families dominated the Commission—so much so that the history of the Commission is largely the history of the rise and fall of the various New York Family leaders. With its intense energy and network of affiliations and rivalries, the city was like a volcano, erupting periodically and spewing its aftermath in concentric circles affecting almost everyone. Unlike their country cousins, who usually lived long and healthy lives and died of natural causes, Family leaders in New York led precarious lives. As a result, most of the Family leaders invoked protective measures, for defensive purposes.

6

Protocol of a
Commission Meeting

*God gave us two eyes and one mouth so we could see more
than we could talk.*

Joe Bonanno

Commission meetings, like the meetings of a Family's Administration, had definitive procedural rules and strict protocol.
Whenever a quorum was present (three when the Commission
had five members, four when it had seven, five when there were
nine), it signified that whatever was decided became policy.

To be a member of the Commission, you had to be the
leader of a Family. Those members, and any other members
they added to the Commission, decided how many and which
Family leaders would be added over the ensuing years.

All the members of the Commission were friends in both
social life and business. They enjoyed each other's company,
and after the business sessions concluded, the meetings turned
into occasions for dinner and drinking. We discussed business
and political issues of the country and the world and exchanged
social information. We might talk about a son who was in col-
lege or had been appointed to the United States Military or
Naval Academy; a daughter's engagement and wedding plans;

or a young grandson or granddaughter about to be baptized. By the time we said *arrivederci*, we shared a sense that tomorrow would bring good things; we were at peace with ourselves and the world.

We held all the formally sanctioned Commission meetings in the homes of people known by members. I never heard of a meeting in a quasi-public or public place. The host was usually someone from the appointed area who had facilities to accommodate twenty to twenty-five people in an easily accessible location, and the location always had security protecting those in attendance from prying eyes. Since Commission meetings were generally held to discuss pending problems or make new policy, the Commission members most affected by the potential outcome could ask for an extraordinary meeting and offer the time and place, after consultation.

The people participating in a Commission meeting would arrive at staggered times, in twos or threes to avoid attracting suspicion. At any formal Commission meeting, I always saw the men in attendance wearing suits and ties. Some always dressed better than others, either because of the way they were built or because of their personality or demeanor. For example, Joe Profaci, a short, stocky guy who worked in the olive-oil business with his shirtsleeves rolled up, paid more attention to business matters than to his looks and manner of dress. On the other hand, Tommy Lucchese—a.k.a. "Three-Fingers Brown" Lucchese—was always dressed to the nines, had a jeweler's eye for detail, and never had a hair out of place. (Contrary to the public's general perception, our members worked long hours in "legitimate" businesses, paid rent or mortgages, paid taxes, took their kids to school, went to church, and did all the things other people did who were not "connected.")

Attendance at Commission meetings depended on the agenda and the matters under discussion. If the meeting involved confrontational matters, all members of the Commission would attend, usually accompanied by their *sotto capos* (underbosses) and highest-ranking members of their Administrations. In less confrontational meetings, only those who had some stake in the outcome might attend, with each *rappresentante* (the Family's leader) bringing two or three members of his Family's Administration. These members were generally old-timers—often including the *consigliere* (the Family's adviser or counselor), who was well-versed in the history of our tradition. The inclusion of old-timers was no accident, for they could be relied on to mentally record what transpired at the meeting faithfully, for future reference. (For obvious reasons, we never took written minutes.)

As the members arrived, they gathered for light refreshments and talked while awaiting the arrival of the full contingent, giving them a chance to catch up on personal matters before the Commission officially convened to discuss business. My father told me that this served an important purpose, at least for him and others brought up in the old-world tradition. When he was chairman, he would arrive a little early to observe how the men would interact. In particular, he would pay attention to which members stepped away from the others to talk in small groups. This gave him insight into alliances he could expect—and to potential conflicts. He used these clues to determine how to accommodate the different interests of each member and to tailor the discussion in the meeting to achieve the results he desired.

His mind worked like that of a chess player, attempting to anticipate the moves of others well in advance. But this was no game; he took his position as chairman very seriously. Decisions on matters before the Commission could have life-or-death ramifications.

After entering the meeting room, the members sat in chairs arranged in a circle or around a circular table. The circle signified our tradition, which has no beginning and no end—

and served as a reminder that each member had equal status. The chairman called the meeting to order by announcing in Sicilian, "Attaccarmu tornu" ("Let's tie the circle"). At that precise moment, the outside world ceased to exist. The only authority for this group of men was its selected chairman, who represented hundreds of years of our tradition. For the duration of the meeting, there would be no drinking, no smoking, and no leaving the circle—for one who left the circle would be creating a weak link within that circle, thereby shattering the bond. (Those not seated at the Commission table—including the *capos* and *sotto capos*—would sit behind their respective leaders, usually in chairs placed along the walls of the meeting room, in much the same way that congressional aides sit behind their representatives during televised congressional hearings, ready for consultation if summoned.)

When the chairman declared "Attaccarmu tornu," it was the signal for the Commission members, and anyone else invited into the circle, to stand and join hands, completing the circle. The chairman would then utter one of two other statements in Sicilian: "En nome del la nostra constitutione, il tornu attacadu" ("In the name of our constitution, the circle is tied") or "En nome del la fratelanza, il tornu attacadu" ("In the name of our fraternity, the circle is tied"). The members would then unclasp their hands and sit around the table.

For the members, this tying of the circle had a stronger significance than the swearing of an oath in a courtroom. On occasion, a nonmember invitee could join the circle if summoned, if what he had to say would be relevant to the deliberations in the matters at hand. Such invitees would understand that their testimony was limited to reporting the facts, not interpreting them.

The circle gave sanctity to what was said, and it was expected that no ulterior motives would compromise a speaker's testimony. In our world, the true *mafioso* was guided by the essence of *omertà*, the admonition to act in a manly way: in the circle, we could say anything we knew about anyone or any situation, whether friend or foe, without fear of reprisal. (In the popular imagination, the concept of *omertà* is understood as a code of silence—but in our world this applied only to outsiders. It is much the same as choosing to remain silent in a criminal courtroom rather than informing on a friend.) In testimony before the Commission, however, complete truthfulness is the only acceptable testimony. He who speaks before the Commission assumes the immense burden of the weight of centuries of tradition upon his shoulders.

The rules regarding talking, leaving the room, and eating apply to all those in the room. No one seated behind the men at the table could speak unless specifically addressed by a Commission member. Their presence indicated their elevated rank within their Family, and served as a reminder of the importance of keeping such trusted members privy to the problems brought before the Commission and educating them on how those problems might be resolved.

The chairman then informed the attendees of why they were gathered, and announced the pertinent matters on the agenda. One of the chairman's most important powers was to decide which subjects were to be discussed, and in what order. Most of the subjects were interrelated, and the skillful chairman would manage to guide the conversation, choosing the order of presentation he believed would result in the best decision for everyone.

By the time the matter at hand was on the table ready for a vote, the chairman would have a pretty good idea which way the members were leaning. Depending on his own point of view, he could then choose to bring it to a vote, or to continue discussions in an effort to reach the result he desired. Before voting, each member would have an opportunity to express his view, so that everyone present would know where everyone else stood on the matter. More often than not, votes were divided evenly between the conservatives and liberals, leaving the chairman as the tie-breaker. It was every chairman's hope to rule by consensus and resolve each matter in a way that was acceptable to the majority, without having to cast his tie-breaking vote.

The person selected as chairman served in a dual capacity: as a *punto di appoggio* (literally, a fulcrum)—that is, as a point person acting as a facilitator for the other leaders—and as an equal among equals, the leader of his own Family. A chairman's leadership experience, and his knowledge of the culture and tradition of our world, were the main factors determining his election, and each chairman was expected to reflect those influences in his decisions.

As the resolution process neared its conclusion, the chairman and each member would negotiate, generally in good faith. This was our forum for dispute resolution, somewhat like traditional court-sponsored mediation. Slowly, an acceptable compromise would take shape. Although each member had an equal say in the matter, one's personal influence, and level of respect within the leadership, would affect the outcome.

After all, some members make dust and some members eat dust.

Adjournment

The meetings of the Commission generally began around eight o'clock at night, and sometimes went as late as four o'clock in the morning. More informal meetings were held during the day, when the agenda called for matters of a less serious nature.

At the conclusion of a meeting, the chairman would formally request whether anyone else had anything to say. If the response was no, the men would stand and join hands, repeating the words of adjournment, "Il tornu e sciolto" ("The circle is untied"). With that, the meeting was officially over.

Body language played an important role in every aspect of our lives, constantly testing our observational skills. When the circle was tied—whether at a Commission meeting or in a Family's Administration meeting—the joining of hands was firm and solid. When the circle was about to be untied, the joining of hands would be slightly elevated; and when the final word was uttered, the hands were emphatically forced downward to emphasize the breaking, or untying, the symbolic "no beginning and no end" of the fraternity.

Immediately after any meeting, the members and their guests would repair to a social hour, enjoying a small repast with hors d'oeuvres and refreshments—another valuable period for me to intermingle and observe how others behaved. As my father was fond of saying, "God gave us two eyes and one mouth so we could see more than we could talk."

7

The 1936 Scheduled Commission Meeting

We don't kill politicians.

A Commission rule

In 1933, Thomas E. Dewey, the future governor of New York and presidential candidate, was chief assistant U.S. Attorney in the Southern District of New York. He was an up-and-coming prosecutor making a name for himself by prosecuting and convicting criminals—including such members of our world as Waxey Gordon, who specialized in bootlegging and illegal gambling.

Irving Wexler (known as Waxey Gordon) had grown up on the Lower East Side of Manhattan, the son of Jewish immigrants. He acquired the nickname "Waxey" because he was so skilled as a pickpocket that when he lifted wallets from his victims, it was as if the wallets were waxed. Arnold Rothstein, the underworld financier, hired Waxey as a rumrunner during the early days of Prohibition. He moved up in rank under Rothstein's tutelage, eventually running all of Rothstein's bootlegging and policy operations on the East Coast. After Rothstein's death in 1928, Waxey aligned himself with the

Luciano/Lansky Combine, but was constantly in disagreement with Luciano regarding the bootlegging business. Indeed, it was widely rumored—behind closed doors—that Luciano himself supplied Tom Dewey with information that led to Waxey's conviction for tax evasion in 1933, resulting in a ten-year prison sentence.

I can't say for sure whether those rumors were true, or a bit of disinformation aimed at helping Dewey gain publicity to advance his political ambitions. If Luciano wanted Waxey out of the way, he certainly had the means to eliminate him without resorting to the law. In our world, giving up someone to the authorities, whether a friend or an enemy, would be a violation of *omertà*. However, Luciano was an Americanized Sicilian. The old Sicilian traditions were not part of his upbringing. And Waxey's fate left one question unanswered: Did Luciano let the government handle this problem for him? If so, was he also trying to build a storehouse of points he could call in later if Dewey was successful in prosecuting him? Luciano's suspected breach of *omertà* was not lost on the conservative wing of the Commission, and it would remain on their minds as they monitored his actions in the months and years to follow.

Dewey was also gaining notoriety through his vigorous prosecution of Arthur "Dutch" Schultz, a Bronx-based gangster who was unaffiliated with the New York Families. Schultz, who was involved in bootlegging and the numbers rackets in Harlem, was known for his brutality and ruthless strong-arm tactics in extorting money from restaurant owners in New York City. Having witnessed the success of using tax laws as a weapon against the likes of Al Capone, Legs Diamond, and Waxey Gordon, Secretary of the Treasury Henry Morgenthau Jr. called upon FBI director J. Edgar Hoover and New York mayor Fiorello LaGuardia to begin a major crackdown on vice in the Big Apple, offering the resources of his office to help.

Early in 1935, New York governor Herbert Lehman appointed Dewey special prosecutor, after a number of prominent Republicans had turned down the assignment. That same year, Schultz defeated two attempts by Dewey to have him convicted of tax evasion. Both trials were held outside New York City, in the upstate towns of Syracuse and Malone. The acquittals further fueled Dewey's and LaGuardia's desire to put Schultz behind bars. A short time later, Dewey filed new charges relating to Schultz's restaurant rackets. The trials were taking its toll on Schultz and his business empire; expecting the Bronx gangster to be convicted in Malone, Luciano was already planning how he would divide Schultz's businesses. Meyer Lansky, in particular, was dead set against Schultz, and that alone was reason enough for Luciano to eliminate him, one way or another.

At the time, Albert Anastasia was underboss (second in command) to Vincent Mangano, leader of the Mangano Family, one of the original five New York Families. Schultz, never one to be genteel, told Anastasia, "I've had enough of Dewey, this transplanted Midwesterner. Tell the boys, if they won't do it, I will." Schultz confided that he had already set a plan in motion, enlisting a confederate disguised as a woman to push a four-wheeled baby carriage past Dewey's home each morning to verify his routine. Even in those days, people like Dewey were concerned with phone taps; the prosecutor left his house each morning accompanied by two bodyguards and walked to a drugstore nearby, going inside to use the pay phone to call his office while the two bodyguards waited outside.

Alarmed at the news, Anastasia quickly informed his *rappresentante*, Vincent Mangano (still serving as Commission chairman), who in turn immediately notified Luciano and the other members of the Commission.

Although Anastasia would have been happy to see Dewey gone, he made Schultz promise not to do anything until he got back to him. As far as Anastasia was concerned, this was the last thing they needed; "we don't kill anyone but our own," the code of the Sicilian tradition went, and such a high-profile assassination would have enormous repercussions.

Nevertheless, Dewey was considered a danger in our world, because of his zeal in prosecuting crime figures, especially men living the *cosa nostra* way of life. His attempts to prosecute Schultz, while unsuccessful, made life unbearable for the Luciano/Lansky Combine.

Indeed, it wasn't long before Dewey targeted Luciano himself as his next prosecution. Dewey considered Luciano the kingpin of vice in New York City; the young prosecutor knew Lucky was smart and elusive, but intended to see him behind bars. Dewey felt his best shot for a conviction was to bring Luciano up on charges of prostitution, for his activities exploiting women and collecting substantial amounts of money from their "professional endeavors." But Dewey's decision appears to have had at least one unintended effect—convincing Luciano to put his differences with Schultz aside and let Schultz get rid of Dewey.

After I was made in 1954, I had numerous conversations concerning Commission meetings with my father. The Luciano prostitution charges, and the shadowy role they played in the 1936 Commission meeting, were one of the examples my father used to illustrate the principles and perils of our way of life. Luciano's motives, and his willingness to bend the rules of our world, were silently questioned by the members of the Commission at this tense moment in our relations with the public sector. The members of the conservative wing weren't sure if Luciano would break from tradition and start targeting for death the kinds of people—politicians—who had always been off limits to those in our world.

Our way of life does not tolerate prostitution. Our tradition considered it immoral to profit from women selling their bodies. We knew that many men in our world did not follow this tradition, but we never condoned prostitution. Luciano's name carried great weight, and my father always believed that any men trying to organize the prostitution racket in Luciano's name were acting without his specific knowledge. The fear of the Luciano name was a way to extort money from the brothel owners. Naturally, these "freelancers" took on great risk by going outside Family sanctioned businesses, which undermined Luciano's authority. And they played right into Dewey's strategy, as he tried to tie the prostitution racket to Luciano himself in order to get a conviction.

When the scheduled 1936 Commission meeting was held, at the home of one of Mangano's group leaders in the Pelham Bay section of the Bronx, one issue dominated the discussion: whether Tom Dewey should be killed.

Our traditions made it clear that a servant of the government, merely doing his job, should not suffer the penalty of death. This rule included police officers, politicians, newspaper reporters, and other public servants. There were practical, as well as ethical, reasons for this: Any visible move against a public servant would turn politicians, law enforcement officers, and the public against us and we were sure to expect fierce retaliation against our Families and businesses. Politicians and police officers, whom we carried in our pockets like so many pennies, would be alienated and come down on us with a vengeance. Even the weekly envelopes of cash they received in exchange for looking the other way would not be enough to neutralize the effect of the public outcry we could expect if we killed such people.

On the other hand, Tom Dewey was an aggressive prosecutor. He was making no effort to hide his pursuit of Luciano. Until he was eliminated, one way or another, it seemed certain that he would be relentless in targeting our way of life. And so the issue became clear. Should we waive the rule and allow Schultz to take out Dewey in an effort to save Luciano?

Albert Anastasia, Mangano's hot-tempered *sotto capo*, was close with Luciano, and he raised the question at the 1936 Commission meeting, pressing for the death penalty for Dewey. Anastasia was from Calabria in southern Italy, south of Naples. He had an eighth-grade Italian education and received his secondary schooling on the streets and the waterfront. The conservatives on the Commission, which included my father, believed that Luciano himself instigated Albert into making the proposal, in order to test the waters. They knew that it might not take as much for Luciano to break with time-honored traditions and promote killing a politician, especially when it was his ox that was about to be gored.

The conservatives dismissed Anastasia's suggestion outright and voted against it. In a sense, while the headline-grabbing Dewey owed Lucky Luciano something for making his name a household word, one could also say that he owed the conservative wing of the Commission his gratitude—for saving his life.

The "Dutchman" wasn't so lucky. Schultz's fervor against Dewey had been growing from week to week, and the Commission decided that the Bronx gangster would have to be eliminated in order to maintain the status quo, which was in the best business interests of the Combine—and he had to go *soon*, before he had a chance to execute an unsanctioned hit on Dewey. Eliminating Schultz, Luciano knew, would also pacify the Sicilians, who were uncomfortable with the constant publicity and media attention. Schultz's fate was left up to Luciano; the Commission pledged not to interfere.

The contract to eliminate Schultz went to Charlie Workman, one of Luciano's most trusted and efficient hitmen. Workman engaged Mendy Weiss, known to be as efficient a killer as Anastasia, to accompany him. On October 23, 1935, Workman and Weiss surprised Schultz and three of his associates at the Palace Chop House in Newark, New Jersey. The extermination that followed was the bloodiest since the 1929 St. Valentine's Day shooting in Chicago.

In keeping with protocol, upon the completion of the Schultz matter, Luciano sent word by personal messengers to each Family leader to inform them that he took complete responsibility for the Schultz matter and for everyone to consider it a Family matter. This procedure established two important positions: first, if any problems developed from the Schultz killing, they were Luciano's to resolve; and second, it established that Luciano was laying claim to all of Schultz's assets. The Commission accepted this, and the Schultz matter was put to rest.

As for Thomas Dewey, he owes at least a portion of his fame to Charlie "Lucky" Luciano. Both men became familiar names to the American public in the 1930s, and Dewey saw this publicity as an opportunity to advance his political ambitions. He was elected District Attorney of New York in 1937 and governor of New York in 1942; he even ran unsuccessfully for president in 1944, before being reelected governor for two more terms, in 1946 and 1950.

Dewey's later career was of dubious distinction. In discussing this era, my father told me that Dewey resisted overtures from Louis "Lepke" Buchalter, who once controlled the garment industry unions on the Lower East Side. Lepke offered Dewey help in prosecuting Sidney Hillman, the president of the Amalgamated Clothing Workers Union and Franklin Roosevelt's main labor adviser and fund-raiser. Lepke figured that Dewey would jump at the chance to cut off political funds that could be used against him by Roosevelt, his chief rival.

By this point, organized labor, empowered by Roosevelt's New Deal, had become a major political force. Hillman had been very close to Roosevelt since the latter's time as governor of New York, and in mid-1936 helped found the American Labor party, along with David Dubinsky of the International

Ladies Garment Workers Union (ILGWU); Jacob Potofsky, Hyman Blumberg, and Luigi Antonini of the Garment-Trades Unions; and Alex Rose of the Millinery Workers. The combined efforts of this new party gave Roosevelt close to 250,000 assured votes in New York alone; with LaGuardia's popularity from introducing labor reform legislation favoring workers adding to that total, Roosevelt had little to worry about.

For some time, the Communists had been making an effort to infiltrate the labor movement, and labor unrest was a common problem. Hillman had used associates of Lepke's to maintain the peace through Lepke's activities as a labor racketeer in the 1920s; Dubinsky, Blumberg, Rose, and Antonini often helped themselves to Lepke's supply of strong-arm men to quell the often dangerous, sometimes fatal confrontations between labor and management.

In 1941, Lepke was tried, convicted, and sentenced to death for the 1926 killing of Joseph Rosen, a garment industry trucker who had threatened to expose Lepke and his criminal activities to Dewey; appeals delayed the sentence from being carried out several times over three years. In 1944, Lepke wanted Dewey to commute his death sentence in exchange for evidence that would help in prosecuting Hillman.

But it wasn't to be. At 11:16 P.M. on March 4, 1944, time ran out for Lekpe. That night, at Sing Sing prison, thirty miles north of New York City, he became the first major underworld leader to be executed—and the last. Just hours beforehand, Dewey refused to commute Lepke's death sentence and that of his two associates, Louis Capone (no relation to Al) and Mendy Weiss. Asked to explain his decision, Dewey commented, "I don't make deals with gangsters."

But Dewey's glib comment hid the real reasons behind his decision—among them Dewey's White House ambitions, which had him courting the same people who had helped Roosevelt. There was even a suspicion that Dewey refused to commute Lepke's sentence as a favor to the Luciano/Lansky Combine, which stood to gain from the takeover of Lepke's businesses. If Luciano had, in fact, supplied Dewey with information that helped convict Waxey Gordon years before, Dewey might have allowed Buchalter's conviction to stand as a way of returning the favor. For further evidence of this theory, one need look no further than the mysterious matter of Dewey's commutation on January 3, 1946, of Luciano's thirty- to fifty-year sentence, granting Luciano parole solely for the purpose of deportation to Italy after World War II, and Dewey's refusal to testify before the Special Committee to Investigate Organized Crime in Interstate Commerce, headed by Senator Estes Kefauver in 1950–51, to explain the commutation.

And, of course, there was the simple matter of money. During one of my many conversations over the years with my father and other old-timers, I learned that the Dewey campaigns had asked our world for contributions. Even despite Dewey's successful prosecution of Luciano, who went to prison in 1936, our world responded by raising approximately $250,000 to aid the Dewey treasury—more than $90,000 of which came from the Luciano/Lansky Combine.

8

The 1941 Scheduled
Commission Meeting

*Boys don't become men by getting older; boys are shaped
into men.*

Vincent Tarantola, *capodecina* in the Bonanno Family

The Luciano Leadership Void
and World War II

In 1936, Charlie "Lucky" Luciano began serving his sentence
of thirty to fifty years in prison. This left an unsanctioned
leadership void in the Luciano Family that could directly affect all five New York Families. In principle, the selection of
a new leader required death (natural or otherwise) of the old
leader, or an election by the members of the Luciano Family.
A temporary leader, or acting *rappresentante*, could take over if
authorized by Luciano.

Luciano sent word from prison that he intended to remain
leader of his Family, and designated Vito Genovese to assume the
position of acting leader until further notice, with Frank Costello
remaining as *consigliere*. As fate would have it, in 1937 Genovese
found himself in trouble with the authorities and escaped to Italy

to avoid prosecution on a murder charge. This only exacerbated the Luciano Family's leadership void—an issue that became one of the key items on the agenda for the 1941 Commission meeting.

In August 1941, the regularly scheduled Commission meeting took place at a rural location near Farmingdale, Long Island. Vincent Mangano, leader of the Mangano Family, presided as chairman, selected to serve in that position at the 1936 Commission meeting. Joseph Profaci, Joseph Bonanno, Gaetano Gagliano, and Frank Costello (on behalf of the Luciano Family) represented the other four New York Families. Paul Ricca of Chicago and Stefano Magaddino of Buffalo were also present. Also present were Joseph "Socks" Lanza and Guarino "Willie" Moretti (a.k.a. Willie Moore), the official bearers of the wishes of Luciano, who continued to be a guest of the government incarcerated in Dannemora, the maximum-security prison near the Canadian border in upstate New York. Luciano sent word through them that Frank Costello was his choice to serve as temporary leader replacing Genovese, and the 1941 Commission members sanctioned and approved Luciano's decision.

In discussions with my father during the 1970s, he recalled a number of other matters raised during the 1941 Commission meeting. A series of heated discussions took place involving the impending war with Germany and Japan, and the possible repercussions it could have in our world.

By this point in the European war, Germany had already invaded Poland, Denmark, Norway, the Netherlands, Belgium, Luxembourg, and France; had absorbed Czechoslovakia; and had established a German-friendly French government in Vichy; and Romania, Bulgaria, Yugoslavia, Serbia, Macedonia, and Hungary were all under Axis influence. In 1941, the Germans were on the move, headed for the eastern seaboard of the United States. In March 1941, the United States established an Atlantic Fleet for protection of convoys in the North Atlantic, and took all German and Italian ships moored at U.S. docks, along with some Danish ships, into "protective custody." In May, the unarmed S.S. *Robin Moor* became the first United States merchant ship sunk by a German U-boat.

In August 1941, around the time of the Commission's scheduled meeting, the first wartime meeting between the United Kingdom's prime minister, Winston Churchill, and President Franklin D. Roosevelt took place at Ship Harbor, Placentia Bay, Newfoundland, Canada. Roosevelt had thus far hewed to an isolationist policy toward the war, and Churchill was unhappy that Roosevelt wasn't doing more to aid England and the other European countries that had been invaded by Germany. Their meetings, held aboard ship, gave birth to the Atlantic Charter, a blueprint for the war aims of the Allied Nations during World War II and a preliminary step toward the formation of the United Nations after the war ended.

In October, a German submarine torpedoed a Navy destroyer, the U.S.S. *Ruben James*, sinking it, resulting in the deaths of 115 of the 159 American sailors; it was the first U.S. Navy ship sunk by hostile action during the war.

In November, and several times the following year, the New York members of the Commission met informally, continuing their discussions of the war and its effect on our world. The discussions centered on the ongoing friction among the government, the Office of Naval Intelligence, and the Longshoremen's Union over control of the docks in New York and along the eastern seaboard and Gulf ports.

Like everyone else, the Sicilian faction of our world felt the tension mounting over the international political situation. For the Sicilians, what was happening in Europe hit close to home; they were extremely concerned about the welfare of their families and relatives on the island across the Atlantic. The Americanized members did not have the same worries.

South Street during the 1940s.

Yet the mood of the Commission as a whole matched the solemn mood of everyone else in the United States. It certainly looked as if war was coming.

As Italian-Americans, we had special reason for concern. At the beginning of the war, the American public looked upon us with distrust, because Mussolini represented the enemy on the Axis side.

Few people today remember that when the United States first entered the war, some Italians living in the coastal areas of the country—many of them fishermen—were rounded up as enemy aliens, much like the Japanese, and placed in internment camps or forced to relocate. Many of these men, or their sons, later enlisted to fight for America against the Axis enemy. The Italian-Americans in our world considered themselves true patriots. When Albert Anastasia was drafted into the Army, everyone talked about how proud he was to be a soldier. One of our group leaders had a son who became an Army general; Tommy Lucchese's son, a West Point appointee, became a full-bird colonel.

After the fall of France in June 1940, the United States government seized the French luxury liner S.S. *Normandie*, which was docked in New York Harbor, alongside the R.M.S. *Queen Mary* and R.M.S. *Queen Elizabeth*, all three ordered to remain in port because of the war. Before long, England gave the United States permission to convert the twin *Queen*s into troopships, refitted to transport troops to the battlefronts. International law technicalities delayed the similar refitting of the *Normandie*, but eventually the legal matters were resolved and conversion work begun. In preparation for its use by the U.S. military, the *Normandie* was renamed the U.S.S. *Lafayette*, in honor of the Marquis de La Fayette, a general who served with George Washington in the Revolutionary War. (S.S. stands for "steamship"; the designation U.S.S. preceding a ship's name indicates a military ship, while S.S. indicates a merchant marine or non-military vessel.)

On February 9, 1942, a mysterious fire broke out on the *Lafayette* while it was being converted from a cruise ship to a troop transport at Pier 88, on the Hudson River. The mysterious fire immediately attracted suspicion, and rumors of sabotage flew in the days that followed. Who had started the fire? The first question was, who had had access to the ship?

After the Japanese attacked Pearl Harbor on December 7, 1941, the United States government had assumed complete control of all U.S. docks. Given the working relationship our world had had with the government for decades, however, it was in the government's best interest to quietly allow us to maintain our day-to-day control over operations on the docks. We controlled the fishermen and the stevedore companies that

The U.S.S. Lafayette, *formerly known as the* Normandie, *burning before she capsized at Pier 88 on the Hudson River in New York on February 9, 1942.*

employed the longshoremen who loaded and unloaded ships on the Brooklyn and New York docks. We also controlled the trucking for delivery of fresh fish to the restaurants and wholesalers, as well as other products shipped into and out of the docks.

The Navy, which was responsible for protecting the ports of New York from foreign attack, immediately suspected sabotage. Fearing further attacks by enemy agents along the waterfront, Naval Intelligence made contact with our world through the attorney representing Joseph "Socks" Lanza, a member of the Luciano Family who headed the United Seafood Workers union at the Fulton Fish Market. Sicilians never spoke or aided government authorities in any way, but Lanza was a Neapolitan, and the government saw him as a potential liaison with the Sicilians in our world. Lanza, who was under indictment at the time, agreed to reach out to our world for patriotic reasons—despite the fact that the government extended no promises of dropping the charges against him.

In the interest of preventing further sabotage along the docks, Lanza helped the government, enlisting the union to serve as the eyes and ears of security. The Office of Naval Intelligence asked us for favors, promised us favors in return, and we were anxious to help.

As for the *Lafayette* fire, there has always been speculation about whether or not the fire that broke out was sabotage or caused by a spark from a welder's torch in refitting the ship. As far as we knew it was not sabotage—and no evidence of sabotage ever surfaced. However, the government's belief in the sabotage theory would prove to be beneficial to Lucky Luciano.

My first recollection of meeting "Socks" Lanza is very clear. When I was ten years old, I was walking down to the East River docks with my father early one winter morning, shivering in the cold, positioning myself so that he blocked the biting wind blowing in from the East River. I remember the mingled odors of fish and cigar butts saturating the air and growing stronger as we approached the Fulton Fish Market. I kept my mouth shut, and breathed hard trying to keep up with my dad's longer steps.

All around us, big burly men were busy wheeling boxes of fish on hand-trucks or moving stacks of fish on pushcarts. They sloshed through fish juices, fish guts, and fish slime that covered the cobblestone streets in lower Manhattan. As fishmongers shouted to each other, men with clipboards made notes weighing and tabulating the fish count before the catch was loaded onto the trucks. When I think of it now, the fish barrels lined up on the docks looked like platoons of soldiers in formation. My eyes darted around quickly, taking it all in. I found it funny that the dockworkers bathed the fish in tons of ice while I was standing there freezing. As we walked, I noticed that some of the men acknowledged my father in one way or another. My father responded, nodding his head in appreciation. I sensed the air of importance and respect my father commanded. When he pulled me over to a vendor of hot roasted chestnuts, the man addressed my father as Don Pepino, handed him two bags of the steaming nuts, and refused payment. My father thanked him, and we continued walking until we

The Fulton Fish Market, 1936.

reached a building with a restaurant on the second floor over-looking the fish market.

Along the way, my father pointed out several Navy men in uniform patrolling the docks with SP (Shore Patrol) brassards on either sleeve tightly bound around their biceps. Two naval officers in uniform were surreptitiously eyeing a man holding a clipboard talking to one of the dockworkers. This man, I later learned, was Socks Lanza.

As soon as the man was alone, the naval officers approached him. I noticed my father watching carefully, without triggering any attention, as this entire episode unfolded. It was apparent to me, even at ten years old, that my father expected me to pay more attention to the people than to the dead fish in barrels. The lesson of observing people and my surroundings, without triggering attention, would save my life in later years.

After the officers left, Lanza approached my father, clip-board in hand, inviting him upstairs to the restaurant. The Office of Naval Intelligence instigated the meeting by solicit-ing Lanza's aid, although they did not know my father would be involved.

My father told me to meet him in front of the restaurant in two hours and left me to fend for myself until his meeting was finished. I spent that time exploring the Fulton Fish Market, lis-tening to workers shouting in Italian and watching the men put-ting fish into barrels. As I shivered, and grew slowly accustomed to the gamy smells of fish and truck exhaust, a private meeting between Lanza and my father was taking place upstairs. Lanza explained that Naval Intelligence was trying to persuade him to enlist the help of Lucky Luciano, whom they believed could pre-vent any further sabotage on the docks. Luciano was willing, and he negotiated a deal that, in return for his cooperation with the authorities, the government would move him from Dannemora to Green Haven Correctional Facility, just up the river from New

York City. That would make it much easier for Luciano to conduct Family business from prison. Later, Naval Intelligence would approach Luciano for another favor, requesting information required for the planned U.S. invasion of Sicily. As a quid pro quo, they would agree to pardon Luciano after the war in exchange for aiding his country.

Luciano knew very little about Sicily, having come to the United States as a young boy, but he knew that the Sicilians in our world had maintained contacts on their home island. So he had Lanza contact John Tartamella, *consigliere* of the Bonanno Family, to arrange this meeting at the Fulton Fish Market with Joe Bonanno.

After his meeting with Lanza, my father set up a meeting with Joseph Profaci and Vincent Mangano. The three of them wanted to help Luciano, in order to give him some credibility with the government and get his sentence reduced. They contacted the other leaders of Families around the country, but none of the others had direct Sicilian connections.

Instead, my father and Mangano both wrote to Mafia leaders they knew in Sicily, who were against Mussolini and wanted the Germans out of their homeland. The letters were in code understood by only the writer and the recipient, using phrases with special meanings known only to them. "Only my *paesano*, a Castellammarese living in Palermo, knew what I meant," my father told me. The messages asked the leaders to ensure that the Sicilian people would offer no opposition to American forces during the planned invasion. Once that was accomplished, secret meetings were arranged between Naval Intelligence and Luciano at the prison. Meyer Lansky acted as a conduit, transporting information in and out of Green Haven to the Luciano Family; he took the information on Sicily we had gathered and fed to Lanza, and fed it in turn to Luciano. Throughout all of these secret meetings, neither my father nor Mangano had direct contact with the government. It was important that all information pass through Luciano, in order to build his case for aiding the United States. It was imperative that the government remain unaware of any involvement of the other Family leaders in order to maximize Luciano's importance.

The information we passed along enabled the Office of Strategic Services (OSS) to gain entry into Sicily with the help of the Sicilian Mafia and steal secret defense information and plans from a safe at a German naval base in Sicily. This gave the United States advance information, enabling the Allies to land in Sicily safely. The Allied invasion of Sicily was one of the largest amphibious assaults in history. Dubbed Operation Husky, the invasion landed roughly 180,000 men on the island in 1943, attacking what Churchill described as "the soft underbelly of Europe." Once in Sicily, the Mafia Families aided the Americans in the invasion. When asked whether his real motive in aiding this invasion was to help Luciano or his country, my father said, "I felt I was an American. I was patriotic because I love the United States regardless if it loves me. I also wanted to help Luciano—because he was a father."

And yet, after the war, Lucky Luciano was shunned by Naval Intelligence. He did not receive the pardon he was offered. Instead, Governor Dewey commuted his sentence and granted parole for the specific purpose of deporting him to Italy. In 1947, he showed up in Cuba. Socks Lanza and Willie Moretti visited him there on the orders of Frank Costello to bring him up to speed on a new problem, this time involving Bugsy Siegel—the primary item on the agenda at the 1946 meeting of the Commission just months before.

9

The 1946 Scheduled Commission Meeting

Suspicion is a powerful motivator. It breeds fear of the unknown. If acted upon without substantiated facts, trust will be eroded in the best case. Murder may result in the worst case.

Vincent Mangano

There were three pressing matters that came before the Commission in 1946: the permanent changing of the guard in the Luciano Family; the growth in narcotics trafficking; and the Bugsy Siegel problem, which had originated as a local issue but had since escalated to a matter of such national concern that it warranted Commission intervention.

By the time of this next Commission meeting, America was celebrating the end of World War II. Travel restrictions had eased, and the nation was feeling good about itself. The Commission decided to hold its scheduled 1946 meeting in December, just before Christmas, in Miami, Florida. The setting would be a yacht owned by Willie Moretti, moored at the dock behind his home. Moretti was an old-timer, originally part of the Buffalo Family led by my father's cousin Stefano Magaddino.

Moretti had a reputation as a strong enforcer. He was one of the two men sent to Jacksonville, Florida, to rescue my father from immigration authorities when he first came to this country from Sicily via Havana, Cuba. Moretti later transferred to New Jersey and became part of the Luciano Family. When Frank Costello became leader of the Luciano Family, Moretti was his muscle.

Lucky Luciano didn't stay long in Sicily before he made his way to Havana. He never gave up trying to return to the United States, but as the chances looked more and more remote, the Commission informed Luciano that it would be in the best interest of his Family, and of all of our world, if he would step down and appoint a permanent leader. Luciano agreed with the Commission's suggestion. In return, the Commission allowed Luciano to continue whatever relationships and businesses he had or cared to make in the future that might benefit the Families or himself.

Frank Costello, acting leader of the Luciano Family, was the logical choice to succeed Luciano. Yet there was another candidate: Vito Genovese, who had served as the Family's acting leader before escaping to Italy to avoid being prosecuted on a murder charge. Genovese had recently returned to the United States after all the witnesses testifying against him mysteriously "disappeared." Now, Genovese wanted to reclaim his erstwhile role as leader of the Luciano Family. Genovese had once overshadowed Costello, the Family's *consigliere*; now their effective rankings had reversed. (I use the word *effective* because the *sotto capo* and the *consigliere* really had no numerical rankings in the leadership. In some Families, the *consigliere* was the second most influential member after the *rappresentante*.)

Still, Costello was Luciano's choice to take over permanent leadership of the Family, and with Lucky's approval Costello

Leadership Realignment of the Luciano Family

	1931	1936	1939	1946	1951
Leader	Luciano			Costello	Costello
Acting Leader		Genovese	Costello		
Sotto Capo	Genovese		* Moretti	* Moretti	Genovese
Consigliere		Costello			
Muscle					Moretti

* Moretti was not given these official titles, but acted in these roles.

appointed Genovese as his *sotto capo*. Moretti, who became very close to Costello during Genovese's absence, remained Costello's loyal muscle.

While Genovese was in Italy, Moretti's influence was elevated in the Family. He was looked upon by the other Family members as Costello's eyes and ears, like a *sotto capo* without the title. His influence diminished when Genovese returned and was appointed *sotto capo*—and that did not sit well with Moretti. The bonds of loyalty between Moretti and Costello were beginning to fray.

For some twenty years, there had been relative peace in our world in most inter-Family affairs. Of course, from time to time there were intra-Family problems: a *sotto capo* here, a *capodecina* there; a soldier who might disappear in Boston, or Kansas City, or Los Angeles. But those were local matters, governed by each Family's hierarchy, not subject to Commission intervention.

The first ripple disturbing the Families' tranquillity began with the return of Vito Genovese from his self-imposed exile in Italy. After Genovese put his legal problems behind him, he began hanging out around town in the company of Tommy Lucchese, of the Gagliano Family. Albert Anastasia, *sotto capo* of the Mangano Family, formed an alliance with Costello and the two of them were often seen tête-à-tête at the Red Devil and Vesuvius restaurants in midtown Manhattan near Times Square, while Frank Scalice and Carlo Gambino from the Mangano Family were rubbing elbows with Lucchese.

Such inter-Family affiliations were common in New York, but they complicated the lives of everyone concerned. With so many personalities and divergent backgrounds, keeping the natives from becoming restless was becoming a full-time job for the Family leaders. The Commission was supposed to alleviate discord and tension among the Families, but as newer faces came into positions of authority and old-world ties began weakening, things seemed to be getting increasingly out of control.

Over the next five years, sparks between Costello and Genovese continued to fly. Adding fuel to the fire was friction in the Mangano Family between Vincent Mangano and his *sotto capo*, Anastasia. The alliances formed within and among Families in these years would soon come to a head at the 1951 Commission meeting.

In the 1940s, American industry was enjoying the handsome profits garnered from the war effort and the postwar boom that followed. Car manufacturers converted their plants to military production and saw profits soar. The U.S. agriculture, business, and entertainment industries entered a period of tremendous growth and prosperity. In our world, however, the opposite seemed to be true. Tensions were rising; people who had once been friends or at least social acquaintances now seemed wary of each other; smaller, close-knit groups were becoming the norm.

The makeup of the Commission was also changing, shifting its ideology ever so slightly toward more liberal attitudes, in part through the influence of younger members who had seen the world and absorbed the philosophies of other cultures. At home, many of our members became wealthy while supplying the needs of a nation at war. In the garment industry, clothing for the troops kept the factories humming. The auto and trucking industries converted their plants to build airplanes, warships, and military vehicles, which they turned out in amazing quantities.

In our world, some profited during the war dealing in ration stamps and black-marketing. Buying fuel for your car required a certain number of stamps per gallon, and the rationing of stamps by classification and specific need was a source of revenue for us. Doctors, police, and workers in essential industries received more stamps than people involved in nonessential industries.

You needed stamps to purchase meat, sugar, bread, butter, and many other grocery items. Nylon was considered an essential item needed for, among other things, the making of parachutes for our fliers. Therefore, when we were able to obtain women's nylon stockings, they brought a high price.

As a youngster, I remember seeing the local bookmaker or neighborhood loan shark come around with packages wrapped in plain brown butcher paper—and the exclamations of delight that followed from the young girls gathered in my grandfather's garage on Jefferson Street, each one hoping to walk away with a pair of nylon stockings. The number of pairs they could buy depended on how much money they were willing to spend. Times were good: the money was flowing, and our world benefited from a laissez-faire attitude. *Let the market set supply and demand*, went the prevailing wisdom. *No interference necessary, from either local governments or law enforcement.*

The end of the war brought about a mixture of new faces, new ideas, and new developing philosophies, in which money and business increasingly became the primary motivation. Friendships, Family ties, and loyalty were beginning to go by the wayside. As we progressed into the middle of the twentieth century, our world also increasingly fell victim to the counterculture developing in our country. The younger generation of our world began losing touch with its priorities, letting the new do-your-own-thing mentality carry the day.

The younger members of our world had been growing up with the values of their contemporaries; the postwar generation saw our time-honored traditions as a quaint throwback to another time. They were entering a period of rampant experimentation with drugs, and trying to emulate the exaggerated portrayals of "gangster" lifestyles as shown in film noir movies produced in Hollywood and New York. The rise of this new generation led to the decay of all the things that had guided us for hundreds of years: prudence, caution, moderation, and respect. As with young American society in general, our people fell into what I call the "opera generation," the me-me-me's and I-I-I's. People did whatever they wanted and didn't take responsibility for their actions.

Narcotics

Our narcotics problem was still in its infancy, but the Commission members were well aware of the growing pressure from some of the members of the Families to engage in this business. The profits could be enormous.

A few weeks after September 11, 2001, my father sat down with me and told me a story he had never discussed before. He was in a nostalgic mood, pained just like the rest of the country after the attacks on the World Trade Center. He knew I was writing a book on the history of our world and wanted me to know something that occurred in 1946 that he had kept secret from everyone since that time.

During that time, FBI director J. Edgar Hoover had worked closely with Naval Intelligence. He knew that it was my father, not Luciano, who had made contact with the Sicilian *mafiosi* to gain information and support for the Allied invasion of Sicily. It was no coincidence that Hoover had denied the existence of the Mafia in the United States until the Apalachin affair in 1957: We knew that Hoover had secrets of his own to hide. In our circles, the rumors were already circulating that photographs existed of Hoover dressed as a woman, and in compromising positions with his "best friend" and assistant, Clyde Tolson. I personally saw the photographs and they were exactly as rumored.

In 1946, my father met secretly with Hoover. The meeting was never revealed to anyone until my father told me about it when he was ninety-six, the year before he died. Joe Bonanno knew that narcotics could be the downfall of the Families and the Commission. He felt strongly that it would ruin the businesses we were involved in, which were nonthreatening by comparison. When he went into the meeting with Hoover, he was seeking assurances about two things: that Hoover would not pursue active legal enforcement against sanctioned businesses of the Bonanno Family and the other Families; and, even more important, that Hoover understood that the Bonanno Family was opposed to narcotics, and that any member of the Family found to be engaged in that business would pay with his life.

Both of them knew that Hoover was not the man in government assigned to pursue the elimination of narcotics. At that time, drug enforcement was under the purview of the Federal Bureau of Narcotics, headed by Harry Anslinger. My father, who was dead set against any of the Families dealing drugs, felt that anyone successfully prosecuted by Anslinger for narcotics violations should get what they deserved. The potential for profits may have been great, but the threat of bringing down "this thing of ours" was too profound to risk.

There was an unspoken understanding that, if Anslinger chose to enforce the narcotics laws against the members of some Family, the Bonanno Family would choose not to intervene. This was a very dangerous position to take, for some might have construed it as a violation of *omertà*—even though my father never actually aided any prosecution against a member of another Family or anyone living the philosophy of *cosa nostra*. Of course, Hoover could make certain overtures to Anslinger, which might stop or slow the ascendency of drugs in our world.

At the 1946 Commission meeting, Joe Bonanno informed the members that he had learned that the government was mounting an all-out attack against narcotics, and warned the Families that they should stay away from this new source of profit. He never revealed the source of his information.

The Commission, at this time, was still governed by the conservative majority, and the members agreed that no Family would engage in narcotics trafficking. But the winds of change were blowing: It would be only a matter of time before the liberals would reverse this resolution—much to the conservatives' surprise.

Benjamin "Bugsy" Siegel

Another festering problem was what to do about Bugsy Siegel, an associate of Luciano's who had been sent to the West Coast to get him away from New York and from problems that had been

brewing between him and Joe Adonis. Adonis, a very powerful man in our world, was having turf wars with some of the
Jewish fellows, particularly Siegel. They were both headstrong
men; Bugsy was hard to control in any environment, and with
Luciano in prison, both men were leaderless and restless. Soon
friction was mounting between these guys and the members of
their respective groups, all of whom had grown up together in
New York City with friends at the highest levels in our world.

There is a public conception that "the mob," or the Commission, sent Bugsy to California. I have always struggled
with this myth. I never understood what the public meant
in using the phrase "the mob": all twenty-four independent
sovereign Families? Everyone in the United States involved
in organized crime or criminal activity? Just as often, the
phrase "the mob" seemed to refer to a single person or Family
that seemed dominant in a given place and time—Luciano,
Capone, or whatever well-known Family happened to be the
news of the day.

The truth is that it wasn't the Commission who sent Bugsy
Siegel to California. The Commission did not have the authority to make that decision. The Jews had their own organization, and Meyer Lansky was its recognized leader—at least,
he was to those in our world. Lansky was smart, financially
sharp, reasonable, and respected by each group.

The Jewish connection to our world was always strong.
Lansky had grown up with Bugsy and Luciano, along with
many other Jews and Italians, and the groups learned to accommodate one another for mutual benefit. We had a saying
that M + M = M, meaning "Muscle" (Italians) plus "Moxie"
(Jews) equals Money. Our Jewish brethren understood the
importance of keeping the peace—and the need to separate
Adonis and Bugsy.

The actor George Raft, another of Bugsy's longtime
friends, had made it big in the movie industry in Hollywood.

Bugsy, with his movie-star good looks, had a passion for being among the rich and famous, so it wasn't hard to convince him that everyone would be better off if he relocated to Los Angeles, at least until things between him and Adonis could cool down. The Jewish contingent made that happen.

Bugsy's vision of Las Vegas, as portrayed in movies and books, was different from what is commonly attributed to him. Siegel had no romantic attachment to Las Vegas. I don't mean to minimize his role in the city's expansion, but Bugsy viewed Las Vegas as a "cowboy town," full of people he considered "rednecks." Like all of us, he looked at the city as an opportunity to make money, not as some stylized "vision" of what Las Vegas might become. What he saw was a chance to entice his Hollywood friends to become big-money patrons, with the aid of his financial backers from the East Coast. He'd already seen how popular gambling was in Los Angeles, using the wire services to clear racetrack betting. When he heard about the little town of Las Vegas and the legal gambling opportunities there, he realized that the hundreds of workers who had settled in the area after construction of the nearby Boulder Dam could provide a ready labor force if the city should expand—and would be customers as well. Back then, the trip from Los Angeles to Las Vegas was a long drive, but legalized gambling would make the trip worthwhile for all those Californians with heavy wallets and appetites for gambling.

But Siegel's relocation out West also caused new problems. He loved being in Hollywood, but he had a way of ruffling the feathers of another Italian. Siegel's penchant for sticking his nose in other people's business, as he mingled with the Hollywood elite, did not sit well with Jack Dragna, the leader of the Los Angeles Family. Given the close association the New York Italians had with the Jewish organization, Bugsy was still the responsibility of the Eastern Commission members—so, before long, Dragna was complaining to the Italians back in Cleveland

and New York that Bugsy was being "disrespectful." As a courtesy, Dragna told them, "Either you take care of this or we will."

The Siegel/Dragna situation alone could have precipitated a war involving Families across the United States. But it was even worse when coupled together with a second problem: it soon became clear that Siegel was racking up massive cost overruns at his pet project, the Flamingo Hotel.

The Commission addressed the Siegel matter with sadness and some reluctance, but it resulted in a step that was taken for the benefit of all.

In our world, words are carefully chosen. Words used incorrectly can result in misinterpretation, and that in turn can have severe consequences. For example: when I first mentioned the Siegel situation above, I referred to it as a "local matter." The problem of Siegel's involvement in the Flamingo Hotel in Las Vegas was a local matter in the sense that, originally, it involved a financial investment by only two New York Families—the Luciano Family and the Mangano Family. As the project wore on, however, the Cleveland and Los Angeles Families were persuaded to invest in Siegel's follies, not only in Las Vegas, but also in other ventures. Before it ended, Chicago, Kansas City, and Minneapolis investors joined in. Soon we were hearing that every time they picked up the phone it was Siegel saying, "Send me another fifty thousand," or "I need another hundred thousand."

The Commission had to find a way to rein Siegel in. Those in our world decided that it was up to our friends in the Jewish organization to solve the problem. Bugsy had come from Lansky's organization, and he and Luciano would have to solve the problem.

The decision reached aboard Moretti's yacht in Miami's Biscayne Bay at this 1946 meeting of the Commission was that our Jewish friends would have to take care of Siegel. The task fell to Meyer Lansky because he was Siegel's boyhood friend and had vouched for Siegel's success.

Frank Costello, now acting leader of the Luciano Family, had the job of letting Luciano know that he and Lansky would have to resolve the problem or the members of the Commission would not be held responsible for whatever happened to Siegel. Costello sent Lanza and Moretti to Cuba to meet with Lansky and Luciano and inform them of the Commission's decision.

As I heard it over the years, the story was that the Siegel decision really had very little to do with money and the Flamingo Hotel, although that was an easy excuse. The Flamingo Hotel situation was merely one of a long line of problems with Siegel, dating back many years. The fact is that Bugsy had begun to believe that he was untouchable. He was overreaching the acceptable boundaries and protocol of our world.

Before adjourning the December meeting, the Commission scheduled a subsequent meeting, to finalize the Siegel decision after hearing from Luciano. This second meeting took place in February 1947 in Fort Lauderdale, Florida. The only item on the agenda was the Siegel matter. Luciano reluctantly went along with the decision. Lansky had no other choice, having given Siegel fair warning and exhausted all efforts to control Siegel's spending habits. Word came back that Luciano and Lansky received the message and that they would take care of the problem.

Moretti again made available his yacht, which could host twenty to twenty-five people in addition to the crew. My father, telling me about that evening, was straightforward. In Sicilian, he told me, "It was a pleasant, breezy Florida night, with gently rolling waves slapping against the hull of Moretti's yacht as it powered out to sea, manned by a hand-selected crew. Frank Costello informed us of Lansky and Luciano's agreement. The mood was somber. The fact that something had to be done about the Siegel problem was ratified, and the formal meeting was adjourned."

Unlike the plots of many old Warner Brothers B movies, such matters just weren't handled by sending two "gorillas" from the East, Murder Inc.–style. In fact, none of the Commission members said that Siegel had to be killed. The Commission merely delivered its decision—that the problem had to be resolved—to Jack Dragna, because he was the victim of the actual insult. It was up to him to decide how to resolve it and to effect the punishment he thought appropriate. Given Dragna's relations with Siegel, of course, it didn't take great imagination to foresee that Siegel would be a dead man. To tell Dragna "Do what you have to do" was, in effect, to recognize Siegel's fate and agree not to interfere.

In our world, a timetable is rarely set to determine when a person marked for death will be dispatched. These things are not done by the clock. The time and circumstances must be right, or some cowboy might botch it up by shooting from the hip. Weeks, months, and, in rare cases, even years can go by before such an order is carried out. The primary concern is the safety of the people who are carrying out the sanction; it is all-important that they are able to prevent any danger to themselves and be able to walk away unharmed. Every precaution is taken. In our world, when you do something of this nature, you're always aware that the same thing could also happen to you. We learn at a very young age not to become creatures of habit. When you leave your house, don't use the same route each day. Being predictable can be life-threatening. Here's a personal example:

The six-hour Showtime miniseries *Bonanno: A Godfather's Story*, the authorized life story of Joseph Bonanno Sr., had three premiere showings. Besides the events in New York and Los Angeles, there was an invitation-only premiere at the Loft Theatre in Tucson, Arizona, on July 12, 1999, with a reception afterward and an invitation-only private dinner the following day honoring my father at one of our favorite restaurants in Tucson, Anthony's in the Catalinas.

By the time of the premiere, my father was ninety-four years old, retired, and living in Tucson. The day before the movie premiered in town, my father instructed me to drive him to the theater so he could see with his own eyes where all the exits were located. Security was so ingrained in his mind that he never left anything to chance. Then, that night, we talked through everything we'd seen, to reassure him that I'd seen what he'd seen. He wanted to be sure I knew the fastest way to the exit if something went wrong. What he didn't know was that several days earlier I had made it my business to go to the theater with a few of my men, because I knew that he would raise the issue with me. You could say about him, even at the age of ninety-four, "Ancora imparo" (he was still learning)—and he was still teaching, too. That's the way my father was, from my childhood until he died at the age of ninety-seven.

Old habits are hard to break. One day, when I was a boy, my father took some sewing thread, wrapped it twice around my hands, and said, "Break it." I did so with ease. He then wrapped the sewing thread four more times around my hands and told me to break it. Although it cut into my skin, I managed to break it again. Then he wrapped my hands once more, but this time he wound the thread eight or nine times around. And this time I couldn't break it! "You see, that's what habit is," he told me. "The first time it's easy to break. The second time it gets a little harder. It keeps getting progressively harder to break the more times it wraps around your hands until it gets to the point where you will not break that habit." Being predictable is a bad habit. Being conscious of your surroundings, though, was a habit that served us both well.

When it came time—for symbolic reasons—Jack Dragna chose an Italian and a Jew from among his men in Los Angeles to "do the Siegel work." On Friday afternoon, June 20, 1947, Bugsy Siegel was in Beverly Hills. His longtime girlfriend,

Joe Bonanno's ninety-fifth birthday at the Marriott University Park Hotel in Tucson, Arizona, January 22, 2000. Note the earpiece enabling Joe to summon one of his men at a moment's notice.

Introducing my father, Joe Bonanno, at the premiere of Bonanno: A Godfather's Story. *My seat is reserved for the aisle; Gary Cantalini from the East Coast is standing in the light-colored suit.*

Virginia Hill, was to return that evening from Europe, his daughters were coming to Los Angeles to spend the summer with him, and the Flamingo Hotel in Las Vegas—which he opened in December 1946, while it was still unfinished—had been completed, reopened, and was slowly turning a profit. Life was good. He had no idea that his impending demise was imminent.

He was at his girlfriend's North Linden Drive home in Beverly Hills. After having a light snack, he busied himself visiting with a friend, Allen Smiley, while Virginia's brother, Chick Hill, was upstairs with his girlfriend, Jerri Mason. At about ten-thirty, he was sitting on the sofa, reading a newspaper and talking with Allen. An oversize glass window framed his upper back and head, and the back of his head was exposed and vulnerable, making him an easy target for assassination. Then a barrage of bullets from a .30 caliber carbine blasted through the window and tore through Ben Siegel's head and upper body.

On the other side of the country, the leaders of the New York Families, along with me and six hundred other guests, were attending a wedding reception that Saturday evening honoring the union of Stefano Magaddino's daughter to the son of his underboss, John Montana, at the Niagara Hotel in Niagara Falls in upstate New York. In those days, when the wedding of a leader's daughter or son took place, it was customary to invite the leaders of all the Families. I was fifteen years old and have a vivid recollection of the events that took place during that trip.

The wedding festivities in New York were winding down. My cousin Peter Magaddino (Stefano's only son), Anthony DiGregorio (the son of Stefano's brother-in-law, Gaspar), and I struggled to stay interested in what was going on in the main ballroom. Peter and Anthony, both somewhat older, had been asked to entertain me, but I could tell they were chafing at the assignment. By the time midnight was approaching, the party was diminishing. While there were many recognizable faces in the room, it occurred to me that all the Family leaders seemed to have left. I mentioned this to my companions. "What else is new?" they responded. "They're up in some suite talking. They're always talking, no matter where they are."

I remembered seeing my father and Uncle Joe Profaci walk out together a while before, and then Vincent Mangano, followed shortly thereafter by Albert Anastasia. Frank Costello and Willie Moretti were also gone from the room. Tom Gagliano and Tommy Lucchese were nowhere to be seen. I later learned they had adjourned to Costello's suite atop the hotel. Looking back, it seems appropriate that Costello's suite would be the meeting place, since it had been Costello's responsibility to get Luciano's and Lansky's agreement regarding the Siegel matter.

As it got closer to midnight, the mood in the ballroom seemed to slow to a crawl and the band was on a break. A group of bored women who had been chattering had quieted down; others were half-asleep at their tables. Then, as if by some pre-arranged signal, the Leaders all reappeared, smiling and ready to party. Instantly the room awoke, the band started playing, the women resumed their chatter, and the party sprang to life.

Word had come down: the Siegel problem had been taken care of the night before. Bugsy Siegel was dead at the age of forty-one.

Contrary to what you see in the movies, men of our world see no symbolism in the way a person is dispatched. There is no elaborate premeditation of the number of shots, no message or code left at the scene for later interpretation. Now, in the old country long ago, the delivery of a dead fish in a brown bag may have had some meaning to a killer who wanted to send a message—but if so, that was a personal message. When someone is marked for death in our world, the only object is to get in and get out quickly and safely.

Logic dictates that the message must be simple: Whoever is marked for death . . . dies.

At least life ended for Bugsy while he thought life was good.

A number of years later, reflecting on the events that occurred that night, I realized that I was too busy as a young man enjoying the music and dancing at the wedding to notice the apprehension on the faces of some of the leaders when all the Commission members were told about Bugsy. Either they were masking their feelings with wedding smiles, I now recognize, or my skills of observation as a young man left something to be desired. Yet even at that age, my training had alerted me to the subtle absence that evening of all the important leadership of our world—even though the reasons were not for me to know at the time . . . and I knew better than to ask.

In the case of Bugsy Siegel, one mystery remains: the identities of the two shooters. In our world, those who execute such an order, and the details of how it is carried out, are rarely known—even by the person giving the order. To the best of my knowledge, the Siegel case is still open in the Los Angeles district attorney's office. I never knew the name of the Jewish shooter. But many years after Siegel's death, over lunch at Mimi's Italian Kitchen in Los Angeles, I did learn one half of the secret: the name of the alleged Italian shooter during a conversation. The other half of the story remains untold.

10

The 1951 Scheduled Commission Meeting

The Mangano-Anastasia-Moretti Insult

*A lapse in protocol can result in the appearance of disloyalty—
a precursor of death, either his . . . or yours.*

Joe Bonanno

In the late 1940s—even as the Cold War was breaking out between the United States and the Soviet Union—another kind of cold war was developing among three of the New York Families: the Mangano, Luciano, and Gagliano Families. These Families, as shown in the following diagram, were cross-pollinated by a number of nurturing alliances across Family lines. But they were also subject to intra-Family rivalries that festered until the next Commission meeting, in 1951.

Vincent Mangano had grown up on the Brooklyn waterfront, gaining a reputation as a tough Sicilian not to be challenged. By 1951, Don Vicenzu, as we sometimes called him, was in his sixties. He was becoming paranoid, convinced that the younger members in his Family were envious of his position. He was especially insecure regarding Albert Anastasia, his *sotto capo*. Anastasia had cultivated a close relationship with

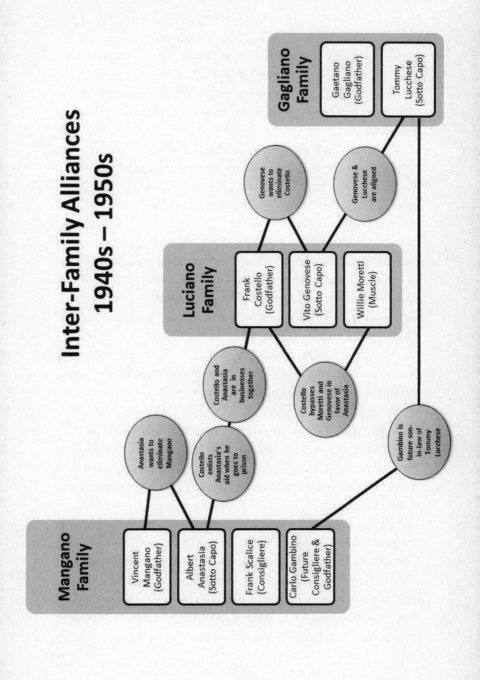

Inter-Family Alliances
1940s – 1950s

Gagliano Family
- Gaetano Gagliano (Godfather)
- Tommy Lucchese (Sotto Capo)

Luciano Family
- Frank Costello (Godfather)
- Vito Genovese (Sotto Capo)
- Willie Moretti (Muscle)

Mangano Family
- Vincent Mangano (Godfather)
- Albert Anastasia (Sotto Capo)
- Frank Scalice (Consigliere)
- Carlo Gambino (Future Consigliere & Godfather)

- Genovese wants to eliminate Costello
- Genovese & Lucchese are aligned
- Costello and Anastasia are in businesses together
- Costello bypasses Moretti and Genovese in favor of Anastasia
- Anastasia wants to eliminate Mangano
- Costello enlists Anastasia's aid when he goes to prison
- Gambino is future son-in-law of Tommy Lucchese

Frank Costello, who by now was the Luciano Family's *rappre-sentate*, and Mangano did not like his number-two man being so cozy with the leader of another Family. Such a situation can plant seeds of doubt—whether justified or not—in an insecure person's mind. Before too long, suspicion and mistrust began taking hold in Mangano's mind. In our world, such feelings of insecurity can be deadly.

Anastasia had also grown up on the Brooklyn waterfront. At that time, he was the most fearsome enforcer in our world. The press had been promoting his reputation as a ruthless killer during the 1920s, crediting him as the prime enforcer of what they called Murder, Inc. This name was a myth, but it made great headlines. But there *was* a group made up of Italians and Jews known for their brutality and willingness to enforce punishment, and Anastasia was a charter member. Anastasia was a no-nonsense, straightforward guy who spoke his mind. You knew where he was coming from at all times. That type of confidence instills fear.

The alliance between Anastasia and Costello strength-ened in the early 1950s. Before going to prison on a con-tempt of Congress charge in August 1952 (for walking out of the Kefauver hearings in New York that month, after testifying for a week in March 1951), Costello asked An-astasia, a member of the Mangano Family, to help Moretti look after the Costello Family's interests. By doing so, he committed three unpardonable sins. First, he bypassed his second-in-command, Vito Genovese, going outside his own Family for help without informing Genovese of what he was doing or why. Second, when he went outside the Family, Costello bypassed the leader of the Mangano Family in favor of Mangano's second-in-command, Albert Anastasia, who at that time was still considered an underling. Third, he also bypassed his own loyal muscle, Willie Moretti, in favor of Anastasia, another Family's *sotto capo*.

In the 1950s, there were approximately 2,700 made members in the New York Families, considered equals regardless of their Family affiliation. Naturally, each Family had its hierarchy of leaders; a clear sense of organization was the only way to manage so many men. And a made guy in one Family was not restricted from doing business with members in another Family. Relationships were born and nurtured, and business transacted with made guys across all Family lines. But this crossover of alliances between Families, especially those involving *rappresentanti*, underbosses, and *capos*, could always be the subject of suspicion, raising fears that a power struggle within a Family might be in the works. Formation of inter-Family alliances, without following protocol, breeds suspicion and stirs up intrigue in our world that is the starting point of possible trouble.

In our world, not unlike your world, confrontations are an inevitable part of life. People and philosophies come into conflict and relationships change over time. Either we do something to resolve the conflicts when they arise, or we wait, allowing things to cool down. In our world, though we may wait, we never forget. This may not always be healthy, because it allows anger to ferment. Sometimes, a new disappointment with an individual can bring back to mind earlier confrontations and reopen old wounds.

In 1951, Vincent Mangano and Albert Anastasia were at a stage where they feared each other. They were like two bull elephants vying for supremacy over the herd. In our world, second place under these circumstances is not an option.

The first battle you fight in any engagement is with yourself. You must overcome all doubts and extinguish all fears about what may happen. Then you look ahead at your enemy and hit him right where you want to hit him.

Anastasia hit first.

In April 1951, Vincent Mangano disappeared. His body was never found. After Vincent's disappearance, his brother,

Philip Mangano, started to cause trouble, threatening to find out what happened and pointing the finger at Anastasia. Not long after that, Phillip was found shot to death in a swamp area in Brooklyn.

The disappearance of Vincent Mangano was an internal matter brought about by jealousy and fragmentation of power within the Mangano Family. But Mangano's disappearance also affected other New York Families because of inter-Family alliances. Maintaining the peace among the Families was crucial in order to avoid war.

Although we continued to hold regularly scheduled meetings of the Commission every five years, at other times Commission members, particularly those in the New York Families, would meet for lunch or dinner whenever it was necessary for face-to-face meetings with their peers. After Vincent vanished and his brother was found dead, we held such a dinner meeting at La Scala, a restaurant on Fifty-fourth Street in New York City. The goal was to clear the air regarding Anastasia's responsibility for the "disappearance" of his Family's *rappresentante*. The Commission also needed to dispel all rumors implicating involvement of other Families. This was the first time since the 1930s that a sitting boss had vanished under mysterious circumstances, so the inevitable conclusion was that he had been killed. And, despite our shared tradition of treating each Family as a sovereign nation, when the head of a nation is assassinated, the other nations get a little nervous.

La Scala was owned by two young Italians, Alberto and Arturo, who had come to this country from Genoa working as seafarers on a merchant-marine ship. After jumping ship in New York, they worked in Little Italy at the Villa Pensa restaurant, and after a few years saved enough money to open a restaurant uptown. Frank Garofalo, the Bonanno Family's *sotto capo*, had helped them get started, making sure that the unions wouldn't bother them and reaching out to the Profaci Family, which was in the linen, liquor, and olive-oil businesses, to "treat them right." As a result, Bonanno Family members felt at home at La Scala. Whenever we needed a restaurant, with our privacy secured, for a special occasion—whether personal or business—that's where we went.

To enter La Scala, you stepped a few steps down from the sidewalk and opened the doors to a small vestibule with a cigarette machine on one side and a cloakroom on the other. The next set of doors led to the main dining room. The walls of the dining room were decorated with pictures of its namesake, La Scala opera house in Milan. There were three rows of tables, one row along each wall and a third one down the middle of the room. The kitchen was in the rear, so all the commotion of a working kitchen was visible right from your table—quite innovative entertainment at that time. There was also a small bar with two or three seats to the right of the kitchen.

To the left of the kitchen was a flight of stairs leading to a private dining room aptly named the Second Act. This room, which could accommodate about thirty or forty people, had its own private outside entrance and private restrooms. We had somewhat more casual business meetings and many social get-togethers in the main dining room over the years, but the Second Act was where the Bonanno Family gathered for important meetings when absolute privacy was required. So, we met upstairs at the Second Act to discuss the Mangano killing and Anastasia's involvement in it (if any), and its potential impact on the other Families. The 1951 scheduled Commission meeting was coming up in November, and the leaders didn't want any surprises to get in the way at that event.

At the La Scala meeting in April, the bond between Costello and Anastasia tightened. Anastasia neither denied nor admitted any involvement in the deaths of Vincent Mangano or his brother. He did inform the members that he had information that Mangano had been planning to eliminate him, and that therefore he had the right to defend himself. Costello vouched for Anastasia, confirming Albert's story. Costello's corroboration was enough to persuade the other leaders to let the matter rest and treat it as an internal Mangano Family matter, outside the Commission's jurisdiction.

At that meeting, the members of the Mangano Family also selected Anastasia as their new leader. But Costello's role as Anastasia's new best friend was an affront to Willie Moretti, who had been loyal to Costello, and now felt undermined. Moretti lashed out by spreading the word that he'd never heard anyone suggest that Mangano had been planning to kill Anastasia. He played on his longstanding role as Costello's confidant, telling others that if Costello had known of such an assassination plot, he surely would have told his loyal right-hand man, his muscle, but that Costello never told him anything of the kind.

In our world, when someone makes statements implying that the leader of a Family is a liar—and, worse, that he has lied to the leaders of other Families—he'd better have clear and convincing evidence, or it's time to get his affairs in order. Moretti must have been insane; he was acting like a woman scorned, as a way of getting back at Costello for hurting his feelings. And in our world, insanity is no defense. Moretti was shot to death in Joe's Elbow Room, a restaurant in Cliffside Park, New Jersey, on October 4, 1951. Vito Genovese ordered the assassination without consulting Costello, although Genovese was prepared for any confrontation with Costello if challenged.

Only after Moretti's death, though, did Genovese realize the strength of Costello's alliance with Anastasia. Genovese would have to establish his own alliances if he intended to replace Costello as head of the Luciano Family. He chose to align himself with Tommy Lucchese.

The regularly scheduled meeting of the Commission took place in November 1951 at the home of Salvatore "Tata" Chiricho, in the Pelham Bay section of the Bronx. Chiricho was an old-timer from the Masseria days, whose home was located at the end of a secluded street near the bay. Built during opulent times, many of the homes in the area had two or three stories with large basements. Tata's house was big enough to accommodate a large group of people, with a side entrance off the main driveway that led directly to the basement. There were three rooms in the basement; one large room with a huge table big enough to seat about fifteen people, and room for more seating along the walls; one smaller room, converted into a fancy kitchen with a small bar; and a bathroom.

The two main issues discussed at this meeting were the Anastasia/Mangano problem and the death of Willie Moretti.

My father, Joe Bonanno (third from left), at a dinner meeting in 1951, his piercing eyes staring into the camera with disapproval.

The Five New York Families
After 1951 Commission Meeting

BONANNO FAMILY	ANASTASIA FAMILY	LUCIANO FAMILY	GAGLIANO FAMILY	PROFACI FAMILY
Joseph Bonanno Sr. Godfather	**Albert Anastasia** Godfather	**Frank Costello** Godfather	**Gaetano Gagliano** Godfather	**Joseph Profaci** Godfather
Frank Garofalo Sotto Capo	**Nino Conti** Sotto Capo	**Vito Genovese** Sotto Capo	**Tommy Lucchese** Sotto Capo	**Joseph Magliocco** Sotto Capo

The meeting of the Commission began with a formal acknowledgment that there wasn't sufficient evidence to prove that Mangano's disappearance was caused by Albert Anastasia, and that Costello's testimony that Mangano had threatened to dispatch Anastasia was a sufficient defense even if Anastasia was responsible. The earlier meeting at La Scala had defused that matter nicely.

The Commission treated Willie Moretti's death with some compassion. Costello pointed out that Willie's strange behavior during the time before his death was probably due to the fact that he was in the advanced stages of syphilis, and stated that Moretti had become an embarrassment to those around him. Thus his illness was offered as the excuse for his jealous-lover reaction to the close relationship between Costello and Anastasia. Nevertheless, Moretti's conduct was considered sufficient reason for his elimination. It was also to Genovese's advantage to get rid of Costello's muscle—even though Moretti's health was failing so badly that he probably didn't have much longer to live anyway. The members viewed his quick death as an act of compassion, and ruled that it was an intra-Family affair that was not the concern of any other Family.

The 1951 Commission meeting established the following principle: "Family business, with consequences within the Family not substantially affecting the other Families, was not a matter for the Commission." This ruling was accepted by every Family in the United States.

There was one footnote to the Vincent Mangano story, in which I played a minor but memorable role.

In April 1951, I was in the Senior Class office on the first floor of the main building at Tucson High School in Tucson, Arizona. I was speaking with the class advisor, Danny Romero, when I received a message that Principal Andy Tolson wanted to see me as soon as possible in his office. Danny and I looked at each other with puzzlement; being summoned directly to the principal's office, without either your classroom teacher or some other staff member being notified, was unusual.

When I arrived at Mr. Tolson's office, I noticed two men in Brooks Brothers suits outside his door. His administrative assistant told me to go right in. Mr. Tolson asked me to close the door and be seated. Then he surprised me. "The two gentlemen outside are FBI agents who would like to speak with you," he said. "I told them that it was your choice whether or not to speak with them, but if you refused, then we would have to contact your parents." He volunteered that both agents seemed to be "put off" when he mentioned speaking to my parents. Then Mr. Tolson, in a very easygoing and paternal manner, walked around his desk, looked into my eyes, and asked, "Are you in any kind of trouble that you want to tell me about? If you are in trouble, maybe

you should contact your family before being interviewed."
I thanked Mr. Tolson and assured him that I wasn't in any
trouble, to the best of my knowledge, and I would have no
problem speaking with the agents. Besides, my parents were
in La Jolla, California, where my father was recuperating
from a recent heart attack.

The agents came into the office. After sitting down, one of
the agents asked if I knew a Vincent Mangano of New York. I
replied that I did. He asked when I'd seen him last. Less than
a week ago, I said. They looked at each other.

"Do you know where he is now?"

"I suppose he's at his home on Tucson Boulevard," I answered.

I sensed excitement in their voices; the mood of the conversation was turning anxious. The agents wanted to know if
I would take them to the location. "Not unless you tell me
what this is all about," I answered. They informed me that
they weren't at liberty to discuss details, but that they wanted
to speak to Vincent about his brother.

Now that didn't make sense to me. I had never heard of
Vincent having a brother.

Then one agent got an idea. "How old is Vincent Mangano?"

"Maybe thirty, or a few years older," I replied.

With that, both agents seemed to deflate. They thanked
me and I was excused.

The Vincent Mangano they were looking for was the leader
of the Mangano Family in New York. The Vincent Mangano I
knew was his nephew, who had recently sold his second home,
on Fourth Street in Tucson, Arizona, to my father.

That ended my association with the Mangano case.

11

The 1953 Extraordinary Meeting of the Commission

Every possession is a burden, and information is a possession.

Joe Bonanno

For twenty-two years, from 1931 until 1953, in a world often described as violent and barbaric, twenty-seven hundred men in the New York–New Jersey metropolitan area coexisted for the most part in peace and tranquillity. The various factions within our world—the Italian/non-Italian group, the Mustache Petes, and the Sicilians—found a way to survive without inter-Family violence.

We had evolved in those decades. By the early 1950s, we had men from almost every Family connected in the garment industry and the entertainment and recording industries. We ran nightclubs, jukeboxes, and vending machines, and controlled trucking as well as shipping and receiving on the docks. We had found success with gambling in Nevada. And we continued to control the labor unions.

By 1953, however, relationships among three of the New York Families—those headed by Anastasia, Costello, and Lucchese—had grown obviously strained. The Commission faced the possibility that these three dominant Families could trigger a war. Such a breakdown would affect the remaining two New York Families, Bonanno and Profaci, as well as the other Families throughout the United States, and the consequences could be dire. Memories of the Castellammarese War loomed in the air; in the words of Yogi Berra, we wondered if this was *deja vu* all over again. The Bonanno and Profaci Families, who operated mainly in Brooklyn, tried to remain aloof from the growing intrigues. But we knew that we would have to get involved if shooting started.

In the wake of the Mangano/Anastasia/Moretti affairs, various alliances were strengthened. Anastasia, now the leader of the old Mangano Family, continued his close alliance with Costello, leader of the former Luciano Family. And Vito Genovese wanted Costello out of the picture so he could ascend to leadership of the Costello Family.

Genovese's alignment with Tommy Lucchese—the *sotto capo* and heir apparent of the Gagliano Family—was getting bolder. The Family's leader, Gaetano "Tom" Gagliano, had been a strong ally of the conservative branch of the Commission. Of all the leaders of the New York Families, however, he is the one who left the least obtrusive mark on history. There are only a few scattered references to him in the history of our world—a testament to his leadership skills. In 1953, Tom Gagliano requested a private dinner with the other four leaders of the New York Families, along with Stefano Magaddino of Buffalo. Gagliano, who was at the peak of his power, asked those assembled if they had any problems they needed to take care of, either with him or any member of his Family. He asked if he had any outstanding obligations, whether social or financial. Then, when the answers came back negative, he declared that he was resigning as leader, effective immediately.

Gagliano announced that his second-in-command, Tommy Lucchese, had his blessing, and the blessing of the subordinate leaders of his Family, to replace him as leader. He further re-

1953 Repositioning of the Five New York Families

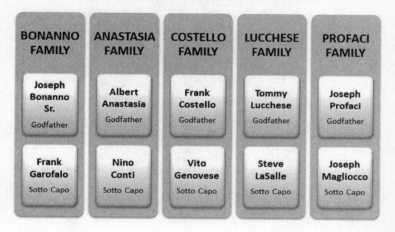

BONANNO FAMILY	ANASTASIA FAMILY	COSTELLO FAMILY	LUCCHESE FAMILY	PROFACI FAMILY
Joseph Bonanno Sr. Godfather	Albert Anastasia Godfather	Frank Costello Godfather	Tommy Lucchese Godfather	Joseph Profaci Godfather
Frank Garofalo Sotto Capo	Nino Conti Sotto Capo	Vito Genovese Sotto Capo	Steve LaSalle Sotto Capo	Joseph Magliocco Sotto Capo

quested that, unless there were any objections, Lucchese would be allowed to take his seat on the Commission immediately. All agreed, and, with that, Tommy Lucchese became a Commission member. A few months later, Gagliano died of natural causes.

As of that meeting, the New York Families took on the names of their new leaders.

The problems among the Families of Anastasia, Costello, and Lucchese were disasters waiting to happen. To try to prevent the inevitable, the Commission decided to hold a special meeting to address the problems.

The 1953 extraordinary meeting took place at the estate of Joseph Profaci's *sotto capo* and brother-in law, Giuseppe "Joe" Magliocco, in Islip, Long Island.

The property had a house with twenty-two rooms, including seven or eight bedrooms, a large living room, a large banquet dining room that could accommodate forty people, and another dining room that could seat at least fifteen, with a

Joseph Maglicco's estate in Long Island, site of the 1953 extraordinary meeting of the Commission.

restaurant-style kitchen that made it easy to prepare meals for a full house. The back porch looked out onto a half-acre lawn with majestic large maple trees; just beyond was the six-stall horse stable, to accommodate Magliocco's passion for horseback riding. Joe Magliocco was not a small man; he weighed close to three hundred pounds. His personal horse was a beautifully configured white Arabian, sixteen hands tall. I often marveled at the ease with which that magnificent animal carried that huge, but proficient, rider. To the north of the stable was a garden where tomatoes, zucchini, and a variety of American and Italian vegetables were grown. One of those Italian delights was *cocuzzi*, long, narrow squash that are among Magliocco's favorite vegetables, and which he grew in his garden with care. When peeled, cut into quarter-inch slices, and cooked, *cocuzzi* make an excellent sauce over either short or long pasta.

The property guaranteed our privacy: a high, solid fence encircled the estate, making the location completely secluded and secure. It was our world's Camp David, a perfect place to spend an afternoon or evening to discuss important business matters.

At the time of the extraordinary meeting, the Commission was facing a serious situation that had the potential to destroy our world if it was not managed successfully. For the first time in our history, one boss (Frank Costello) was accusing a second boss (Tommy Lucchese) of threatening to kill a third boss (Albert Anastasia). The situation was made even more difficult by the huge egos of the players.

On that balmy early summer day in May, the men of the Commission assembled, with concern on their faces and some anxiety in their hearts, and seated themselves around a table to test one another's willingness to maintain the peace. To do this, they needed to draw on their talents for brinksmanship to resolve this unprecedented situation.

Costello had been informed by two men that Lucchese was planning to eliminate Anastasia. Now burdened with that message, Costello announced that he was obliged to inform the Commission and request an investigation. He was doing what he had to do.

Those present at the meeting included my father's cousin Stefano Magaddino, leader of Buffalo; my father's *sotto capo,* Frank Garofalo (we called him Don Ciccio); the Bonanno Family *consigliere,* John Tartamella; and of course my father, Joseph Bonanno. Although I was not yet a formal member of the Family, I was made just a short time later, in 1954, and after that I had this meeting described to me many times, in great detail—as an object lesson in how to avoid potentially volatile and dangerous confrontations using intellect rather than muscle. What I am about to describe is drawn directly from those firsthand accounts.

Everything in our world is calculated. Nothing, no matter how seemingly insignificant, is overlooked. We are taught from an early age to watch out for the little things because they will trip you up. The big things will take care of themselves . . . with a little guidance.

The decision to hold the meeting at Magliocco's estate was not a random choice. The main house, which was well hidden from the road at the end of a long driveway, provided a measure of safety that could be crucial if tempers flew out of control. When one Family leader levels such an accusation at another as Costello was making toward Lucchese, there is no better formula for mayhem. And if mayhem were to ensue, then the utmost seclusion was essential.

When Costello asked the Commission to investigate the alleged Lucchese murder plot against Anastasia, he did so under the guise of preventing another Mangano-style "disappearance"—or, worse yet, a volatile multiple killing in response from Anastasia. By acting preemptively, Costello hoped to have the Commission censure Lucchese—a verdict that carried a heavy weight in our world, possibly even leaving open an opportunity for Lucchese's enemies to move against him.

But there were other motives for Costello to finger Lucchese. Costello was known in our world as the Prime Minister, for both his eloquence and his connections with politicians. Lucchese, too, cultivated relationships with politicians and government officials, and he was also a persuasive speaker. Underlying this whole affair, then, was a subtle rivalry between these two leaders concerning their relative influence with those outside our world in the political arena. Costello's move to demean Lucchese in front of the other members of the Commission thus served several purposes: It would diminish the competition over who would control the politicians, leaving Costello as the undisputed liaison between our world and these government officials. The embarrassment might also weaken Lucchese's alliance with Costello's underboss in the Luciano Family, Vito Genovese, whom Costello recognized as a threat.

Those of us in the unaffected Families, like unaligned nations in a fast-spreading war, were forced to take a stand. There could be no fence-sitting, no ambiguity or neutrality. You listened to the evidence, made your decision, and backed it up. If a consensus was reached, there would be no bloodshed; if not, beware.

After the usual exchange of greetings, Joe Magliocco announced that the meeting room was ready. In marked contrast to the Commission meetings of the past, an undercurrent of uncertainty charged the atmosphere.

The Commission members who were present—Frank Costello, Albert Anastasia, Joe Profaci, Stefano Magaddino, and Joe Bonanno—entered the room first. Although the outcome would affect our entire world, the decision of the New York Families always predominated on any issue. Anthony Accardo, the Commission member from Chicago, had been invited to the meeting, but he had decided not to attend, taking the position that this was a New York problem and agreeing in advance to endorse the majority ruling. This was a typical Chicago Family reaction—sitting on the fence, wanting to stay out of the politics of the New York Families. Magaddino from Buffalo attended reluctantly, only at Costello's request. All the leaders brought their *sotto capos*; some brought the Family's *consiglieri*, who seated themselves behind their respective leaders.

As usual, Costello looked dapper in his well-tailored suit and with his manicured fingernails. He was a man of stature: intelligent, fluent, alert, and conscious of everything around him. For this meeting, he brought along Vito Genovese, his second-in-command. Genovese, who was not a Commission member, had no vote at this meeting. But inviting him along was a shrewd move on Costello's part: it would give him a chance to watch how Genovese and Lucchese interacted. If the rumors of their close relationship were true, Costello might take preemptive action to avoid being the next victim. For all he knew, Lucchese and Genovese might have been scheming together to eliminate both Anastasia and Costello. After all, Costello's elimination would make Genovese the leader of the Luciano Family.

Tommy Lucchese had more than one motive to eliminate Anastasia. Primary among them was his desire to have Costello replaced as the top dog among the Families in the political arena. But he also wanted to open the door for Carlo Gambino, Anastasia's *consigliere*, to become leader of the Anastasia Family. An alliance of three families led by Genovese, Lucchese, and Gambino would make for a powerful trinity on the Commission. This could easily occur because Lucchese and Gambino were close, and in the not-too-distant future would be related by their children's marriage. But if such a plan were actively in the works, any slip of the tongue, even a telling facial expression, at the Commission meeting could have exposed them, giving Costello an opportunity to embarrass Genovese and neutralize Lucchese.

Vito Genovese had dark hair and rugged good looks; he dressed well, although somewhat on the flashy side. He always wore yellow-tinted glasses. His only obvious flaw was his voice, which was a bit higher than those of the other men.

Albert Anastasia was a strong presence in the room, along with his second-in-command, Frank Scalice. Albert was taller than most in our world, and handsome, with wavy hair. But he dressed modestly, and in manner he was artless and plainspoken. When he spoke, it was with the authority of one who could, and would, back up his words with action. Despite his pugnacious reputation, though, Albert could be open-minded; he was capable of compromising for the good of all. There was no facade to Anastasia's personality. What you saw is what you got.

Seated next to him was Joe Profaci—the second-longest-tenured Family leader, along with Stefano Magaddino of Buffalo. Profaci was of medium height, paunchy but not fat. He was never one for exercise, and he certainly never showed much care about what he was wearing. His interest in Family politics and intra-Family fighting took a distant second place to his first love, which was running his olive-oil business. Joe Magliocco, the host, was Profaci's number-two man and sat behind him.

Stefano Magaddino was short, stout, and very hardheaded. He always appeared as a cantankerous old man, obtuse but far from stupid. He had an uncanny instinct for survival. Accompanying Stefano was his number-two man, John Montana.

Seated between Magaddino and Profaci was my father, Joe Bonanno, the youngest member of the conservative wing of the Commission. Seated behind him was his second-in-command, Frank Garofalo, and next to him was Bonanno *consigliere* John Tartamella.

Tommy Lucchese, on trial for his life, waited in an anteroom just off the meeting room, accompanied by Stefano LaSalle, his second-in-command. Once everyone took their seats around the table, the chairman called in Lucchese, who took his place at the table, with LaSalle sitting behind him. Tommy was a short, fair-haired man with a clean-cut look who dressed with studied care; we called him "Tommy Brown" after the baseball pitcher Mordecai "Three-Fingers" Brown, who as a boy had mangled his fingers in a corn grinder on his uncle's farm. When Tommy was a kid he ran around with a gang whose leader was Lucky Luciano. Tommy's parents, worried about his gang connection, demanded he get a steady job, and he did, in a machine shop. While working, he suffered a bad accident that sliced off the thumb and forefinger of his right hand, so the comparison and nickname were well-grounded. As he took his seat, Lucchese displayed no sign of nerves; finesse and opportunism were his trademarks. He always seemed in control of himself. Nothing in his manner betrayed the predicament he was facing.

Tommy "Three-Fingers" Brown Lucchese showing his famous fingers as he is sworn in to testify before the Senate Labor Rackets Committee, 1958.

The first order of business was to ratify the action taken at the last Commission meeting, confirming that the chairman who had been selected at that time would serve for all subsequent meetings held in the next five years. Only two years had passed since the Mangano-Anastasia matter, and at the 1951 meeting the Commission had selected my father to serve for the next five years. So the dubious honor of chairing this extraordinary meeting fell to him.

The gamesmanship began the moment my father addressed the Commission. Having been away from New York for some time, he announced, he had not been privy to many of the situations facing the Families of New York. So he preferred, with the consent of those assembled, to prevail on Joe Profaci to act as chairman for this meeting. This move was not a show of humility; nor did it reflect any indifference to the problems of the New York Families. Rather, it was a calculated move to set him apart from the others, while preserving the chance to cast the deciding vote, as was the chairman's right.

Up to now, the members of the Commission's conservative bloc had always voted the same way. At this meeting, a quick glance around the table revealed two conservative members, Magaddino and Profaci, and two liberal members, Costello and Anastasia. Lucchese, who had replaced the conservative Gaetano Gagliano, could be swayed, depending on the issue— but at this meeting, since he himself was "on trial," he would have no vote. My father, the third conservative, could influence the vote if he saw the need.

My father had not forgotten that Lucchese had been instrumental in Maranzano's downfall; on a personal level, he considered Tommy sneaky, a weasel. Still, if the vote went along "party lines," my father's instincts warned him that he should put his personal feelings aside and find him innocent of the charges brought by Costello; in his view, it was the only way to avoid a shooting war. That is why he chose to hand over temporary chairmanship to Profaci: as chairman, he would have been restricted in his ability to sway the room, but as just another Commission member he was free to maneuver, manipulate, and persuade his fellow members as he thought necessary.

Frank Costello, as the individual bringing the charges before the Commission, spoke first. In a concise opening statement, he reviewed the case against Lucchese, including the damaging testimony from two of Lucchese's own men, who contended that Lucchese was preparing to move against Anastasia. In the interest of peace, Costello explained, he himself had an obligation to bring the matter before the Commission for investigation.

Costello disclaimed any bias in the matter, maintaining that his only concern was that justice be served. He reminded the members that the Families had been at peace for two decades, and that in all that time, this was the first such major inter-Family problem to be brought before the Commission.

As Costello spoke, his eyes shifted from Lucchese to Genovese, looking for the slightest change in Lucchese's demeanor. Lucchese remained expressionless, countering Costello's eloquence by appearing to remain above the fray. Genovese, too, remained stoic as he watched the drama unfold, determined not to display any reaction to his leader Costello's allegations against his confederate, Lucchese.

If Costello intended for his blunt accusations against another Family leader to rattle either Genovese or Lucchese, his plan was not working. Lucchese's very willingness to appear at the meeting demonstrated that he wasn't concerned with its outcome. He could have refused to appear, and instead might have retreated to marshal his forces for a fight. But Lucchese was too smart to do anything of the kind. He realized that such tactics would diminish his chances of retaining power and the leadership of the Family.

After Costello finished, Profaci asked Lucchese to answer the charges brought against him by Costello. This was Lucchese's opportunity to refute the allegations or mount an affirmative defense. To everyone's surprise, he chose to do nothing. He remained mute, almost imperious in his refusal to deny *or* confirm the charges.

Costello pushed for an immediate decision by the Commission based on the only evidence submitted—the testimony of Lucchese's two men. Taken alone, their word would have required a verdict of guilty. It was an uncomfortable moment for all the Commission members. This wasn't amateur hour; they recognized that bringing a guilty verdict against a sitting leader, without an adequate explanation, would be likely to result in war.

The fact was that the Commission members had come to the meeting expecting Lucchese to defend himself. Profaci and Magaddino took his silence to be an admission of guilt.

Neither of them particularly liked Lucchese, and they were not inclined, nor did they want, to probe further.

My father, however, recognized that if Lucchese was eliminated it could tip the balance of power on the Commission from conservative to liberal. It would mark yet another real step away from the conservative traditions toward the priorities of the new generation. He was not ready to permit this to happen. Even though we saw Lucchese as a liberal replacing the conservative Gagliano, my father reasoned that if the conservatives could save Lucchese's life, he would owe them a debt of gratitude—one he could be counted on to repay in the future.

The dilemma was, how do you protect someone, disliked in the first place, when he refuses to protect himself? My father needed time to come up with a strategy.

Bonanno made eye contact with Profaci. A short time later, the temporary chairman suggested a brief recess to stretch their legs, use the facilities, and have some refreshments—a rare but necessary departure from the rule that nobody leaves the room during a Commission meeting. My father was convinced that Lucchese was holding back—that he had something on his mind. Costello and Lucchese were engaged in a deadly game; Genovese's stoic silence, the bluntness of Costello's accusations, and Lucchese's calm refusal to answer just didn't add up.

As John Tartamella, the Bonanno *consigliere*, later related, my father excused himself and motioned to Frank Garofalo, his *sotto capo*, to join him. The three of them got some refreshments and went into the living room area to talk privately. When my father asked what he thought, Garofalo said he felt that Genovese was up to no good—that he was using Lucchese to further his own ambitions. "Why did Costello ask for Magaddino to come?" he mused. As Tartamella pointed out, the New York Families alone constituted a quorum; they would have been able to conduct business and issue binding decisions without Magaddino.

Together, my father and Tartamella concluded that Costello had insisted that the entire conservative wing attend in order to force them to take his side. The conservative wing had no love for Lucchese because of Lucchese's involvement in Maranzano's death. We knew it was Lucchese who had channeled information to Luciano about Maranzano's office habits, thus setting up Maranzano's assassination in 1931. Costello might not have had much luck with some of them; Profaci and Magaddino weren't the kind of men to be moved by incidents from a quarter century ago. My father was different. He had been close to Maranzano, a member of Maranzano's elite fighting force. Costello knew that those old memories might have brought back lingering doubts about Lucchese's loyalty—doubts that might help Costello now, as he tried to capture the conservative vote.

At first, Costello had been pleased when my father relinquished the chair for the meeting. But he soon began to sense trouble, and wondered what my father had up his sleeve. Having made a pretty strong case against Lucchese, he wanted a decision, believing all that was left to do was for Lucchese to fess up and accept the Commission's decision.

Still, there was one unanswered question: Why would Tommy remain silent in the face of a probable death sentence? Was Lucchese trying to tell them something with his silence?

The only thing that would save Tommy Lucchese was the same self-defense argument Anastasia had used when Vincent Mangano, his *rappresentante*, mysteriously disappeared in 1951. If Tommy had evidence that Anastasia was planning to kill him first, Tommy would have had license to act in self-defense.

If Lucchese made this argument, of course, Anastasia would immediately have demanded proof. Did Lucchese have any such proof? If so, was he at liberty to explain where he got the information? Then, if Lucchese *were* to admit plotting against Anastasia, Costello would surely jump in to ask how Lucchese knew this—hoping to draw out whatever involvement Vito Genovese may have had in the matter. Costello knew that, if Lucchese had indeed been plotting to move against one of the New York leaders, he would have needed the support of someone else—and the only logical candidate would be Genovese, Costello's underboss. (The other three Families were content to live and let live as long as their territory of Brooklyn was not disturbed.)

Although Costello failed to ensnare Genovese as he had hoped, he was still confident that the Commission would at least censure or remove Lucchese. Growing impatient, he urged the Commission members to go into the adjoining room and cast their votes. My father, though, wanted to know the truth about Lucchese. However, he knew that if he suddenly objected and asked to speak to Lucchese alone, it would look suspicious. He had to retain the appearance of impartiality. He could not afford any suspicion that he was sticking up for Lucchese.

My father then addressed the group. He reminded them all that they had come a long way to discuss and resolve a very important issue. And he argued that, in the interest of fairness and justice—and knowing the weight the Commission's decision would have in our world—the Commission's temporary chairman, Joe Profaci, should talk to Tommy privately. In that way, he suggested, Profaci might be able to get some information from Tommy that would make our decision easier. "Let's give Tommy the full benefit of the doubt," he added. "After all, the goal, as Frank Costello announced, was to accomplish justice for everyone."

Profaci was taken by surprise. He had not seen the suggestion coming, and had no idea why my father had made it. But he went along with it, figuring he would soon find out.

As Costello mulled this turn of events over in his mind, the others indicated their agreement; after they appealed to his sense of fair play, he assented to the idea. If he had refused, it would put him in a bad light. Furthermore, Costello was sure the others had not figured out his real motive, which was to nail Genovese. After Costello agreed, Profaci invited Tommy to follow him into the adjoining room—still unsure what good it would do.

Once they were alone, Profaci made some small talk with Lucchese, expressing his sympathy and concern, and asked if Tommy had anything to say. Tommy said no.

Profaci threw up his hands. He returned to the meeting room and announced that Tommy had nothing to say. Then, as a last resort, he suggested that my father might have better luck getting Tommy to open up, since they had known each other much longer and had worked together.

Costello was beside himself. Genovese looked extremely uncomfortable. Magaddino, who was feeling left out of the intrigue, was about to say something when Costello said, "Okay, but let Magaddino go with Bonanno." It was a canny move on Costello's part: He knew Magaddino didn't like Lucchese, and he knew that Lucchese knew it. Lucchese wasn't likely to talk freely with Magaddino in the room. Costello felt that Profaci and Magaddino had probably made up their minds concerning Lucchese's guilt, whereas he wasn't too sure where my father stood and saw the risk of allowing him to talk to Lucchese alone.

Magaddino grumbled at Costello's suggestion. Talking to Lucchese was a waste of time as far as he was concerned. But since Costello had asked, he magnanimously agreed.

The two men stepped outside to speak with Lucchese alone. Once again, Tommy refused to speak. My father prodded Lucchese to speak to them, but after one or two refusals, he and Magaddino returned to the meeting room, with nothing gained.

But Magaddino was intrigued by my father's persistence. *What's my cousin Joe up to?* he wondered. *Does he know something I don't? If he does, I want to know, too.* Taking a seat at the table,

Magaddino said, "Tommy won't talk, but since everything else seems to have failed, maybe Bonanno should speak with Lucchese alone." Magaddino's curiosity had gotten the best of him—and played right into my father's hands. Of course that's what he had wanted all along—for someone else to suggest that he meet with Tommy alone, so that he himself wouldn't seem to be siding with Lucchese. And since it was Costello who had asked Magaddino to attend the meeting, Costello could hardly reject Magaddino's suggestion.

When my father stepped outside alone to talk with Tommy, he finally opened up. He told my father that he'd learned that Anastasia was planning to kill him, and he was preparing to defend himself. The problem was, everyone would know that the only person who could have given him such information was Vito Genovese—and he couldn't give Genovese up. If he did, Costello would have the right to eliminate Genovese on grounds of disloyalty—and Lucchese would probably be the next leader killed for conspiracy.

There was only one way out for Lucchese: He would have to find a way to neutralize Costello's eloquence, and answer the evidence he had presented. The wind had to be taken out of Costello's sails.

To help him accomplish this, my father suggested a bold and unusual strategy: Lucchese would have to bite the bullet if he wanted to avoid a bullet to the head. The plan was to defuse Costello's allegations by *admitting* them—and then to ask Anastasia, who suffered the insult, for mercy. Addressing Anastasia directly and bypassing Costello, who brought the charges, was the only way out.

My father would only have suggested such an action if he felt confident that he could anticipate the result with reasonable certainty. To do this, he had to know Anastasia's character very well—and he did. Albert Anastasia had been a social friend of my father's for years. I grew up calling him Uncle Albert. In fact, it was Anastasia who had told my father when it was time to bring me into the Family. "If you don't make Bill, I'll bring him into my Family," he said, "and he'll become a made guy." If anyone knew Anastasia, it was Joe Bonanno.

My father knew that a direct appeal to Albert's sense of justice, and a request for mercy, were the only things that could save Lucchese's life. Albert may have been a ruthless enforcer, but he killed only when he was angry or provoked. A request for mercy would humiliate Lucchese, but it was the only way left to save his life.

Bonanno and Lucchese returned to the meeting, and Lucchese announced that he wished to address the Commission. Looking Anastasia straight in the eye, he admitted that he'd made a mistake and that Albert was in the right. As a man of honor, Lucchese acknowledged that he would have to pay whatever penalty Albert decided. This act of contrition left his fate in Albert's hands rather than that of the Commission.

It was a plea for mercy, and it worked. "Albert Anastasia does not kill people who beg for his mercy," Anastasia responded. Lucchese's humiliation was a small price to pay for his life.

But it would soon turn out to be a bad decision—for Anastasia.

12

The 1956 Scheduled Commission Meeting

Living this lifestyle is like teaching your child to drive: hours and days of boredom interspersed with moments of terror.

Joe Bonanno

One evening, while having dinner with some of our group leaders at La Scala, my father told us that the 1956 scheduled Commission meeting would take place in a small town called Apalachin, New York, near the Pennsylvania border. He would announce the traveling crew within a few days.

Going to one of these out-of-town meetings placed a burden on the traveler, but my father's leadership style included involving his Administration in inter-Family relationships. He felt that if members of our Administration had social and working relationships with the leadership of other Families, it would help to foster a healthy rapport among us all.

On the way home, my father instructed me to be available to shuttle some of the men who were coming in for the meeting. Beyond simple convenience, this served a number of purposes. The primary one was to facilitate developing my relationship with other leaders of our world, but it also served to instill in me a sense of discipline and commitment.

In October 1956, two cars left for Apalachin. I drove one car, with my father and Johnny Morales, a Bonanno Family group leader (and my father's driver and bodyguard), as passengers. Carmine Galante drove the second car, carrying Frank Garofalo and my uncle Giovanni "John" Bonventre (my mother's brother).

At that time, there were several routes available to get to upstate New York. We chose to drive up via Route 17, winding our way through the beautiful Catskill Mountains. In those days, in order to leave as little to chance as possible, we never traveled with more than three people in a car; nor did we travel in tandem with other cars. A lone car with three men never attracts as much attention as a procession of cars traveling together. We decamped for the night in the Arlington Hotel in Binghamton, where Joseph Barbara had made reservations for us. The next morning, we had something to eat at the coffee shop and then left for the meeting.

From left to right: Sal Profaci, Joe Barbara, and my father aboard Profaci's boat Rosalia, *named after his daughter, my future wife. (The photo was taken in 1951; Sal Profaci would later be killed on the boat when the engine mysteriously exploded.)*

*The home of Joseph Barbara,
Apalachin, New York, 1957.*

Getty

*The meeting and entertainment room at the
estate of Joseph Barbara.*

The meeting was to be held at Joseph Barbara's hilltop estate in the little town of Apalachin. Not far from the house, a New York state trooper stopped the car driven by Carmine Galante for speeding. The trooper recognized the occupants of the vehicle, and problems ensued: not only was Galante speeding, he was using the driver's license of a fugitive wanted by the Federal Bureau of Narcotics as well. He was arrested and pled not guilty at his arraignment. The New York State Police later alleged that a West New York/New Jersey police captain and a detective, on behalf of the West New York police commissioner, interceded on Galante's behalf, securing his release after taking a bribe of $1,000 to keep Galante out of jail. (Eventually, the New Jersey Law Enforcement Council opened an investigation into the bribery charges. The police captain and the detective were suspended from their posts. The commissioner, who earned an extra $5,000 per year handling pistol permits for Hudson County, was also suspended from that job. According to the *New York Daily News,* Galante—whose vending-machine business was formerly in West New York—"had a direct line to police headquarters.")

As we pulled up to the estate, Joe Barbara came out of the main house, smiling from ear to ear and welcoming us to his home.

Barbara, a native of Castellammare del Golfo like my father, had made a fortune with his soft-drink bottling and distribution business, Mission Beverage Company, and owned a bottling plant, the Canada Dry Bottling Works, outside of Endicott, a larger town a few miles from Apalachin. His house sat on a sloping hill overlooking the town, reached only by a private dirt road. A large parking area made it convenient to park your car and go directly to a huge stone-faced garage.

The garage also served as an ad hoc entertainment area, with bathrooms, a small kitchen, and an area large enough to set tables for at least thirty or more people. Barbara controlled the local police, whom he paid off to leave him alone. He confirmed that his home would be a safe place to meet. As was my father's custom, we arrived at the meeting before the other Commission members, even though Carmine's interlude with the law had caused some delay.

When the other leaders and members of their Families arrived, we gathered in one of the dining rooms to socialize and enjoy some light Italian dishes. I had been made two years before, in 1954, and this was my first formal Commission meeting. I knew some of the members quite well, including Anastasia and my father's cousin, Stefano Magaddino. And, as a new attendee, I was especially vigilant, looking out for possible alliances between members that might indicate future trouble.

After a while, Barbara signaled to my father that the other, private meeting room was ready. The seven members of the Commission repaired to that room for their private meeting, where they reaffirmed their commitment to continue the Commission for another five years. After their private meeting, they summoned the others from the dining room to join them. I paid particular attention to Tommy Lucchese, who, at least from his body language, gave no indication of any lasting scars from the deep trouble he had found himself in at the extraordinary meeting three years before. He was careful to socialize with everyone, doubtless trying not to draw attention to his closeness with Vito Genovese or to antagonize Anastasia. He was cordial to Carlo Gambino, Anastasia's *consigliere*, but not to the point of suggesting anything might be awry or that the relationship of their children, who would marry six years later, had any influence on the business matters before the Commission.

Lucchese was clever. His practice was always to take sides or switch sides depending on which way the wind was blowing. I had no reason to expect him to change now. As far as I was concerned, he was sneaky, and that made him dangerous. My father cautioned me to watch my back—and his.

The 1956 Commission meeting was supposed to be routine. Except for the recent Mangano-Anastasia affair, our world was relatively calm. At the upper levels of the Family Administrations, there was an understanding nationwide that there would be no breach of the peace.

The meeting began with Chairman Joe Bonanno speaking the words "Attaccarmu tornu" and completing the ritual formality of tying the circle. The seven took their seats at the table reserved for the Commission members. I sat behind my father, giving me a frontal view of Anastasia sitting across from my father. Counterclockwise from Albert sat Joe Profaci, Magaddino, Lucchese, Frank Costello, my father, and the newest member, Sam Giancana, completing the circle. Vito Genovese sat behind Costello, and the rest sat behind their respective leaders, maintaining strict silence.

The Insult

The first item on the agenda was the introduction of Sam Giancana to the members of the Commission and the other high-ranking attendees. Giancana, former *sotto capo* of the Chicago Family, had been chosen by the Chicago Family as its new leader. The sitting leader, Anthony Accardo, had indicated his plans to retire in the near future, and appropriately set the stage for a smooth transition for his successor. Giancana took Accardo's place at the table.

The chairman then asked if anyone had anything to say. And then, out of nowhere, the fireworks started.

As best as I can recall, Giancana looked directly at Anastasia and asked him, "How do you plan the death of Frank Scalice?"—

in other words, When and how are you planning to eliminate him? This came out of nowhere. Scalice was an old-timer, a ranking member in the Anastasia Family. But we had all heard rumors that Anastasia and Scalice were having problems; word on the street was that Scalice was raking in a handsome profit running a secret side business selling memberships in the Family to wannabes. Giancana, like Anastasia, was known for his temper; both were prone to act first and deal with the consequences later.

Still, whatever Scalice's infractions, Giancana—a brand-new member of the Commission—had just questioned Anastasia's leadership, in front of the leaders of all the other Families. It was an outrageous affront, a breach of a fundamental principle: the autonomy of each Family. Anastasia's face grew red; his eyes looked as if they were about to fire bullets. I looked around the room. The other leaders were clearly disturbed, even frightened at what might happen next. Profaci and Magaddino glanced at each other as if hoping the other would say something. This was a major insult, to both Anastasia and the Commission. Was this son of a Sicilian so Americanized that he didn't realize what he had done?

Before anyone else could step in, Anastasia started screaming, "What the hell is this? Who the hell are you? Why, I have every right—"

Magaddino cut him off midsentence. "Albert, calm down." But this only enraged Anastasia more. He rose to his feet and continued: "You—the new boss of Chicago. You come out here and you want to know about *my Family*! Why, I'll send you back to Chicago! Don't anybody dare to stop Albert!" he cried, referring to himself in the third person. "Nobody should interfere in my Family. I say nobody!" Anastasia lunged across the table at Giancana.

At that point, my father took charge. He stood up, protecting Giancana while trying to shout Anastasia down. "Albert, sit down! You are out of order!"

"All right, you're the chairman," Anastasia answered, never taking his eyes off Giancana. "I'll shut up." And then, with great hesitation, Albert sat down.

We were now in a situation where somebody was going to lose face. As the tension mounted, Giancana held fast, unwilling to appear intimidated. After my father restored some semblance of order to the meeting, Giancana then said apologetically, "I meant no disrespect." The situation, for the time being, was defused. It was the only time I can remember Giancana displaying any form of capitulation. That didn't fit his reputation, and it wasn't his style. My mind wandered uneasily to the prospect of what might follow between them after the meeting was adjourned.

Eager to lower the emotional temperature in the room, my father quickly changed the subject, raising the matter of adding two new members to the Commission: Joe Zerilli of Detroit, and John LaRocca from Pittsburgh. This would bring the total number of members on the Commission to nine. From time to time, the Commission might drop or add a city this way; indeed, not long thereafter LaRocca would retire to Sicily, and the Commission would replace him with Angelo Bruno from the Philadelphia Family, reasoning that continued representation from that part of the country was important.

After Giancana affronted everyone, the meeting calmed down—at least on the surface—but I noticed clear undercurrents suggesting that the inter-Family alliances were growing stronger. Vito Genovese and Lucchese were already allies. If Costello were eliminated, Genovese would take over that Family. If Anastasia was eliminated, Carlo Gambino, who had familial ties to Lucchese, might be his logical successor. There was no question now that Giancana would risk few repercussions if Anastasia were to have an unfortunate accident.

Narcotics

Such considerations weren't merely academic. If the balance of power among the New York Families were to shift from conservative to liberal, the Commission's position on narcotics trafficking would surely change with it. The subject of narcotics was the next item on the agenda at the meeting.

The problem of narcotics had been a thorny problem confronting the Commission for some time. After World War II, worldwide narcotics production and trafficking had become big business—partly as a source of income for war-ravaged countries and their governments, and partly as a prodigious source of personal income for the many people involved in the growing, production, and distribution of drugs in their various forms. Throughout the Middle East, South America, and the Far East, narcotics were a flourishing and profitable business. People in our world took notice of this situation, and some of them logically saw potential there.

However, that led to a dramatic schism among the leaders of our world. The liberal faction openly pressed for the Families' participation in narcotics trafficking, pressing the Commission to revisit the anti-narcotics resolution passed at its 1946 meeting. The conservative faction, however, opposed involvement just as strongly. This issue would be the subject of many meetings, debates, and positioning until it finally took its toll, weakening the fabric and structure of our world.

At first the debates were contained within the Luciano Family, by now rechristened the Costello Family. Frank Costello, the Family's leader, was against our participation in drug trafficking. But Vito Genovese, who spent most of World War II in Italy as both a "friend" of the Italian government and an unofficial adviser to the American occupation forces, advocated for it.

165

From the time Genovese returned to the United States, the friction and unrest in this important and large Family was obvious enough to cause concern among the other New York Families. As time went on, factions within the other Families— both in New York and nationwide—began jockeying for position on the issue. Narcotics were the single most dividing issue to face our world since Prohibition and the Castellammarese War of 1930–31.

By 1956, the issue had completely divided our world, with each side staking out strong positions. The majority on the

Commission Members' Ages

1931 Average Age 36 Years Old			1956 Average Age 56 Years Old		
Member	Territory	Age	Member	Territory	Age
Luciano	New York	34	Costello	New York	65
Profaci	New York	34	Profaci	New York	59
Bonanno	New York	26	Bonanno	New York	51
Gagliano	New York	47	Anastasia	New York	54
Mangano	New York	43	Lucchese	New York	57
Magaddino	Buffalo	40	Magaddino	Buffalo	65
Ricca	Chicago	34	Giancana	Chicago	48
			Zerilli	Detroit	59
			LaRocca	Pittsburgh	46

Commission still voted with the conservatives that year, confirming the Commission's position that narcotics was not an approved business. Yet the younger generation, eager to expand the operations of the Families and to profit from the growing narcotics traffic, was beginning to test the resolve of the old-timers.

One important factor was age. In 1931, the average age of the Commission members had been thirty-six. By 1946, the average age had risen to fifty-six.

Before the 1956 Commission meeting adjourned, we conservatives would be left with a sense of trepidation over what was to come. Our fears were warranted.

In 1956, my father was at the apex of his career. He was a man of substance, with three homes: one on Long Island; a second in Tucson, Arizona; and a third, a fourteen-room Colonial in upstate New York, surrounded by 280 acres of pas-

*My father (seated between men standing) toasting
at dinner with workers at his Sunshine Dairy Farm in
Middletown, New York, 1946.*

tures and hills. The Bonanno Family had numerous business interests, including a funeral home, garment factories in New York, cheese factories in Wisconsin and Canada, a working dairy farm in Middletown, New York, a bakery, and a cotton and cattle ranch in Arizona.

He was on top, economically, personally, and professionally, and was highly respected by leaders both in New York and across the country. The other leaders often turned to him for advice, because of his reputation for being able to bridge the gap between the old Sicilian traditions and how we were trying to make them work in America. He was one of the few American leaders who was able to approach leaders of the tradition in Sicily.

The event that enhanced my father's prestige among the Families more than any other was the wedding he threw for me and my bride that year. Every Family leader but two attended. The reception was held in the Grand Ballroom of the Astor Hotel in New York, and there were three thousand guests.

Beyond a social occasion, the wedding symbolized unity and peace—although it was a fragile peace at best. Vito Genovese and Albert Anastasia still harbored their longstanding animosity toward each other. Anastasia and Costello alike were still watching Lucchese with caution. But they all attended my wedding, making an effort to put on a good front for the visiting Families.

My wedding reception in the Grand Ballroom of the Astor Hotel in New York, 1956. More than three thousand guests were in attendance.

With my bride, Rosalie, cutting our six-tiered wedding cake.

13

1957: The Year of
Turmoil in Our World

You can never be a good captain on smooth waters.

Joe Bonanno

Trouble in Sicily

In late 1956, my new bride, Rosalie, and I went to Italy for our honeymoon.

Upon our arrival at the Palermo airport, my uncle John Bonventre from New York, a group leader in our Family, was there to meet me, accompanied by a couple of men from our world. After greeting us, Uncle John told me that my father had contacted him and left instructions for me to call him as soon as I arrived at the terminal. When I called, my father told me that he wouldn't explain any further over the phone, but that he didn't want me to go anywhere near Villabate, the home town of Rosalie's family.

He told me that my uncle John would fill me in further. When I asked Uncle John, he explained: "I just had a conversation with Uncle Joe," referring to Joe Profaci. "Profaci told me about some problems and suggested that neither of us go to his town." Fine, I said; I was curious, but I didn't ask any questions.

• • •

That evening, after dinner at a local restaurant, we all went to the Mondello Palace Hotel in the town of Mondello, just outside of Palermo. Uncle John and I went outside to a terrace and spoke confidentially. Over espresso, biscotti, and some anisette, he explained that there was a battle raging in the Palermo underworld for control of the marketplace.

On our honeymoon in Sicily, 1956.

My father (left, with shotgun) with group leader John
Bonventre at the farmhouse of Uncle Lucio Labruzzo,
my mother's brother, in Bullville, upstate New York.

In Sicily, much like in the United States, some underworld factions were vying for power within the unions that controlled citrus, fishing, construction, and other industries. Although ten years had passed since the end of World War II, Sicily was still trying to recover: Most of the postwar reconstruction money had gone to the North, which was more industrialized, and little cash seemed to trickle down to Sicily.

The situation had grown serious enough, Uncle John explained, that people were getting killed. Only a few days earlier, Joe Profaci's cousin Antonio Catoni had been murdered. I was content to stay away—but Rosalie was anxious to know why we couldn't go to see her father's hometown, and this created the first little friction between us. In true Sicilian fashion, I told her to leave it alone, and nothing more was said about it. When I returned to the United States, I gave my father a full report on the trouble in Palermo regarding the unions, as well as the debate over narcotics in Sicily, which paralleled the situation in the United States.

May 1957: The Attempted Assassination of Frank Costello

As the 1950s wore on, Vito Genovese continued building alliances both within and outside the Costello Family. Genovese, who always believed that he should have been the one to take over the Luciano Family after his return from exile, gave the order to Vincent "The Chin" Gigante to take out Frank Costello, his rival.

On May 2, 1957, the assassination was attempted. Fortunately for Costello, the assassin's bullet only grazed his scalp—but that was enough. The message was clear. Genovese, who had cultivated strong relationships within the

Costello Family, was prepared to take control. The warning was enough to drive Costello into retirement, and Genovese took over the Family.

Albert Anastasia was furious at Genovese's power play. He wanted to restore his ally Costello to power—by eliminating Genovese.

Anastasia tested the waters by approaching the conservatives—Profaci, Magaddino, and my father—making his case for war and asking if they would try to stop him. If the conservatives were willing to remain neutral, Anastasia said, he planned to kill Genovese and his allies. But my father took a strong position against Albert's plans. If war broke out, he explained, there would be no winners. Ultimately, he persuaded Anastasia to listen to reason. Albert backed off; he and Genovese even met, reconciled their positions, and declared a peace. But there was another, more profound result from all this: from that point forward, the burden of securing and preserving the peace had been shifted to the shoulders of the conservatives.

June 1957: The Killing of Frank Scalice

A further indication of unrest in our world came with the killing of Frank Scalice on June 17, 1957. Scalice had been a controversial figure in our world ever since Vincent Mangano had replaced him as leader of one of the original five New York Families back in 1931. After Anastasia stepped into Mangano's shoes in 1951, Scalice was elevated to the position of *sotto capo*. But one day in June 1957, Scalice was buying fruit in the Bronx when a couple of men came in and sent him to meet his maker. With Scalice out of the way, the door opened for Carlo Gambino to step forward and begin the era of what would soon be the Gambino Family. His son's marriage to Tommy Lucchese's daughter, in 1962, would tighten the bond between these two powerful Families.

September 1957: Joseph Bonanno's Trip to Sicily

Later in this same turbulent year, my father traveled to Palermo, primarily for a non-business trip—to attend the dedication of an orphanage in Ribera at the request of Fortunato Pope, the editor of *Il Progresso*, the largest Italian-American newspaper in the United States. Pope's father had a long history of association with the Bonanno Family.

In preparing for the trip, my father—who was still the sitting chairman of the Commission—had a bon voyage luncheon with Genovese and Lucchese. As he filled them in on his travel plans, they asked, "Who should we contact while you're in Sicily in the event of a crisis?" He said, "Contact Stefano Magaddino. He's the oldest member on the Commission, and he knows more than the others about our tradition." As my father would find out after returning to the United States, however, the question Genovese and Lucchese asked wasn't so innocent.

In our life, there is no such thing as a total vacation. Even during the most personal of times, you are always working. When word got around that Joe Bonanno was in Italy and heading to Palermo, some of the Sicilian Family leaders reached out through the Castellammare Family to ask for my father's help. They arranged a get-together for about sixty at Spano's Restaurant on the waterfront there, including many well-known members of our world.

At the gathering, some of the Sicilian Family leaders approached my father asking for guidance in resolving the issues they had with one another, in hopes of putting an end to the Sicilian marketplace killings. They told Bonanno that Lucky Luciano and Santo Sorge were in town meeting with people in Palermo, and that they "would like to have a discussion about our problems and about a professional relationship between the United States and Sicily." As a courtesy, my father said he would be happy to discuss the problems with them. The discussions that followed were informal; there was no specific agenda, and no tying of the circle, because he had no authorization for such a meeting. To try to invest such a meeting with some kind of official status or formal agenda would have been like members of the U.S. Congress going to Italy and trying to pursue a shared, but unsanctioned, governmental agenda with members of the Italian government.

Rather, this meeting was an opportunity for a number of people involved in this lifestyle in Italy to hear some insights and suggestions from someone whose experience might benefit them. The Sicilians we met in Palermo were a group of people with a common background, trying desperately to resolve problems they did not know how to handle. In attendance were Santo Sorge from Sicily, representing Lucky Luciano (who, contrary to published reports, was *not* present); Carmine Galante; John Bonventre; Frank Garofalo; Toto Greco; my father, Joseph Bonanno; and Tomas Buscheta, along with the heads of other Sicilian Families such as Nino Badalamenti of Cinisi and Salvatore "Totò" Riina of Corleone, who were fighting each other. Rumors later suggested that this was a formal meeting held for the specific purpose of discussing narcotics, but that is not true. The rumor probably came about because some of those in attendance, such as Sorge, had narcotics convictions— and narcotics always made for good gossip.

The discussions covered several issues that had recently come to a head in the old country. The group knew that in America, at least since 1931, the Families had coexisted in

Our ancestral home, Castellammare del Golfo, Sicily.

relative peace. The heads of the warring Families wanted to hear firsthand how they maintained that peace—from someone who faced the same problems they were facing.

The Madonie Mountains and the Castellammare del Golfo region of Sicily were dotted with small towns, each of which might have one or two small Families, from three or four up to ten or fifteen people per Family.

Palermo played host to five or six larger Families. Some of these Families formed allegiances, but for the most part they were disorganized, much as they had been in America before the Commission was formed. If the marketplace murders in and around Palermo were to stop, what better solution than to form an American-style Commission, which my father suggested.

The Italian Families were also plagued by the rise of factions that were at odds with their Families' officially sanctioned businesses. Just as in the United States, the postwar years saw some of the younger members beginning to give the old-timers problems—especially over their interest in the narcotics trade— and the old-timers were looking for guidance in how to resolve the situation. The Italian Families were fragmenting; some of these younger members were becoming involved with the Turks and others in the Middle East, attracted by the potential for easy money. The result was constant fighting—not just between the

176

Families, but also within each of the Families, over this narcotics business.

The Sicilian Families' representatives also expressed their desire to develop closer ties with the Families in the United States. Italian law enforcement was in close contact with American law enforcement, and the Sicilian leaders recognized that there might be opportunities to learn from their American counterparts how to deal with the kinds of challenges they too would soon be facing. If Italian officials could learn from their American counterparts, they figured, why shouldn't they learn from us as well?

To facilitate such matters, they suggested creating a formal alliance between the Sicilian and American Families in our world—a kind of international Commission.

As my father later recalled to me, he politely but emphatically responded that he was in no position even to entertain such a question on behalf of the Commission in the United States. The concept of a Commission was strictly an American invention; no such body even existed in Sicily. As my father saw it, an alliance between our Commission and the fragmented Families in Sicily—beyond the usual courtesies extended to those in our world—was out of the question. (Later, the Italian Mafia *would* form a Commission, loosely patterned on ours. The primary difference was that the *consigliere* of each Family was also a Commission member, which was not the case in America.)

And there were other problems we faced in 1957, at home and abroad. One international challenge was that we were losing our grip in Cuba. Fulgencio Batista, who looked kindly upon our control of the casino business in Cuba, was being threatened by a communist insurgent movement led by Fidel Castro, his brother Raul, and Che Guevara, who were hiding out in the hills surrounding Havana, preparing for revolution.

My father, second from left, inspecting Cuban fruit. His bodyguard (and future sotto capo), Johnny Morales, is in the dark suit, far right.

Meanwhile, back in New York, the Profaci Family was beginning to have trouble with the Gallo brothers, who began muscling in on Profaci businesses, claiming they weren't getting their fair share of the profits. Tommy Lucchese was having some troubles in the Bronx. Vito Genovese had not yet solidified his hold on the old Costello group within his Family. Albert Anastasia was dealing with some rumblings of discord within his Family, in both New Jersey and Manhattan. The only Family that didn't seem to have any internal problems was the Bonanno Family—and soon that, too, would change.

October 1957: The Palermo Meeting at the Grand Hotel et des Palmes

A month after my father's arrival in Sicily, another meeting was held in Palermo, Sicily. My father attended that meeting

The Five New York Families as of Mid-June 1957

BONANNO FAMILY	ANASTASIA FAMILY	COSTELLO FAMILY	LUCCHESE FAMILY	PROFACI FAMILY
Joseph Bonanno Sr. Godfather	**Albert Anastasia** Godfather	**Frank Costello** Godfather	**Tommy Lucchese** Godfather	**Joseph Profaci** Godfather
Frank Garofalo Sótto Capo	**Frank Scalice** Sotto Capo	**Vito Genovese** Sotto Capo	**Steve LaSalle** Sotto Capo	**Joseph Magliocco** Sotto Capo

with Frank Garofalo and John Bonventre. Others mentioned as being there were influential members of the Sicilian Mafia including Santo Sorge, Tommaso Buscheta, and Gaetano Badalamenti. Some books and articles by outsiders have suggested that others attended, but I don't recall my father naming any of those others in any of our conversations. Sicilians alive today, relatives of those who attended, may have secondhand knowledge of that meeting—but, despite the fact that it occurred more than fifty years ago, it remains true that revealing anything about who attended, or what occurred, could have terrible repercussions. What is known now about this meeting may be all that will ever be known.

I will tell you what my father told me. At this meeting, the Commission's ban on narcotics trading—ratified just a year earlier—was put to a dramatic challenge. And it soon became apparent from the Sicilian *mafiosi* in attendance that many of the Families in the United States considered the "ban" nothing more than lip service, a way to pacify the conservatives for the time being and keep things amicable among the Families. By now, heroin was flowing freely between Sicily and the United States. Several of the New York Families were involved heavily in the drug trade and reaping enormous profits. And they could no longer be persuaded to honor the ban; instead, they spoke in an almost unanimous voice in favor of sanctioning drugs.

In an effort to explain to the Sicilians why he opposed drug trafficking, my father addressed the subject directly at the meeting. My father found narcotics and prostitution despicable, beneath the dignity of real men of honor. The Bonanno Family made money from gambling, liquor, the garment industry, and other businesses that were not regarded by the politicians as hurting people. If the Families got deep into narcotics, he argued, we would lose the support of the politicians we had cultivated so carefully over the years, and law-enforcement officials would no longer be our silent and forgiving partners.

But my father's words fell on deaf ears. Faced with such broad opposition, he informed the Sicilian leaders, "What businesses you elect to engage in is your Family's decision and will not be interfered with by the Bonanno Family. However, Bonanno will not deal in drugs. And any member of our Family caught doing so will pay the penalty of death." From that time on, narcotics and the other operating businesses in most Families in our world were treated the same.

Beyond his personal distaste for the narcotics trade, there was another reason my father did not want the Bonanno Family involved. He didn't want the federal government poking its nose into our affairs. We knew the local politicians and law-enforcement officials, and we paid them handsomely to look the other way. This allowed us to preserve our low profile. Becoming known for drug trafficking would be like waving a red cape in front of a charging bull.

But the other Families were unable to resist the temptations of the drug trade. This created a schism within the Commission, but more than that, over the years it gave rise to a broad public assumption—one that was blithely spread by the press and law enforcement alike—that the Mafia was a drug-trafficking organization. By the late 1960s, thanks to Mario Puzo's bestselling novel *The Godfather* and other influences, this impression spread like wildfire. To those of us who had fought the spread of narcotics in our world—only to be lumped in with more liberal members as "drug lords"—watching this cultural shift was like watching Josef Goebbels, Adolf Hitler's infamous minister of propaganda, use his Big Lie strategy to spread hatred throughout prewar Germany. In postwar America, the same techniques were used by Madison Avenue, now rebranded as "dominant imagery." And in our world they were used to neutralize, or at least minimize, elements of our world, by unjustifiably painting everyone with the same broad brush.

During the roughly sixty-year war my father fought with the authorities, and the almost thirty-five years I fought with them, a great deal was proclaimed and written about the Bonanno Family's alleged involvement in various crimes. But no one has ever presented a single piece of factual or credible evidence indicating that either my father or I personally approved any narcotics enterprises.

The now famous meeting at Palermo on October 10–14, 1957, offers one example of this culture of misrepresentation. One so-called expert, Claire Sterling, describes in her book *Octopus: The Long Reach of the International Sicilian Mafia* the meeting at the Grand Hotel et des Palmes in apparently authoritative terms. Sterling, who of course was nowhere near the meeting, states flatly that "every man in the Sala Wagner [an ornate suite named after the German composer] was a drug trafficker." Where did this claim come from? It came from an Italian judge who decided to indict those attending the meeting for "organizing the drug traffic to the United States through Sicily." "Bonanno was very big in junk," Sterling writes. She makes no attempt to offer proof; it's just one of many statements in a book based on the opinions of individuals with no firsthand knowledge.

Since in our world we treated all members as equals, even the *rappresentante* stayed out of the business affairs of his Family's members, as long as they had no harmful repercussions to the Family.

Upon my father's return to New York from Palermo, he called a meeting of all the group leaders in the Bonanno Family. All agreed that no one in our Family would deal in narcotics. His explanation to the Family in that meeting was plain:

> When things become a little hard, about narcotics, I pass[ed] a law in my Family. I don't have to tell Luciano. Who deal with narcotics, you die. I give you three months of time. Pack up, close, no more business; the benefit of the doubt. Anybody fool me, they're gonna get killed. Men of tradition approve that. They don't like. In Charlie [Luciano's] Family, and in [the] Lucchese Family, look like there was some that didn't like the idea. My personal law. The cops will come in and they will destroy us and destroy the tradition and the system.

In other words, any member caught doing so would be held responsible for his transgression—and be given three months to leave. If, after that time, such a member was still around, my father gave clear instructions: "You don't have to come see me. I don't have to give the order. Shoot him and kill him! I can do anything I want in my Family for the good of the Family and for the purpose of what's right."

Everyone who knew my father well knew exactly how he felt about narcotics. From late 1978 into the 1980s, while I was

Outside the U.S. Penitentiary at McNeil Island, before I returned to prison on charges of violation of probation, 1978.

With Anthony Tarantola near a bullet-riddled sign outside Camporeale, Sicily, hometown of both the Tarantola family and my mother's family, the Labruzzos.

serving time in prison, my father came to rely on my number-two man, Anthony Tarantola.

They were so close that my father even referred to Anthony as "my son" or "my nephew" in interviews and newspaper articles—and indeed the Tarantolas were related to the Bonannos.

Regarding the narcotics issue, Anthony recalls my father's position clearly: "When discussing the heroin involvement of certain Families after the war, and primarily when things heated up in the mid-1950s, there is no doubt in my mind Joe Bonanno was dead set against narcotics trafficking and was never personally involved with it. When the subject of narcotics came up, his eyes—which were piercing to begin with—would look like they were on fire."

After my father laid down his ultimatum in 1957, we did learn that some members of the Bonanno Family were dealing in this "side business." The greed for fast money was the new intoxicating elixir, too lucrative for some younger members to resist. The risks were high, but the profits were even higher, and some considered the risks worth taking. For the most part, they were right: only a small fraction of those involved in narcotics were ever caught. Some were even members of the Family's Administration—and they received envelopes of cash from time to time in exchange for keeping quiet. As always, money flowed upward. No one asked questions about where this money came from or how it was earned. To do so would have been like asking for a bullet in the head.

One Family member found to be dealing in narcotics was Carmine "Lilo" Galante, a group captain, who was dealing in Montreal and who was subsequently involved with the French Connection trafficking scandal. By the time my father learned about his activities, however, things had already gone too far. My father recognized that Galante was a lost cause. "It didn't matter anymore," he said. "Killing Galante now . . . wouldn't kill the problem. But my order still stands!" Galante did become persona non grata in the Bonanno Family after we became aware of his narcotics dealings. He was out of favor for roughly twenty years, despite repeated requests for others in the Family to intercede on his behalf. He was a stain on the fabric of our tradition and the Bonanno Family.

In 1960, Galante was indicted on violation of federal narcotics laws; in 1962 he was found guilty and sentenced to thirty years in prison. He was incarcerated in Alcatraz pending appeal and released on parole around 1974. In 1979, members of the Family killed him after he gorged himself on a sumptuous lunch at Joe and Mary's Italian-American Restaurant in Brooklyn.

October 25, 1957:
The Murder of Albert Anastasia

My father returned from Sicily on October 27. Only then did he learn that Albert Anastasia had been gunned down two days before, on the morning of October 25, in the barbershop of the Park Sheraton Hotel on Fifty-sixth Street and Seventh Avenue in New York City. It was Genovese—in concert with Tommy Lucchese, now head of his Family—who ordered Anastasia killed. They claimed that they had tacit approval from Stefano Magaddino of Buffalo. I say "tacit approval" because Magaddino wanted to be known as the most senior and most significant member of the Commission. (This isn't to say that Magaddino wanted to be made *capo di tutti capi*; as before, that was a position only journalists and law-enforcement officials used, not those in our world. I never met anyone who thought he was the *capo di tutti capi*.) The Commission worked precisely because it was decentralized—because of our policy that each Family must stay out of the internal affairs of the others, as confirmed by the outcome of the 1956 Commission meeting, after Giancana insulted Anastasia.

Over the years, many writers have characterized various men as boss of all bosses: Charlie Luciano, Vito Genovese, Frank Costello, even my father, Joe Bonanno. None of these men ever showed the slightest inclination toward that kind of posture. I remember meeting Vito Genovese at the Waldorf-Astoria; he looked more like a bellboy than anyone claiming such a grand title. Neither he nor any other Family leader ever showed the condescension you might expect from someone claiming such a title. And I personally met every one of them during the 1940s, 1950s, and 1960s.

November 9, 1957:
Meeting in Livingston, New Jersey

After Anastasia's murder, the threat of a shooting war was in the air once more. The meeting that prevented such a war was held on November 9, 1957, at the home of a Genovese captain named Ruggiero "Richie" Boiardo in Livingston, New Jersey. It was not a Commission meeting, but the Anastasia Family did invite some Commission members to attend—including Stefano Magaddino, Tommy Lucchese, Angelo Bruno, myself, and my father, whom they asked to chair the meeting. The Anastasia Family had split into two groups over whether Albert had "stepped over the line" and deserved what he got. At this meeting, each group had the opportunity to state its case.

One group, the Anastasia loyalists, was represented by Aniello Delacroce and Tommy Rava. The other group was represented by Carlo Gambino, *consigliere* of the Anastasia Family. As always, Gambino was aligned with Tommy Lucchese, head of the Lucchese Family. At the meeting, Lucchese suggested that my father, as chairman of the Commission, appoint a temporary leader of the Anastasia Family. This was a shrewd move by Lucchese, because a temporary appointment that was approved by the Commission was unlikely to be challenged. But it should be noted that the Anastasia Family had to grant the chair of the Commission this authority, or the Commission would have no power to act. And that is exactly what happened: The opposing parties—as well as Nino Conti, who had replaced Frank Scalice as Anastasia's *sotto capo*—agreed that my father, as chair, should name the temporary leader. Bonanno and the Commission accepted their decision, and the groups declared a truce.

Although some speculated that Carlo Gambino may have had a hand in Anastasia's murder, there was no hard evidence against him, and my father chose Gambino as temporary leader of the Family, for a three-year term. However, he did so under

The Five New York Families as of November 9, 1957

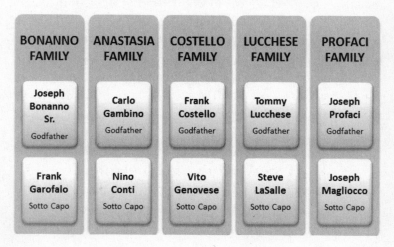

BONANNO FAMILY	ANASTASIA FAMILY	COSTELLO FAMILY	LUCCHESE FAMILY	PROFACI FAMILY
Joseph Bonanno Sr. Godfather	**Carlo Gambino** Godfather	**Frank Costello** Godfather	**Tommy Lucchese** Godfather	**Joseph Profaci** Godfather
Frank Garofalo Sotto Capo	**Nino Conti** Sotto Capo	**Vito Genovese** Sotto Capo	**Steve LaSalle** Sotto Capo	**Joseph Magliocco** Sotto Capo

three conditions: First, that Gambino report to a Commission member from time to time. (Tommy Lucchese, future father-in-law to Gambino's son, would fill this role.) Second, that neither Gambino nor any other group leader could arbitrarily be removed or replaced without Commission approval. And, third, that at the end of his probationary term, if everyone was happy, Gambino would become the permanent leader. That's exactly what happened.

Some years later, I had the opportunity to ask my father why he'd chosen Gambino despite the suspicions that he may have been involved in Anastasia's assassination. My father's answer was short and blunt: "One needs much more than his masculinity to survive in this world of ours. One needs friends. We considered Gambino a generally peaceful person, somewhat servile, but one who would go out of his way to avoid conflict. We needed someone who could bring the various warring factions together and not tear them further apart. We did not need guts—what we needed was brains. Brains he had."

As it turns out, my father's analysis was correct. In 1960, at a meeting in Ontario, California (we were in the state to attend that year's Democratic National Convention), we officially sanctioned Gambino as the head of the Family. Years later, in 1968, Gambino's diplomatic personality would serve us well, when—mindful of his own accession to Family leadership—he voted to declare peace between the Bonanno Family, newly torn by internal conflict, and the Commission.

November 14, 1957:
The Apalachin Meeting

When my father returned from Sicily on October 27, 1957, he learned that, in his absence, Tommy Lucchese and Carlo

otbara's home in Apalachin. My father was opposed to the idea.
He saw no reason to hold another national meeting so soon
after the 1956 scheduled meeting, and he knew that Barbara
no longer felt he could vouch for the security at his home. The
police had been demanding more money from Barbara to keep
quiet about goings-on at his house, and they were reluctant to
let anything further happen there after the bribery allegations
made against the New York police officers in relation to Carmine Galante's speeding arrest.

Lucchese and Gambino may have conceived the meeting—
and recruited the support of my father's cousin Stefano
Magaddino—but their reasons have been misrepresented
through the years. There has been much speculation regarding the purpose of the Apalachin meeting. The FBI
files suggest the following nine different theories for the
meeting:

1. That Genovese wanted tribute for a fund
   used to bribe corrupt public officials

2. That Barbara was acting as a banker, using
   his large fireproof vault to store cash used
   to settle accounts of various business transactions between the members

3. That the meeting concerned the manufacture, distribution, and sale of liquor and
   arrangements for procuring sugar for the
   manufacture of illegal alcohol

4. That the "money men" were meeting to con-
   fer about future legal or illegal ventures

89

5. That the meeting was to discuss ways to counter adverse publicity regarding the McClellan Committee investigation into trade union corruption and exploitation for criminal purposes

6. That we were discussing plans to gain control of the garment industry

7. That we were discussing plans to get further involved in narcotics trafficking

8. That we were discussing gambling in Havana

9. That we were meeting to settle who would control the rackets after Anastasia's murder

The FBI was wrong on all counts.

The 1957 Apalachin "barbecue," as it's sometimes called, was never intended to be a Commission meeting in the first place. It was a social get-together, with two ancillary business purposes. The November 9 meeting in Livingston, a few days earlier, was where the important business was discussed.

The real goal of the Apalachin meeting, as Lucchese and Gambino intended it, was to put a stop to the turmoil in New York, and to let the other Families know that the Anastasia Family had reached a successful truce, in order to prevent further fallout from Albert Anastasia's killing. The new leaders of the Anastasia Family wanted to "cool the nerves of all the Families across America" and let them know they would be seeking no reprisal for Anastasia's death.

There was also a second item on the agenda: to abolish drug trafficking once and for all among the Families, and to punish any Family member who was proven to be involved in that kind of business. So that is the ultimate irony of this second, infamous Apalachin meeting: that both of our agenda items were designed to promote peace and to prohibit certain illegal activities among our members—not the opposite, as described by law-enforcement officials and Estes Kefauver, the senator from Tennessee and head of the Senate Special Committee to Investigate Crime in Interstate Commerce in 1950–51.

If Apalachin had been intended to be a Commission meeting, my father, as chairman of the Commission, would have been present. As it happened, however, he did not attend the meeting. He did send two of his men—Gaspar DiGregorio and John Bonventre—but while they were out hunting in the area, the police stopped them at a roadblock designed to snare the attendees.

Before leaving for Sicily, my father, who needed to have his driver's license renewed, had given instructions to his brother-in-law Frank Labruzzo to take care of it, since at that time anyone could get it renewed on a local level. New York State required driver's license renewal every year for a five-dollar fee. Frank renewed it and asked Gaspar DiGregorio (a former Maranzano group leader who had become a group leader in the Bonanno Family) to give it to my father, who was staying in Endicott a few miles away.

When he was stopped by the police, Gaspar showed my father's license to the police, which is why the FBI files report Joe Bonanno among the names of the men at the Apalachin meeting. And this was by no means the only error in those records. When I reviewed the FBI files, I was surprised at how little they knew about our world, or at least how little of what made it into the official reports was true. It seems as though the FBI agents' primary purpose was to gather raw "information" from every source they could—including newspaper clippings written by reporters based on secondhand sources, rumors, and pure conjecture. This material was voluminous, academic, interesting, but inherently flawed—due to the lack of direct experience on the part of those who collected it. Nevertheless, the theory of dominant imagery prevails: if inaccurate information is written up and passed on often enough by apparently "authoritative" sources, the public will believe it.

On November 13, 1957, two New York State Police officers, Sergeant Edgar Croswell and his partner, Sergeant Vincent Vasisco, happened to be at the Park View Motel in Vestal, New York, investigating claims that the owner had been plagued by bad checks. For some time, Sergeant Croswell had been tracking the movements of gangsters through Binghamton, New York, which was about twelve miles east of Apalachin, where Joseph Barbara lived on his hillside estate. As fate would have it, while they were there, Barbara's son, Joe Jr., walked into the motel and made reservations for six rooms, telling the clerk that his father would pay for them. The troopers had been watching Joe Barbara Sr. since his bootlegging days years earlier. His previous run-ins with the law made him the object of police suspicion. The officers decided to make a trip to Barbara's estate.

When they got there, they saw four expensive cars in the driveway, with New York, New Jersey, and Ohio license plates. Not knowing what was happening, they did nothing more that day. The next day, November 14, they waited until the guests began arriving and then drove to Barbara's estate accompanied by agents from the Alcohol Tax Unit of the Internal Revenue Service. There they found about forty Cadillacs, Imperials, Lincolns, and other high-priced cars parked on and near the estate. The police set up a roadblock around the estate and began writing down license-plate numbers. Barbara's wife, Josephine, spotted the officers and sounded the alarm, setting off a mass exodus into the surrounding woods. It was just after 12:30 in the afternoon, as the barbecue was just starting, when about sixty high-ranking Mafia members from around the country began running to escape the officers. Some were caught in the surrounding fields, and others were intercepted after reaching the highway posing as hitchhikers while trying to escape; some of the unfortunates were easily spotted, their white hats and streetwise clothing not exactly standard fare for a stroll in the woods.

The raid on Joe Barbara's Apalachin house began a new, painful era in our world. After the subsequent grand jury indictments of various figures, those in leadership positions grew reluctant to travel, leaving most decisions to less experienced, lower-echelon men.

A view of Joe Barbara's estate and the surrounding woods.

14

The 1962 Commission Meeting

The Gallo/Profaci War

When we find ourselves in dire circumstances, we realize that the only power we ever truly had in life was not power over events nor power over other men, but power over ourselves. True power is the talent for self-control.

Joe Bonanno

Fallout from the 1957 Apalachin meeting continued, with the federal government returning conspiracy indictments against twenty-seven of those whom the authorities believed had attended the meeting, and for giving false, fictitious, and evasive accounts before the grand jury about the purpose of the get-together. In what is believed to be the first criminal case of its kind, the Justice Department attempted to penalize those indicted for invoking their Fifth Amendment rights. In a sense, the Justice Department was using what they knew as the Mafia code of silence against the Mafia.

Around 1960, the charges against the men were ultimately dismissed by the Court of Appeals. In the intervening four years, we kept as low a profile as possible; the leaders of the

Families actually ceased close contact, fearing that any substantial communication would be likely to provoke more scrutiny from the Justice Department. After Apalachin, we were all targeted by the media as "big news." Our years of working under the radar had come to an end.

In late 1961, the Gallo brothers approached Carlo Gambino and requested an audience to discuss internal "leadership problems" they were having with their *rappresentante*, Joe Profaci. The three brothers, Albert, Larry, and Joseph "Crazy Joey" Gallo, were unhappy with the profit split they were getting from their "work" for Profaci, whom we called Don Piddru. Gambino honored the Gallo brothers' request for an audience and then called a meeting of the Commission in early 1962 to discuss it.

This meeting early in 1962, although initiated by Carlo Gambino, was really promoted by Tommy Lucchese. Gambino and Lucchese, who were now related by the marriages of their children, were closely aligned, and both were part of the liberal wing of the Commission. They saw this as an opportunity to replace the conservative Profaci with another liberal member at the expense of the Gallo brothers—especially Larry Gallo, the most likely to assume leadership of the Family. The 1962 Commission meeting dealt solely with this internal revolt in the Profaci Family, which is known today as the Gallo/Profaci War.

In 1962 there were nine members on the Commission. However, Vito Genovese was in prison on a narcotics charge and one of his stand-ins represented his Family. The other members attending were Carlo Gambino, Tommy Lucchese, Joe Profaci, Joe Bonanno, Stefano Magaddino, Sam Giancana, and the two new members selected at the 1956 Commission meeting, Joseph Zerilli of Detroit and Angelo Bruno of Philadelphia. I attended that meeting along with some of the other top echelon members of the respective Families.

Profaci was an original member of the Commission, a conservative whose old ways and stingy habits the Gallo brothers and their followers now considered unacceptable. Profaci's underboss was his brother-in-law Joe Magliocco, who—although he lacked Profaci's influence—was his contemporary and shared his conservative views. The Gallo brothers had a close relationship with Gambino; they wanted him and other influential members of the Commission to intercede and resolve problems in a "legislative" way, through a Commission ruling. The Gallo brothers really wanted more money, and more territory, and to muscle in on the businesses of other members within and even outside the Profaci Family. Joe Profaci was old, they argued, and in failing health; he should retire quietly to spend his remaining days in Florida, and let them take over as the new guard. Of course, the Commission had no authority to remove the leader of a Family—but, the way the ambitious Gallos saw things, that was only a technicality.

By this time, we all knew that the Gallo brothers had been the shooters in the assassination of Albert Anastasia in 1957. On that matter, we decided to look the other way; time had passed, and after all the government prosecutions we didn't want to bring any further attention to ourselves by trying to punish them for the shooting. But our decision not to retaliate against them only seemed to empower them, as this attempt to try to persuade the Commission to oust Profaci demonstrated.

Gambino asked my father to chair the meeting. There had been no Commission meeting in 1961, where the affirmation of continuance of a Commission for another five years would customarily be put to a vote. Although the five-year meeting intervals were not exact, technically the failure to confirm continuance could be construed as rendering the 1962 meeting "unofficial"; if the result were unfavorable to either Profaci or the Gallo brothers, and an accommodation could not be reached, the meeting could be dismissed as illegitimate, prompting an all-out war among the Families.

As the chair in the 1956 meeting, my father was the most logical member to continue in this capacity; his attendance could be construed as a waiver of the five-year renewal, adding legitimacy to this Commission meeting. He was also a longtime ally of his fellow conservative Profaci, and was related to him by my marriage to Profaci's niece Rosalie. Since Magliocco was Rosalie's grandmother's brother, he was also Rosalie's great uncle. If anyone was the right person to avoid bloodshed by reaching some type of an accommodation, my father would be the one.

My father believed that any attempt on the Commission's part to meddle in the affairs of the Profaci Family would break thirty years of precedent. In the very act of granting the Gallo brothers an audience to air their "Family" gripes, he felt, Gambino had violated the 1931 promise of autonomy of the Families. This was a major affront to Profaci, a leader who was compromised by Gambino's decision to side with Profaci's underlings over the leader himself. Such a request would never even have been considered by the original, old-school members of the Commission.

Gambino's action in calling this 1962 Commission meeting went even further in defying established policy—it violated the no-interference rule confirmed at the 1951 meeting, when the Commission refused to consider whether Albert Anastasia should assume leadership of the Mangano Family after Mangano "disappeared," allegedly at Anastasia's order. The Commission had ruled that Mangano's disappearance was a Family matter, and that determining the new leader of a Family was, likewise, a Family matter beyond the jurisdiction of the Commission.

Nevertheless, my father had no choice but to attend the 1962 meeting, because of his longstanding relationship with

Profaci and his desire to allow the ailing leader some dignity in his last years.

Gambino and Lucchese had been aligned for years, even before they both became leaders of their Families. Lucchese was also becoming closer to my father's cousin in Buffalo, Stefano Magaddino, by stroking his vanity and his need to be considered important by the other members of the Commission. If Profaci were forced out, the liberals would have a majority on the Commission—and engaging in narcotics trafficking would be permitted. If Magaddino refused to go along, that would make him the odd man out. Seeing an opportunity to exploit Magaddino's need for feeling important—and especially his longtime desire to eclipse his younger cousin, Joe Bonanno—Gambino and Lucchese figured that Magaddino's defection could be accomplished with a little finesse.

Thus the stage was set for the 1962 meeting of the Commission.

This meeting was held at a Brooklyn poultry distribution warehouse owned by Paul Castellano, Gambino's brother-in-law. After the chair called the meeting to order, with the usual formalities, the Commission members were seated.

My father called on Carlo Gambino to give an opening statement. Gambino was careful not to embarrass or demean Profaci, who after all was still in the room—as was Joseph Zerilli, the leader of the Detroit Family, whose son Anthony Joseph "Tony" Zerilli was Profaci's son-in-law. Gambino praised Profaci for "serving all of us so well" for so many years. He acknowledged that Profaci had been a "father" from the inception of the Commission—but then declared that the older man was "getting old and out of touch deserving of a rest to attend to his health issues." He added that the issues that had arisen within his Family, and the dissension in the ranks, could escalate and threaten the peace. For the good and welfare of all the Families, he concluded, now would be an opportune time for Profaci to step down and turn the leadership over to another.

My father then asked Joe Profaci to leave the room so that an open discussion could begin. Profaci did so without saying a word or questioning the request. The chairman next asked if Tommy Lucchese would like to speak first to express his opinion.

Lucchese, a polished and diplomatic speaker, began by continuing the praise offered by Gambino, but in a more eloquent manner. He focused on the need for unity, eliminating rebellion and conflict within the Profaci Family, and about strong leadership. He seconded Gambino's comments about Profaci's health issues, and suggested that Profaci would be wise to put his interests aside for the benefit of all the Families. Now, Lucchese himself was almost sixty-two, and, as I recall, far from the picture of health himself. Perhaps for that reason, he limited his remarks on Profaci's age to a simple observation: "We all know that one day none of us will be the big dog—just the old dog. And old dogs that have been loyal and obedient to their masters deserve to enjoy their final years." Lucchese didn't speak with his customary zeal—his face had aged and grown pale—but he made his points with the grace we had come to expect.

After Lucchese finished, my father looked around the room to see who would speak next. But the assembled men all kept their silence, avoiding eye contact with my father.

Then my father shouted out: *"Don Piddru should stay!"*

That got people's attention. Everyone was now hanging on my father's next words.

In all the comments made that day, my father continued, not a word had been spoken about the Gallo brothers. Instead, both Gambino and Lucchese had argued that Profaci should step down simply because of his age. But the real issue had nothing to do with getting older, my father insisted; rather, it was one of trust and experience versus distrust and greed. After all, everyone in the room was more than fifty years old; most, in fact, were in their sixties. Responding to Lucchese's respectful comments concerning old age, he said, "We are all aging warriors and we all deserve a rest, but a father does not leave his sons in the midst of turmoil. He first resolves the problems and then retires to look after himself."

My father had made one thing clear: the Bonanno Family would not allow Profaci to be dismissed on any opportunistic claims of age or obsolescence. If push came to shove, Joe Bonanno would go to war to protect his ally. He asked again if anyone would like to say anything else, and was greeted again by silence. Then he called for a vote of confidence for Joe Profaci. All voted in the affirmative.

After the vote, Profaci was called into the meeting and given the news; it was unanimous that he should remain as the leader to resolve the problems within his Family. The meeting was adjourned, and we all enjoyed a sumptuous Italian dinner of seven or eight courses—a meal that might have been planned as a victory celebration for Gambino and Lucchese, but which was now a unity dinner where the guests all made cordial conversation.

About six months later, June 6, 1962, Joe Profaci died of cancer. After a poll among the Family members, Profaci's underboss, Joe Magliocco, was elected by the Family's *capos* to assume leadership of the Family. He also inherited renewed hostilities brought about by the Gallo brothers. Unable to resolve the conflicts within the Family, Magliocco proved much weaker than Profaci. The Gallo brothers' actions plunged the Family into such turmoil that his election was called into question by their allies, including Lucchese, Gambino, and other leaders—including Zerilli of Detroit, who, despite his relation to Profaci (as father-in-law of one of Profaci's daughters), had no loyalty to Magliocco. These leaders supported the Gallo brothers; another faction supported Joseph "Joe" Colombo, a Profaci group leader.

Given the division among the captains, Lucchese argued that the election was a fraud. Magliocco lacked the support Profaci had enjoyed, and even the Bonanno Family would not go to war for him, although we still backed his conservative views.

To address the matter, Magliocco was summoned to Camden, New Jersey, for a Commission meeting—one that was more like a card game with a loaded deck. Only those Commission members staunchly opposed to Magliocco's election showed up for the meeting, and among them they decided that Magliocco's election had been "fixed." They declared that Magliocco had thirty days to hold a new election, and fined him forty thousand dollars for the perceived offense.

In our world, when a leader is fearful of being assassinated, his only real defense is to strike first—as Anastasia had done in 1951, when Mangano disappeared, and again in 1953, after Frank Costello accused Tommy Lucchese of planning to kill Anastasia. What happened next is one of those uncertain things that sometimes happen in life.

In the summer of 1963, I was living with my wife, Rosalie, at Magliocco's estate in East Islip on Long Island while waiting for our home to be completed. By now, you must recognize that this lifestyle of ours can easily destroy any semblance of a healthy relationship between husband and wife, and at this juncture Rosalie and I were having problems that needed time to repair; although I really didn't have the time, I wanted to work on them together with her.

One day, Magliocco asked me to drive him to the Brentwood train station because his regular driver was unavailable. He had a shotgun across his lap and I asked him if I should get my piece. I wasn't sure what was going on, but my training had prepared me to be ready at any time for a possible ambush. Magliocco told me he was just meeting someone from Brooklyn. When the train arrived, a man I recognized as Sally "the Sheik" Musacio walked toward our car. The Sheik, who got his information from group leader Joe Colombo, was someone Magliocco could trust to keep him informed about what his enemies inside the Profaci Family were thinking. Like Profaci before him, Magliocco blamed Gambino and Lucchese for his troubles with the Gallo brothers:

"Is everything ready?" Magliocco asked.

The Sheikh replied in the affirmative.

"Okay, let's start."

To an uninitiated onlooker, such an exchange might have seemed innocent. When the speakers involved were the leader of a Family and a trusted underling, it usually means a death sentence for someone. In this case, the targets were Carlo Gambino and Tommy Lucchese.

The Sheik reported the news to his inside source, Joe Colombo. When he learned of Magliocco's decision, Colombo decided to switch sides: He told Gambino and Lucchese what Magliocco was planning—and that I, Bill Bonanno, had driven Magliocco to the train station. To them, this clearly implicated the Bonanno Family in Magliocco's plans to assassinate Gambino and Lucchese. With that, Colombo became Gambino's and Lucchese's new darling, replacing the Gallo brothers in their affection.

Armed with Colombo's story, Gambino and Lucchese accused Magliocco of plotting to kill them, and declared that they no longer recognized him as head of the Profaci Family. They told Stefano Magaddino of Colombo's disclosures—including the fact that I had driven Magliocco to the train station. Magaddino didn't hesitate to betray his cousin, Joe Bonanno, by aligning himself with Gambino and Lucchese.

It was through this incident that a false and damaging rumor started: that my father intended to kill the leaders of the Commission, with the aim of becoming *capo di tutti capi*, the boss of all bosses. I would be less than forthright if I told you that the thought of eliminating Gambino and Lucchese never crossed my father's mind. By that time, however, he was seeking to retire; indeed, he had already told his cousin Magaddino as much (in strictest confidence). My father had never formed the same kind of personal relationship with Magliocco as he had with Profaci, and was not about to risk his life for the Family's new leader. And my father, who had been instrumental in eliminating the concept of a boss of all bosses when the Commission was formed in 1931, had no designs on such a role himself.

As the situation heated up, my father instructed me to visit Lucchese and to take along Johnny Morales, the Bonanno Family underboss, and group leader Gaspar DiGregorio to dispel Magaddino's insinuations that the Bonanno Family was aligned with Magliocco, and to express that we had no plans to assassinate anyone.

We met over espresso and biscotti at Lucchese's home in Long Beach, on Long Island, to discuss the matter. Lucchese appeared to be satisfied with our explanation, and, in our minds, the issue was resolved. Then, on December 28, 1963, a higher authority brought further resolution to the matter when Magliocco died of a heart attack. After Magliocco's death, my father distanced himself from the Commission and began stepping away from Family matters in New York City. Consistent with the "rule of three" in Sicilian culture, he chose a triumvirate—consisting of Johnny Morales, Gaspar DiGregorio (his oldest friend and best man), and me—to attend to Family matters, and stipulated that we adhere to the tradition of assuring a majority vote by requiring two of the three to agree for any decision to be carried out.

After Magliocco's death, Joe Colombo brought two of the three factions in the Profaci Family together and was elected to the position of leader. The Gallo brothers were out; Gambino, Lucchese, and Colombo were allies; and Magaddino was moving closer to abandoning his conservative position. The new makeup of the Commission was now positioned to destroy the conservative faction. The Bonanno Family, the only real conservative Family left on the Commission, was the next to be challenged.

The Five New York Godfathers as of 1964

BONANNO FAMILY	ANASTASIA FAMILY	GENOVESE FAMILY	LUCCHESE FAMILY	COLOMBO FAMILY
Joseph Bonanno Sr. Godfather	Carlo Gambino Godfather	Vito Genovese Godfather	Tommy Lucchese Godfather	Joe Colombo Godfather

15

The End of
the Commission

*Tradition never dies, as long as there is someone left to
remember.*

Anthony Tarantola

Around April 1964, consistent with his plans to retire, my
father traveled to Montreal. While there, he was invited to
invest in the Saputo cheese company. In those days, the New
York Families had certain understandings regarding the right
to do business in Canada. The Bonanno Family had a relationship in Montreal, and the Magaddino Family of Buffalo
had the same understanding in Toronto. Magaddino, who had
already started losing face by implicating the Bonanno Family
in the attempted coup to kill Gambino and Lucchese, viewed
my father's investment as a stepping-stone to an eventual bid to
take over Magaddino's business relationships in Toronto.

Magaddino's paranoia impelled him to move closer to
Gambino and Lucchese. The expression "Where there's
smoke, there's fire" is hard to overcome in our world. Although
my presence with Magliocco at the train station was easily explained, rumors of assassination plans are almost completely impossible to dispel. Magaddino wanted my father out

of the picture, and he persisted in spreading the rumor that Joe Bonanno was planning to eliminate the heads of the other New York Families.

On the advice of his attorney, my father applied for Canadian citizenship in an effort to make it easier to get credit for his new business venture. The Canadian immigration authorities called him in for questioning, accusing him of lying on his immigration card application: When asked if he had ever been convicted of a crime, he had answered "No." But in 1941, one of his companies had been charged with a wage-and-hour violation in the United States, and the company had paid a small fine to clear up the matter. However, this explanation was insufficient for the Canadian government, who detained him and sent him to prison.

At around the same time, John Tartamella, the Bonanno Family's longtime *consigliere*, suffered a stroke and could no longer function. Although I was not actually named *consigliere*, I had helped Tartamella during his illness that preceded the stroke, and now I assumed his duties on an interim basis. The Family's group leaders sent word through Johnny Morales to my father in Canada, advising him that they wanted to elect a *consigliere* to replace John Tartamella now that he was completely incapacitated. My father agreed, and two names were suggested: mine and Gaspar DiGregorio's. Gaspar nominated me, and I asked Angelo Caruso to place Gaspar's name on the ballot. The full vote was held at La Scala, our preferred restaurant in Manhattan. When the captains polled their crews by secret ballot, I was elected.

This did not sit well with Gaspar DiGregorio. Although it was he who had placed my name in nomination, he had never expected me to be elected. He was convinced that I was too young and too inexperienced to hold the position, and felt it should have gone to him. When Gaspar complained about the election to his brother-in-law, Stefano Magaddino, the Buf-

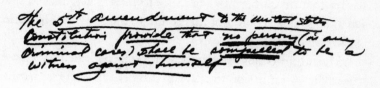

My father's handwritten note with the language of the Fifth Amendment, which he took with him into Federal Court in 1964.

falo leader saw another opportunity to divide the Bonanno Family, by reaffirming the rumors that my appearance at the Brentwood train station with Magliocco confirmed that the Bonanno Family was planning to kill Gambino and Lucchese. Gaspar had somehow convinced himself that my father had used his influence to arrange for me to get the *consigliere* position as my reward for siding with Magliocco. Nothing could have been further from the truth: the position of *consigliere* was an elected one that cannot be influenced by a Family's leader.

After my father had spent a few months in Canadian prison, the authorities agreed to release him if he volunteered to go back to the United States. He did, abandoning his investment plans there. After his release in August 1964, he immediately boarded an aircraft bound for Chicago. The moment he stepped off the plane, he was served with a subpoena to appear before a federal grand jury investigating crime in New York City. He did so, but frustrated the U.S. attorney by invoking his Fifth Amendment rights.

He then called each of his group leaders and asked for personal meetings with each of them. Gaspar DiGregorio did not return my father's call.

During my father's time in Canada, Magaddino had been scheming to replace my father with his brother-in-law, Gaspar, encouraging Gaspar to defect while gaining support from Gambino, Lucchese, and the other Commission members.

Aware that my father was planning to retire, Magaddino saw a chance to seize control of the Bonanno Family if DiGregorio became my father's successor.

Magaddino's next step was to attempt to "call" my father before the Commission to answer trumped-up charges that he had somehow interfered in my election as *consigliere*. This was a setup designed to put my father on the defensive, forcing him to account for his actions, and thus to trap him into confirming the rumors that he intended to eliminate the heads of the other New York Families. Of course, the naming of a *consigliere* was strictly a Family decision, and Magaddino was not part of the Bonanno Family. The principle of Family autonomy was still understood by the members of the Commission, and I believe they saw Magaddino's actions for what they were: merely an attempt to wrongly discredit my father. Instead, Magaddino had undermined his own credibility before the Commission.

Yet Gambino and Lucchese still needed Magaddino as an ally, and they appeased him by agreeing to bring Joe Bonanno before the Commission.

By this point, my father was viewed as a renegade by most of the Commission members. The only member he might have been able to count on was Detroit's Zerilli, a former Profaci ally. Magaddino was not the most educated man, but he was street-smart; he had effectively taken DiGregorio, once a loyal Bonanno group leader, and made him his puppet. The Commission sent a "committee of three"—consisting of two Commission members, Zerilli from Detroit and Angelo Bruno from Philadelphia, along with Simone "Sam the Plumber" DeCavalcante from New Jersey—to deliver a formal request that my father appear before the Commission. Because my father was not in New York at the time, Johnny Morales (his underboss) and I carried the message to him.

When my father returned to New York, he arranged to meet with this committee of three, together with top men in

The Airport Motel near the Newark airport.

the Bonanno Family, at a motel he owned near the Newark airport (fittingly named the Airport Motel).

By that time, however, Zerilli had returned to Detroit—and so, technically, the committee of three never actually delivered its message. Since the Commission had ordered all three to contact my father, he was not technically bound to appear before the Commission.

My father made it clear that any decisions that occurred inside the Bonanno Family were a Family matter. He also declared that he no longer recognized the Commission's existence, on the grounds that the members had never formally agreed to extend the five-year term beyond 1961. Magaddino argued that Bonanno was being evasive and inaccessible, and that his position represented an affront to the members of the Commission. But this argument was discredited after Bonanno agreed to meet with these envoys from the Commission. This was apparently conveyed to Gambino and Lucchese by Angelo Bruno and Sam the Plumber, and the matter of my father appearing before the Commission was dropped.

In September 1964, my father called a meeting of his Family. Gaspar DiGregorio refused to attend, telling some of the other Family members that Magaddino—my father's cousin and rival—had instructed him not to talk or make contact with my father, and that he was now under the protection of the Commission. With absolutely no authority to do so, Magaddino now declared Gaspar the head of the Bonanno Family. This was more than DiGregorio leading a dissident faction within the Bonanno Family: He was attempting an all-out

The wedding of Gaspar and Vita DiGregorio (from left to right: my father, Joe Bonanno; Gaspar DiGregorio; Vita DiGregorio, and Fay Bonanno).

coup. Magaddino sent one of his cousins, a made guy in the Buffalo Family, to New York to lend DiGregorio support in his new position. (Ironically, that cousin, recognizing Magaddino's treachery, defected to the Bonanno Family and never returned to the Buffalo Family.)

The Bonanno group leaders labeled DiGregorio a traitor and declared that his punishment should be death, but my father interceded. He called Gaspar directly to let him know that he was willing to meet with him and Magaddino to try to resolve their differences. My father would not allow Gaspar to be executed, for several reasons: first, because he was my father's oldest friend; second, because my father was best man at Gaspar's wedding and my mother was the maid of honor; and third, because the fact that Gaspar was my *compare* (my baptismal godfather) brought too much emotion into the equation. A man's *compare*, in the Sicilian culture, is closer than his blood relatives.

Moreover, my father realized that if he could persuade DiGregorio to come back into the Family fold, it would demean his brother-in-law Magaddino, which might completely destroy any influence he was trying to build within the Commission. It was a decision born of leniency, and one that turned out to be potentially deadly.

In October 1964, my father was once again subpoenaed to appear before a federal grand jury in New York City. On the evening of October 20, the night before he was slated to appear, he met with his lawyers to prepare for his court appearance. After dinner, they left by taxi to go to the apartment of my father's attorney, William Maloney, where they would stay the night, since it was close to the courthouse. When the taxi stopped in front of the apartment building, my father stepped out—only to be grabbed by two men who forced him into a car, pushed him onto the floor, and sped away. The two abductors were none other than Nino Magaddino (Stefano Magad-

DETECTIVE DIVISION, BUREAU OF CRIMINAL IDENTIFICATION CIRCULAR No. 68	POLICE DEPARTMENT CITY OF NEW YORK	LIMITED TO DEPARTMENT CIRCULATION PHOTO UNIT No. 43060

WANTED AS THE ALLEGED VICTIM OF A KIDNAPPING

THE ABOVE PHOTOGRAPH IS ONE "JOSEPH BONANNO" MALE, WHITE, 59
YRS., WANTED AS THE ALLEGED VICTIM OF A KIDNAPPING.

AT APPROXIMATELY 12:20 A.M., OCTOBER 21, 1964, "JOSEPH BONANNO"
OF 1847 EAST ELM STREET, TUCSON, ARIZONA, WHILE IN THE COMPANY
OF HIS ATTORNEY, WAS REPORTED PHYSICALLY SEIZED IN FRONT OF
35 PARK AVENUE, MANHATTAN BY TWO (2) UNKNOWN WHITE MALES AND
FORCED INTO AN AUTOMOBILE WHICH THEN SPED AWAY.

DESCRIPTION OF PERPETRATORS AS FOLLOWS:

#1 - MALE, WHITE, 6'2", 210 LBS., WEARING BLACK RAINCOAT, A DARK
FEDORA, ARMED WITH A GUN.

#2 - MALE, WHITE, 6'0", 200 LBS., DARK CLOTHES.

GETAWAY VEHICLE WAS A BEIGE 2-DOOR SEDAN OF RECENT MODEL OF
UNKNOWN MAKE, BEARING NEW YORK REGISTRATION PLATES.

ANY INFORMATION ON THE ABOVE, NOTIFY THE 13TH DETECTIVE SQUAD
FORTHWITH: OREGON 4-0770 - OREGON 4-0771 - 777 3290.

*The wanted poster issued for my father as an alleged kidnapping
victim (Library of Congress).*

dino's brother) and Peter Magaddino (Stefano's son). To the
outside world, it appeared that my father had been kidnapped.
Newspapers reported the kidnapping, speculating that my father had been captured by rival bosses and would soon be a
dead man, if he wasn't already.

This was not a kidnapping in the true sense of the word.
It was, more accurately, a bid for reconciliation between my
father and his seventy-three-year-old cousin, who still demanded respect as an elder as if he thought he would live forever. My father was never sure who was behind the action,
but suspected that Gambino and Lucchese had instigated it
to scare him into retiring as leader of the Family on his own
volition, before he was "retired" by force. At the time, some
speculated that my father arranged his own kidnapping to
avoid testifying in court. Even the Police Department of the
City of New York wondered whether this "kidnapping" was
contrived—as evidenced by the caption beneath his picture on
the wanted poster, which read that he was "wanted as the *alleged* victim of a kidnapping."

Nino and Peter Magaddino took my father to a secluded
farmhouse in upstate New York, where he spent six weeks,
most of which was devoted to talking with his cousin Stefano.
While there, he was never treated as a kidnapping victim.
There was no security at the farmhouse, only acres and acres
of woods, with tall trees blocking any chance at surveillance or
prying eyes. My father was free to leave any time he wanted.
But he didn't want to leave, and Stefano didn't want him to—
at least not yet. In truth, the incident was more of a respite
for my father, an escape from subpoenas, courtrooms, and interrogation. It was also an opportunity for my father and his
cousin Stefano to try to understand why things had gone awry
between them. Such conversations require reliving the past,
trying to find the sources of long-dormant feelings of distrust
or resentment. Under such circumstances, total honesty is a

matter of perspective: truth is no more than what each party believes.

During the weeks my father spent at the farmhouse with his cousin, Stefano came and went according to his own schedule. By the end of his stay, however, Stefano was still not convinced that my father simply wanted to retire. Perhaps things just had gone too far with Gambino and Lucchese; it may be that Stefano had been backed into a corner, that the only way out was for him to stand with the liberals and finally get the revenge he craved by showing that he had taken control over his younger cousin at last—something he had desired ever since my father decided to stay in Brooklyn rather than follow Stefano to Buffalo. Stefano had initially lived in Brooklyn upon arriving in the United States around 1909, which was where the largest of the Castellammare group settled. No one had expected my father to rise so quickly to such a position of power and respect and at such a young age, or that his cousin would rule a less important Family on the fringes of the real action.

During this period of prolonged contact, the cousins accomplished little more than venting, trying to get off their chests the complaints they had both harbored for more than thirty-five years. Magaddino remained distrustful, envious, and leery of the truth as my father told it. My father, in turn, finally realized that he could be in danger—not so much from his cousin, but from the leaders of the other Families, all of whom had been convinced by Magaddino's assassination rumors that my father was planning to eliminate the heads of the other Families. Magaddino could easily have killed my father in this remote wooded area—and, regardless of the fact they were cousins, probably would have if it hadn't been clear to him that war would certainly have followed.

Instead, after six weeks, my father's captors were instructed to drive him anywhere he wished to go. My father left, knowing that whatever bonds he and Stefano once shared were now nothing more than loose strings of memory. It was the end of their relationship.

The Invisible Cloak

Joe Bonanno asked that his captors drive him west, away from New York City. When they arrived in El Paso, Texas, he informed them that he had reached his destination and they could leave him. He did this to confuse Magaddino—and to buy some time to think about his next move. El Paso was an unlikely place to exit—unless, of course, he was trying to give Magaddino the idea that he was planning to cross the border into Mexico.

In the weeks since his kidnapping, much of the world had assumed that my father was dead. Instead, for the next nineteen months, he hid in plain sight in Tucson, Arizona; New York City; and elsewhere. He was a master of disguise, able to impersonate anyone from a beggar to an old man or even a Hassidic Jew. Once, I was having breakfast at a diner on Merrick Avenue in East Meadow, Long Island, and he was within ten feet of me and I didn't know it. This cloak of invisibility allowed him to navigate back and forth across the country from Tucson to New York at will. It gave him the freedom to survey his enemies, avoid the government, and plan his next move when the time was right. Meanwhile, he was letting things cool down in New York—including the Family rivalries and the government prosecutions.

The first contact I had with my father was through his underboss, Johnny Morales, who told me that he'd received a phone call and that he was safe. A similar call was placed to my sister Catherine. My sister and I, in accordance with my father's instructions, were told to be at a specific phone booth at a specific hour on a specific day each week. Many weeks might go by with no call, but we had to be there anyway, just in case. It was a method we depended on in that period, one that ensured safe and reliable communication between us and our father.

During his time in hiding, my father avoided direct contact with our immediate family, in order to protect us from his enemies and from the government. At his home in Tucson he had a secret room no larger than a jail cell, where he could hide if required. In New York City, he stayed at the homes of his most trusted friends and kept moving to avoid detection. He communicated only with a very select group of people, the only ones who knew he was still alive; none of them knew where he might be staying or going when he departed after visiting them.

Of course, all this secrecy was a drain on Magaddino, who viewed it as more evidence that the Bonanno Family was preparing for war against the other Families. Magaddino encouraged Joe Colombo, leader of the Profaci Family since 1962, to side with him against Joe Bonanno and to promote further defection. Colombo had no qualms about doing so; indeed, he would welcome any chance to exploit a weakening in the Bonanno Family to swoop in and take over Bonanno businesses in the Brooklyn territory they shared.

The year 1965 saw violence touch several members of both factions in the Bonanno Family. The result was dubbed the Banana War by the press, named for my father's unflattering nickname "Joe Bananas." Whether or not the Banana War was truly a war is a matter of interpretation. In my mind, a war demands that both warriors go for the throat, intent on totally destroying the other. In our situation, this was not the case. It was more a matter of surgical strikes, with each side retaliating after being hit—but underlying the violence was a real hope of reaching mediation short of all-out war.

At the height of the conflict, I had my own chance to kill Gaspar DiGregorio. I even went so far as to stick my .38 snubnose in his mouth at a chance meeting at a tavern in 1965. But I gave Gaspar a pass—much to the dismay of our group leaders, who ridiculed me for failing to pull the trigger. My excuse? After all, he was my *compare*. My justification? I am not sure I could have handled living with the guilt of having him die by my own hand. On reflection, maybe I should have dispatched him. I soon learned that he would not have given me the same clemency.

The Attempted Assassination of Bill Bonanno

In January 1966, my uncle Frank Labruzzo told me that Sorino Tartamella, one of the Bonanno group captains who had defected to Gaspar DiGregorio's side—and the son of our longtime *consigliere* John Tartamella—had called to say that Gaspar, wanting to mend the hostilities between the two Bonanno factions, had requested a meeting with me at a location of my choosing. Other group captains had also conveyed similar overtures.

I found DiGregorio's willingness to meet suspicious. It was possible, I supposed, that this was his way of extending an olive branch. But it could just as easily have been that Stefano Magaddino was behind the invitation, and in that case it was likely to be treacherous. I chose to meet my *compare* at Vito Bonventre's house on Troutman Street in Brooklyn, which was in a familiar neighborhood where we felt protected. It was a working-class Italian neighborhood with houses lining both sides of the street and a small market and other small busi-

The home of Vito Bonventre, Troutman Street, Brooklyn, New York.

nesses along nearby Knickerbocker Avenue. Most houses had small basements with about three steps leading up to a stoop at the front door.

Vito was my father's uncle and father-in-law to Johnny Morales. On the night of the meeting, Johnny was sick with the flu. The meeting was scheduled for 11:00 P.M. on a Friday in late January 1966. A number of Bonanno made guys decided to show up early, just to keep an eye on the proceedings. I drove to the meeting place with our group leaders Frank Labruzzo, Joe Notaro, and Carl Simari, parking several blocks from Vito's house so we could walk there and alert ourselves to any possible danger along the way.

More than an hour passed, and Gaspar did not show. Sorino Tartamella phoned, apologizing for being late, but saying that Gaspar was ill and couldn't make it. He asked to reschedule the meeting, again on our terms. Although some of us smelled a rat, we also thought it could be a tactic to make us more anxious to settle when we did meet, so we agreed to reschedule.

The view from the stoop of the Bonventre house, showing the stair-wells across the street, where assassins were hiding below street level behind the railings, waiting to attack me and my crew.

It was getting late, and we decided to leave. Outside it was dark and deserted, with rows of cars parked along both sides of Troutman Street. Always cautious, we left in twos, so that others would be ready to cover us if hostilities erupted. I walked out the front door onto the stoop with my men following as I descended the steps to the street. We turned right, walking toward Knickerbocker Avenue. Directly across the street were houses similar to Vito's, with railings along the sidewalk to keep people from falling into the sunken space between the house and the basement. The space, about three feet wide, could be used as a foxhole or trench to conceal men crouching down.

Carl Simari noticed a slight glare of light across the street, as if a piece of metal was catching the light from the streetlamp, and instinctively pushed me to the pavement.

At that instant, a barrage of machine-gun fire and single shots erupted from across the street as we glimpsed the shadows of several men standing up behind the railings. We ducked behind the cars and started moving as fast as we could

*Bullet holes from the shootout
during our escape survive today.*

*Carl Simari, who saved my life during
the ambush. Shown here in 1966.*

*In 1966, five months after the attempt on
my life.*

*After he had been missing for eighteen months, my
father appeared at Federal Court after unexpect-
edly turning himself in to the U.S. Marshals. Here he
leaves the U.S. federal courthouse with his attorney
Albert Krieger, having posted $150,000 bail.*

along Troutman Street toward the corner, all the while firing back at our ambushers.

The aluminum siding on a house two down from Vito's was riddled with the holes of machine-gun bullets in a rising pattern. Those bullet holes are still there today.

The only reason we weren't killed was that the machine gun had probably kicked up and to the left when the shooter pulled the trigger. Crouched behind the parked cars, we made it to Knickerbocker Avenue, turned right, and scattered in different directions. We had escaped.

Once we regrouped and calmed down, we had to decide what to do next. We were prepared for war, but first we had to find out whether Gaspar DiGregorio was acting alone or at the behest of Stefano Magaddino—or, more important, were the other New York Families behind it?

The Troutman Street incident thrust our Family discord into the public eye. The authorities immediately ordered a grand jury investigation into the incident, and the New York police, the Brooklyn D.A., the U. S. Attorney, and the FBI all put men on the case. We used one of our media sources to plant information about the shoot-out, anxious to read the reactions of the other New York Families and see if they were involved.

When my father learned about the attempt on my life, he sent word that he was coming out of hiding. On May 17, 1966, Joe Bonanno turned himself in at the U.S. Federal Courthouse in New York City. He was arrested by U.S. Marshals, and released on bond. He then resumed personal control of the Bonanno Family.

Defectors from DiGregorio's group and Magaddino's Buffalo Family—including some of his relatives who believed that Gaspar and Stefano were demeaning themselves by the rumors and could not be trusted—provided us with inside information about their thinking. We sent a message to the remaining members of the Commission, including Magaddino, Carlo Gambino,

Tommy Eboli (for the Genovese Family), Joe Colombo (now head of the Profaci Family), Joe Zerilli (head of the Detroit Family), and Carmine Gribbs (for the Lucchese Family). By this time, Tommy Lucchese was suffering from brain cancer, and thus was no longer a factor in our world. The carefully worded message we sent asserted that Joe Bonanno remained head of the Bonanno Family, that he sent his best wishes, and that the problems with Magaddino were simply Family matters between cousins that they would resolve themselves. In the past, Magaddino's strongest supporter had been Lucchese. Now that Tommy was gone, and the others were unwilling to back Magaddino in a war against Bonanno, the Commission passed a resolution declaring peaceful intentions toward the Bonanno Family and Joe Bonanno.

In the months that followed, however, the killings between the DiGregorio/Magaddino and Bonanno factions continued. Magaddino believed I was the troublemaker preventing peace, and of course I was still a prime target for DiGregorio.

The Commission, now missing its strongest leaders, had lost its ability to function as it had in the early years. Around September 1966, thirteen Family leaders from around the country came to New York in an effort to help settle the problems brought on by the Banana War. They included Carlo Gambino, Mike Miranda (enforcer and *consigliere* of the Genovese Family), and Santo Traficante from Florida. Their meeting at La Stella, a restaurant in Queens, would soon become known as Little Apalachin: They were all arrested and nothing was accomplished. They were freed after posting bond of $100,000 each for a total of $1.3 million.

In July 1967, Tommy Lucchese died of brain cancer. By then, Vito Genovese was on his deathbed in prison. Carlo Gambino had a heart attack. And the Banana War continued to be a source of business for the grim reaper.

By 1968, the Bonanno Family was less than half its size before the split with DiGregorio. We were down to fewer than two hundred men. With my father's permission, Johnny Morales decided to form his own group comprising some of the remaining men from the Bonanno Family.

The handwriting was on the wall. Too many men were dying on both sides. My father was getting older, he wanted to retire with dignity, and he wanted peace on terms he could live with—before his eldest son became the next victim.

In 1968, one of the Bonanno soldiers was shot by a member of the Colombo Family. Within days, a *capo* in the Colombo Family was killed in retaliation. With the war threatening to spread to other Families, Carlo Gambino called my father and offered peace, on terms my father could dictate.

A meeting was held to negotiate this new peace with honor. The meeting, which took place over several days, included Carlo Gambino, Joe Colombo, three Bonanno Family representatives (including me), and—representing the Lucchese Family—Stefano LaSalle and Carmine Gribbs. The terms they negotiated were simple: My father would officially retire. Before he did, he would name a new Administration for the Family; after he left, this Administration would have complete authority to elect whomever it desired to run the Family, without interference from outside Families or the Commission. No Family or member of any Family would commit any acts of retaliation for past acts. And the war would be declared over.

It was a legitimate settlement. In retrospect, however, it also represented the end of an era—the three decades in which the Commission, founded by Charlie Luciano, my father, and their peers, served to preserve equilibrium among the members of our world.

There were three main reasons for the downfall of the Commission. First, human nature dealt us a hand we just couldn't handle. We were greedy, vain, and power-hungry, and we became short-term thinkers needing instant gratification.

We lost our grasp of the principles that had enabled the Commission to flourish for all those years, a time when the Families had agreed to live and let live in peace.

The Sicilian and Italian members of the Commission had realized that they could make money if they lived by a code of honor. The degeneration of the Commission really began after World War II, when some of our younger members went overseas to fight for our country and were exposed to narcotics. As narcotics crept into society, these members recognized that dealing in drugs was an easy way to make much more money than we ever did by producing and distributing liquor during Prohibition. At first, the Commission's conservative wing was able to convince the members of the Commission to institute a no-drugs policy. But that position began to weaken as the younger generation of Americanized Italians began replacing the leaders of the conservative wing on the Commission. Some leaders mandated a death sentence for any member who was trafficking in drugs, but as the younger generation evolved, they refused to follow this mandate.

With that decision, my father and I felt we were inviting the government into our business. Honor went out the window. Lawyers were now our partners, except that we didn't split the fees with them—we just paid them. Federal and state prosecutions drained our war chests, as the legal community had a field day collecting enormous fees from those in need of their services. And the more we paid to try and stay out of prison, the more we relied on narcotics as a source of revenue—a vicious circle in every sense of the phrase.

The second blow to the Commission came in those wars of the early 1960s, when certain members decided to ignore the time-honored rule that the Commission would not interfere with internal Family matters. When the Commission breached this no-interference rule, it undermined one of the cornerstones of strength agreed to by the original members of the Commission in 1931 and ratified again at the 1951 Commission meeting. This breach of protocol deprived the Families of their autonomy—the very condition that allowed the original heads of the New York Families to live in peace.

The third blow was that we failed to nurture a new generation of leaders. The leaders of the previous generation were short-sighted, forgetting that the old-timers wouldn't be around forever to enforce the philosophy of *cosa nostra* that undergirded our strength and success. I recall once being reprimanded by Johnny Morales, whom my father appointed as his number-two man, for expressing my opinion that our current leaders were getting too old and somewhat complacent. The wise thing to do, I felt, was for some of the older leaders to step aside and put younger, abler men into leadership positions, giving them the benefit of wise counsel and technical support while administrating the affairs of the Family. I was quickly and effectively admonished to keep my opinions on such matters to myself, if I didn't want to raise suspicions that I was planning a coup.

But history proves that my idea might not have been a bad one. The early 1970s saw what was called the "opening of the books" in our world: recruitment was extended to men who were thoroughly Americanized, most—if not all—born in this country and largely uneducated in our cultural traditions. While tough in physical strength, most of these men were neither the best nor the brightest. The intermarriages among the Families (which in the past had strengthened our world, much as such arrangements had bolstered the European aristocracy) also eroded, allowing distrust to fester across all of the Families.

The bogus Commission that presided during the time of the Banana War remained at nine members until the late 1960s, when it faded from our world altogether. In that last, disputed Commission era, seven or eight men were designated by various New York Families to act as pro tem representatives to the Commission; they designated one another as Commission members. But the rest of the country's Families opted out of this false arrangement; indeed, they sat back and snickered, aware that New York was always on the verge of eruption and discord.

As the various New York Families sparred for supremacy, we had what developed into a Commission Member-of-the-Month Club. The *esprit de corps* of the well-oiled, functioning machine known as "this thing of ours" was in the throes of convulsion. A war was developing between the Mafia as we knew it and America at large, and we failed to recognize that the two cultures couldn't exist in the same space at the same time: one would either absorb or eliminate the other. The ability to come to terms with reality is what distinguishes those who grow through adversity from those who are destroyed by it—and our way of life was, quite nearly, destroyed by it.

Over time, the Commission was no longer like the palm of your hand, its extended fingers representing the Families, working independently but unified by attachment to the palm. Instead, the Families were now like sections of galvanized piping: still joined together, but with moisture seeping in, corroding the network from the inside.

People of our world came from a tradition that taught us how to survive. They developed a system that, while it may not have guaranteed survival, certainly made survival more likely. This system included learning how to make peaceful accommodations with those in control of the society. In doing so, they accomplished their goals while leaving that society in a restful state of tranquillity. After 1970, no one leader has ever been able to achieve the success or longevity of any of the original leaders in our world during the preceding thirty-seven years—a tribute to the tradition of the original Sicilian men of honor who established the Commission.

Book III

The Family

16

The Structure of
the Family

The root of the kingdom is in the state; the root of the state is in the Family; the root of the Family is in the person of its head.

Sicilian organizational concept

The Family is like an artichoke. Just as the heart of an artichoke is protected by layer upon layer of leaves, the leader of a Family is protected by its members. As long as the artichoke stays intact, everything works smoothly and everything fits together. When you start pulling out the leaves, you get into trouble—unless, of course, the leaf you're removing is rotten.

Each of the original twenty-six Families established within the United States was an entity in and of itself. Each Family was composed of Italian, Sicilian, and sometimes Greek-Sicilian men whose families had been in Sicily for hundreds of generations and had common thoughts and ideological beliefs. Although American law enforcement chose to label the head of a Family "The Boss" or "The Godfather," we did not use those designations in our world during my involvement through the mid-1960s.

To us, the head of a Family was more a father figure than a boss. To people outside our world, after all, "boss" is a term for someone who tells you what to do during an eight-hour work-day; and you follow the boss's instructions, or risk being fired. After work, however, you can do what you want; your boss has no say in your personal affairs. In our world, the obligation to the Family is twenty-four hours a day, but what a member does during the day is his own business and under his own control. The Family is less a place of employment than a network of relationships for the protection and welfare of the group.

Each Family's Administration sets the boundaries for the type of conduct deemed permissible within each Family. A member's minute-to-minute and day-to-day activities are not controlled by a boss. If a member gets into trouble after straying outside the boundaries, however, that member cannot expect protection from the Family. If a Family bans involvement in narcotics trafficking and a member gets caught peddling heroin, for example, he is on his own.

The formal word for "leader," and one that goes back hundreds of years in our culture and tradition, is *rappresentante*. That title signifies that a leader of a Family is a representative of those who select him to the position of leadership. Sometimes the leader is referred to as *il capo*, or "the head." An informal, but more accurate, word for the leader of a Family would be *padre*, for *padre di famiglia*—because the relationship between a leader and his Family members is more like one of father and son. The father, from experience and wisdom, sets boundaries as guidelines for the son to follow.

If the term *padre de famiglia* ever penetrated into the consciousness of law enforcement and the media, however, they may have found it too long, or lacking in sex appeal. It was only after Mario Puzo's novel *The Godfather* was turned into a movie in 1972 that "Godfather" became the most common designation for leader. A godfather, at least in the religious context, is effectively a baptismal sponsor, or "little father"—a second, if you will.

A traditional Sicilian kiss showing respect to my father. In background are actors Costas Mandylor and Martin Landau, both of whom appeared in Bonanno: A Godfather's Story.

My father wearing his blue star sapphire- and diamond-encrusted Godfather ring.

The Godfather of a Family is traditionally presented with a pinky ring by high-ranking members of his Family or other Families out of respect for him, his title, and generally on a special occasion. In my father's case, he was presented with the ring shown in the photo by members of the Commission when he was elected chairman in 1951. The symbolic "kissing of the ring" in the movie *The Godfather* was a sensationalized version of showing respect. This Roman Catholic Church ritual is a tradition that goes back centuries. It is used as a sign of respect for the pope or other high-ranking clergy such as bishops or cardinals and is a form of fealty practiced by lower-ranking clergy or other Catholics. Just as the pope is considered a father to his flock, in our world the Godfather is father to the members of his Family. However, recognition of respect for the Godfather by others is shown by kissing the cheek. I never saw anyone kiss my father's pinky ring, or for that matter, the pinky ring of any of the other leaders.

Most leaders were elected to the position of *rappresentante* based upon respect. Respect, in our world, involved an acknowledgment of power and place—yours and somebody else's. Although *rappresentante* was an elected position, in some cases the position was assumed by force, or agreement, or temporary appointment as "acting head" to represent the interests of the Family.

From the 1930s into the 1960s, the interests of the *soldate* (soldiers or workers, the initial level in the rank of made men) were not generally seen as paramount. Therefore, they needed a buffer, someone knowledgeable in the unwritten rules of our tradition, who could be relied upon for advice and counsel. No *rappresentante* could be expected to talk with four hundred people individually, and on some matters the members did not wish to talk with the Administration or *capi*. And so the role of *consigliere*—the second of the two elected positions—was invented to serve as a liaison between the members and the *rappresentante.* The *consigliere* was like a father confessor: The members could confide in him without fear that confidences would be revealed that might harm them. The *consigliere* would then frame the issues to the *rappresentante* in the way he believed most effective and efficient.

The *consigliere* was also expected to step in to assume temporary leadership of a Family if the *rappresentante* could no longer serve. (This was one of the many things my father and I found amusing about the movie *The Godfather*, in which Robert Duvall's character, Tom Hagen, was *consigliere*: In our world such a thing could never happen, because Tom Hagen was neither Sicilian nor Italian. No *rappresentante* would ever have installed such a man in a position where he might some-day—even temporarily—take over a Family.)

Consigliere is an extremely powerful position, because he serves as a receptacle of information. He could manipulate a group of people within the Family—for good or bad. One of the serious functions of a *consigliere* was to protect the interests of the soldiers, and toward this end he was responsible for maintaining a Family's war chest. A war chest, to us, had

My father, Joe Bonanno (left), and John Tartamella Sr., consigliere of the Bonanno Family from 1941 to 1962, at Lake Ronkonkoma, Long Island's largest freshwater lake, in Suffolk County, New York, 1934.

nothing to do with buying weapons for wars among Families: It was our equivalent of a bank. We regularly loaned money to our members—without interest of course—for business purposes, or when a member was in trouble with the law. Each captain and his crew voluntarily contributed money from time to time to be used in the event one of the members needed it. In the Bonanno Family, our longtime *consigliere*, John Tartamella, kept the money in an old tin box. The money was always repaid . . . in one form or another.

The only time I remember our Family extracting a nonvoluntary payment was in 1958, when the Commission requested each of the Families to contribute ten thousand dollars to a defense fund for the twenty-seven men indicted in the Apalachin affair. Other Families handled their affairs differently; some even taxed their members, although after Apalachin that practice fell out of favor.

The *sotto capo* is a position often described in your world as underboss or "second in command." The *sotto capo* is appointed by the *rappresentante*; he serves at the leader's pleasure and can be removed by him at will. His role is to act as the *rappresentante* would act in any given situation, and in his place. If the *sotto capo* meets with the group captains, for instance, it is as if the *rappresentante* is meeting with them; he is paid the same respect as the leader. Many outsiders assume that, if something should happen to the "Godfather," the underboss takes over. While this may be possible under some circumstances, it is by no means automatic. If something should happen to incapacitate the *rappresentante* permanently—such as a serious illness, an inability to serve as leader, or worse—then the *sotto capo*, as his alter ego, would generally be expected to step aside as well. The *sotto capo* would only be expected to step in as temporary leader in circumstances where the *rappresentante*'s inability to serve was purely temporary. When Charlie "Lucky" Luciano relinquished his leadership role, his *sotto capo*, Vito Genovese,

*My father (right) with Joe Venza,
group leader, Tucson, Arizona, 1949.*

did not replace him; rather, the position of *rappresentante* went to Frank Costello. Anthony Arcardo, the leader of the Chicago Family, was replaced by a group leader, Sam Giancana. There are many other instances where a Family's underboss did not ascend to the leadership position. After Maranzano's death in 1931, my father was elected *rappresentante* and Maranzano's *sotto capo* became a group leader, serving in that capacity for more than twenty-five years.

A Family's Administration is made up of its *rappresentante*, its *consigliere*, and a number of *capodecini*, literally translated as "head of ten" or "captain of ten" —a division similar to that within ancient Roman armies. Although the word *decina* refers to ten, in our world the *capodecina*, or group leader, could be the head of a group of five, ten, fifteen, or twenty or more men. Today these men are also referred to as the "crew," and are *soldati* (soldiers). In fact, everyone in the Family, including the *rappresentante*, is technically a soldier.

Working together, a Family's Administration takes full responsibility for its decisions and subsequent actions. A *capo-decina*'s primary responsibility is to maintain discipline within his crew and to make sure the Administration's wishes are carried out. Another little-known function of any competent group leader is to see to it that each member of his crew makes a living for himself, his personal family, and anyone else for whom he may be financially responsible.

I became a group leader in 1959. My effectiveness and strength as a group leader involved a total commitment to being available for any reason and at any time, day or night, for members of my crew. If a member of my crew called me on the phone, or rang my doorbell in the middle of the night, I instantly responded, no matter what the reason. My theory was, if his feet are on fire, you don't ask how the fire started or who's to blame—you put out the damn fire! It was my job to put some salve on his burns, wrap them with gauze, and call one of our doctors. If I had to go out and buy a gallon of olive oil to pour on his feet—at sixteen dollars a bottle—that's what I'd do. Money was not important. The welfare of the members came first. If the soldier's predicament was his own fault, there would be plenty of time later to admonish him.

Often, in my time, there were four or five *capidecini* who had no crews. In effect, these men were the *rappresentante*'s crew; they reported directly to him and only to him. These men had a special relationship with the *rappresentante* and were perceived to have a little more prestige than the captains with crews.

The *sotto capo* (underboss) had no official capacity at an Administration meeting; he served only as the alter ego of the *rappresentante*, and two heads cannot preside at the same meeting. Likewise, the *consigliere* had no vote at the Administration meetings; his primary function was to observe, mentally record what went on in the meetings, and confirm the conclusions reached by the *rappresentante*.

The movie *The Godfather* and its sequels were responsible for at least three other myths about the organization of the Families.

First, the characters Santino (Sonny) and Michael both referred to a "wartime" *consigliere* to replace Tom Hagen because he wasn't tough enough during the inter-Family wars. In real life, there was no differentiation between a peacetime and a wartime *consigliere*.

Second, and in the same context, Michael tells Tom Hagen, "You're out," replacing him with Marlon Brando's character, Don Vito, as *consigliere*. Since *consigliere* is an elected position, a true *rappresentante* would never usurp the power of the Family members by arbitrarily firing one and appointing another. Such an act would undermine the purpose and concept of the position of *consigliere*.

Third, the movies left the impression that a *consigliere* must be an attorney—another incorrect assumption. No attorney ever served as *consigliere* in the Bonanno Family, or any other Family, to the best of my knowledge.

How did these mistaken ideas about the power, role, and potential "appointment" of a *consigliere* arise? We assumed there were at least three reasons for the confusion. For one thing, the concepts being explained to outsiders may have been imperfectly translated from Sicilian to English; the explanations may have been susceptible to different interpretations; and the writers may have used poetic license to make the characters and events onscreen appear more intriguing and dramatic than anything in our world.

The Family Structure

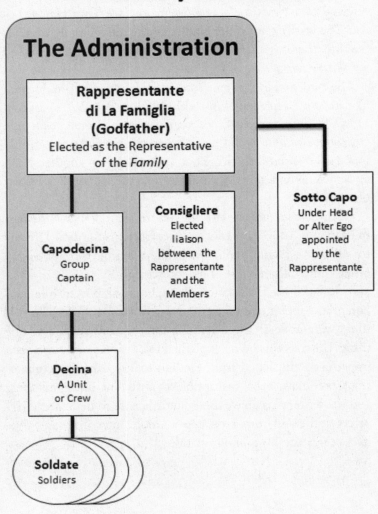

The Administration

**Rappresentante
di La Famiglia
(Godfather)**
Elected as the Representative
of the *Family*

Capodecina
Group
Captain

Consigliere
Elected
liaison
between the
Rappresentante
and the
Members

Sotto Capo
Under Head
or Alter Ego
appointed
by the
Rappresentante

Decina
A Unit
or Crew

Soldate
Soldiers

Bonanno Organization 1931–1968

Rappresentante
Joseph Bonanno Sr. (1931–68)

Sotto Capo
Angelo Caruso (1932)
Frank Garofalo (1932–55)
Johnny Morales (1957–68)

Consigliere
Frank Italiano (early 1930s)
Phillipe Rapa (1932–39)
John Tartamella (1940–64)
Salvatore "Bill" Bonanno (1964–68)

"Made Guys" of the Bonanno Family. From left to right, Martin Bonventre, Sal Profaci, Joe Bonanno, Gaspar DiGregorio, Lilo Galante, and Vincent Danna.

A candid photo of Bill Bonanno relaxing, taken by Gary Abromovitz during a writing session (August 25, 2000).

Enjoying dinner together at Agostino's Italian Restaurant in Casa Grade, Arizona. From left to right, Bill Bonanno, Anthony Tarantola, and Joe Bonanno, circa 1995.

17

Instruments of Death

It was rare that someone was killed in our world who didn't deserve it—or didn't know it was coming.

Joe Bonanno

The Five New York Families
Prior to October 25, 1957

Blood-soaked facial towels, which moments before had been steaming the face of Albert Anastasia, now lay beside pools of blood from his body, which had fallen slumped against the pedestal of the barber's chair. The date was October 25, 1957. The place was the barbershop of the Park Sheraton Hotel in New York City. In 1951, Anastasia had replaced Vincent Mangano of the original Mangano Family of New York, who had "mysteriously" disappeared. Now, six years later, that same Family's second *rappresentante* had made a violent exit, continuing centuries of evolutionary drama in our world.

And what happened next? We moved on.

The dispatching of leaders has always been an infrequent, but not unprecedented, occurrence in our world. But the method of execution had advanced from the early 1900s to Anastasia's time. Where once the Sicilians in the old country and the Black Hand had employed "stiletto justice," now revolvers were the preferred instruments of death.

In the Bonanno Family, violence was a means of last resort, used only if there was no other way to resolve a situation. However, sometimes there was no other way. In that case, the way to handle it was *bota e resposta*, which means "response with a bang . . . but a little louder." We cautioned members in the Bonanno Family that they should carry guns only for defensive, not offensive, purposes. On occasion, somebody was "marked to go." But we were taught that the human animal is the toughest animal to kill. If you are going to kill a human being, you'd better make sure that he is dead. This requires getting close enough to touch the other person. In Sicilian, the saying was "Savva brucharno la carne," or "The meat must burn." If you wanted to be sure to kill your target, in other words, you had to put the gun right next to the skin—close enough to burn the skin.

Killing at close range was also a way to avoid hurting innocent people—an integral part of our rules of engagement. When we sent a crew to do a job, we always discussed it with the group leader, to be sure we took all precautions to prevent innocents from being harmed.

One day, two of my men and I lingered in a car on an intended victim's street for three days, staking out his house, detailing his every move. Every night, we noticed, he took out the garbage at the same time—always alone. On the fourth night, he was marked for execution. But when that fourth night arrived, out he came with his wife and child! My crew and I were in jeopardy just sitting in a car loaded with armaments; if the police had happened by, we would have been history. As leader of the crew, I gave the order to abort the execution; there was just too much of a chance that the wife or child might accidentally get hurt. For this one man, justice would have to wait—for another place and time, when it could be carried out properly.

There were times when we sent several crews out to do the same job, with none of them knowing the other was tapped for the same mission. At the last minute, one crew might be called back. In 1950, a fellow by the name of Charlie Binaggio, a mobster with ambitions to secure political power by placing his candidates in office—thereby positioning himself to control the police departments in St. Louis and Kansas City, Missouri—was killed in Kansas City. The reason? He had borrowed money from several Families, promising that if his candidate for governor won, he would open up gambling operations in Missouri, affording a safe haven for us to operate casinos there. Binaggio's candidate won, but then the politician double-crossed him and Binaggio had to answer for it. Four different Families sent crews with orders to dispatch Binaggio; in that particular case, whoever saw him first had authority to dispatch him.

In such cases, when several crews are sent to do the same job, the member who actually commits the murder is rarely known—thus concealing the actual perpetrators for purposes of security. Sometimes even the person who orders the hit never knows who fires the fatal shot. A group leader might simply call several members of his crew together and tell them, "This has to be done." The crew members assign the job or contract, then decide on their own whether it will be done independently or jointly. Once the order is given and delegated, those to whom the job is assigned are responsible for its success or failure. Preserving maximum deniability is especially important, because information is temptation: somewhere down the road, a person who knows too much just might crack, implicating others or himself. This simple but effective form of insulating the Family members made it difficult for prosecutors to get convictions in the 1940s and 1950s.

How did we procure these weapons? Simple: Most of the longshoremen belonged to one Family or another, so we controlled the docks. Vincent Mangano and Albert Anastasia controlled the Longshoreman's Union on the Brooklyn docks, and Lucky Luciano and Joe Adonis controlled the union on the Manhattan docks. Arms shipments were constantly passing through the New York docks on their way to Europe or South America, and there would always be a case or two that would "fall off the dock" along the way. There were also people in the military willing to sell their weapons for the right price; we were even able to obtain some M–1 rifles from ROTC programs at universities. (Actually, I could never figure out why anyone would use this rifle. It weighed eleven pounds and was difficult to conceal. No one in our world ever used an M–1, to my knowledge; it always seemed like an unnecessary resource.)

When it comes to equipment, there are just as many misconceptions as there are concerning our leadership. Despite countless portrayals on film and TV, for instance, I've never heard of anyone in our world using a .45 caliber revolver—because the .45 was always a problematic weapon. It's a sensitive piece of equipment. If you don't grease it properly, or if a speck of dust gets in it, it's liable to jam up on you. There's nothing worse than pulling the trigger and having nothing happen. The best revolver was a six-chambered .38: no matter what you did with it—whether you got water or dust in it or otherwise abused it—this weapon was always effective. As long as that chamber was free to turn, the firing pin would set off the charge.

The .38 snub-nose revolver was preferred because of its size, which made it easy to conceal. However, the short barrel decreased both velocity and accuracy: the shorter the barrel, the closer you had to get to your target before firing. A six-inch barrel was a lot more accurate, but killers using weapons with longer barrels tended to stay further away from the victim—which raised the problems described above. It was always better to go right up to the victim and use a snub-nose—as in *The Godfather*, when Michael Corleone killed Sollozzo and Mc-Cluskey at the Luna Azura restaurant in the Bronx. (This was one thing *The Godfather* got right.)

My Colt .38 Detective Spec Special CTG snub-nose revolver.

Of course, there were other choices. You could use a .32 caliber gun, but it had only five chambers and, because of the smaller caliber, you usually had to empty the whole damn thing to make sure it did the job. Among rifles, the .30 caliber carbine was probably the best; you would cut off a little bit of the stock, which some of the men would replace with a special carrying handle. This was the rifle that was used to assassinate Benjamin "Bugsy" Siegel in 1947.

The double-barreled 12-gauge sawed-off shotgun, known by the Sicilian name Lupara (or Lupa for short), was originally carried by sheepherders in Sicily to protect their flocks of sheep against wolves and other predators. It was favored for other uses—specifically for vendettas by those adhering to the philosophy of *cosa nostra* in Sicily. Because of its high lacerating power at short distance, killing with the Lupa is known as *lupara bianca* ("the white death"), a term referring to a Mafia murder when a body is not found. There are no sites or scope on the Lupa. None were needed. It was used at close range with a sniper's surprise.

We also used 20-gauge and 16-gauge shotguns, but the 12-gauge sawed-off shotgun was our preferred weapon: it was convenient, because you could carry it under your suit jacket or overcoat, and it was vicious. But you had to be careful, because if you sawed the barrel off too short, it could blow up in your face.

A 12-gauge sawed-off shotgun. Known as "the white death,"
this gun could easily be concealed under a topcoat.

The barrel had to be cut clean and beveled, which is not that easy. We had members or associates who knew exactly where and how to cut the barrel. You had to make sure the pellets or 00 slugs came out of the barrel nice and clean; if the barrel wasn't filed down just right, it could peel back the end of the barrel into several segments. (This was one thing those old movie cartoons got right!)

In the late 1960s, the .22 caliber automatic came into fashion as the new weapon of choice in our world. You loaded the .22 with a convenient clip, rather than single bullets; it made relatively little noise; and if you held the trigger back it would continue to fire rounds until the clip was empty. It left a smaller hole, but when you empty twelve rounds into somebody in a tight pattern, the hole is big enough. Some favored the small, lightweight, and trustworthy .25 caliber Baretta, with an 8-round magazine for .25 caliber cartridges. And there were times when the .30 caliber carbine was much better than the .38 revolver, although even then you would normally be within a few feet from the victim. The movie industry got it right when they showed mobsters shooting someone at a distance, then coming up to him and shooting him again to make sure he was dead. A man doing a job for us might typically carry a "hit kit" in-

A "hit kit" with an assortment of revolvers.

cluding .38 caliber revolvers with various barrel lengths, a .22 caliber six-shot *piccolino* (little one) capable of being concealed in his palm, a barber's straight razor (common in the old days), and an Italian stiletto.

The choice of weapon was a personal thing. Since our top priority was always to avoid killing or injuring innocent people, our rule of thumb was the simpler the better. I was never a big advocate of knives, but we did have some guys who were so good with a stiletto that they could cut your throat in two seconds and you wouldn't even know it until you started

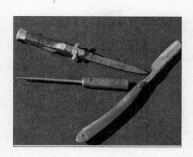

Traditional weapons included the stiletto, ice pick, and barber's straight razor.

gagging on your own blood. Some specialized in throwing the Sicilian stiletto, an art that required a blade of just the right thickness. Others, including one professional called Ice Pick Willie, were known for their ability to take someone out quickly by inserting an ice pick in a victim's ear and thrusting it into the brain. We chose not to sanction the use of bombs because

An Italian .22 caliber
six-shot piccolino.

we felt there was too much risk that innocent people could get hurt. The only Family I know of that used bombs routinely was Cleveland and, sure enough, an innocent man and a couple of children were killed by a bomb that was not intended for them.

Most of the Family leaders took the precaution of employing protective measures, for defensive purposes. My father had suits made with special pockets with snaps for attaching a holster and concealing a revolver.

He also had several bulletproof Cadillacs made for him, with hidden pockets for guns behind the seats and inside the doors. Johnny Morales, a group leader and then a *sotto capo* in

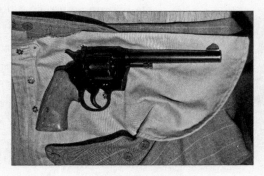

A pants pocket specially designed to
carry a .38 long-barrel revolver.

the Bonanno Family, was my father's personal driver at one time; with its armor plating and bulletproof glass, the car weighed roughly three tons.

My father's bulletproof 1941 Cadillac.

Our people also practiced shooting in farms we owned in upstate New York, and at a gun range in a specially built soundproof basement in Louie Drago's home on Long Island. The basement had a big pile of dirt at one end. The idea was not so much to become a marksman, but rather to get a feel for the weapon you were using—because even identical weapons handle differently. Sometimes it has to do with the pressure you put on the trigger: It's important to take a couple of practice shots with any gun so that you know just how much pressure to put on the trigger before the firing pin will drop back. We had one guy who used to file down the sear, which holds the hammer back, until he created a

My father eyeing a kill while hunting in upstate New York, 1940.

hair trigger. On a .38 revolver, if you filed the sear down, you had to put a good taped grip on it so your hand wouldn't slip from the heel of the gun. You had to be sure that what you were pointing at was what you really wanted to shoot—or it could take your leg off.

We had everything from mortars to Browning Automatic Rifles (BARs). We stored our weapons in the attics of homes of our friends and relatives so they would be readily accessible. We couldn't go driving around New York City with a car full of guns. I was always puzzled that the police didn't stop us more often; after all, the police and the FBI knew what was going on with us. Their defense was that they had to have probable cause to arrest one of us, but to me it always seemed like they were looking the other way. Maybe they were just happy if we killed each other off!

This may surprise you, but in our world, no matter who had to go, no one relished killing another human being. It was never an easy thing to do, although those doing the killing often had to rationalize to themselves that it was the right thing to do, under the circumstances. We all knew the rules, and what would happen if they were broken. In our world, dying was a part of living, and you accepted it as such. It was rare that anyone was killed in our world who didn't deserve it—or didn't know it was coming.

18

Being Made: Initiation, Ritual, and Oath

There are, within any society, certain kinds of jobs that need to be done that are dependent upon trust and a handshake alliance among the few men who can and will perform them.

Charlie "Lucky" Luciano

There is no Sicilian equivalent for the phrase "being made" to signify the induction of a new member into our world. Being made, or being a "made guy," are just more words used in Hollywood movies and books written about gangsters and organized crime. But the American public now recognizes "being made" as the term for being accepted into the criminal organization popularly known as the Mafia—and the term has crept into the vocabulary of our world. Though I have reservations about perpetuating yet another myth, I'll reluctantly use the term here myself, in recognition of its near-universal acceptance.

A man can live his life in the *mafioso* way, being true to his own concept of right and wrong, without ever belonging to any organized group. In our world, such a man may or may not be selected to become made. Even if he is never so chosen, we may still reach out to him for our own purposes. And we will still come to his aid if he should ever need help.

This symbiotic relationship between made members of a Family and others who aren't made can exist only when both parties have a mutual trust based upon the same ideology—if each side can truthfully tell the other, *I will come to your aid if you need help, because I know you will come to my aid if I need help.* This is the way it was in our world, at least in the years before 1968: Much as you can be a Christian or a Jew without belonging to a church or synagogue, you could participate in our world even without becoming a formal member. And it may surprise you to know that you didn't even have to engage in illegal activities to be considered a part of our world. We were really all one group—at least among those who thought that way. That kind of solidarity was one of the reasons it was so difficult for outsiders to penetrate our world.

There were certain demanding qualities that were required for membership into our world. The principal ones were obedience and loyalty to a select group of men of Sicilian or Italian heritage. Still, there were always men who possessed these qualities but to whom we did not extend membership for other reasons. It might be best to explain some of these qualities to you by example.

In 1955, Tony, a tough little Sicilian kid from Cleveland, moved to Arizona. He was one of those men who would say, "My mind and my body are yours. You tell me what to do and I'll do my best to do it." He was the type who thought in terms of *all for one and one for all.* If you said jump, he didn't ask why; he asked, "How high?" No questions asked. That is one of the things it takes to be a made guy—unquestioned obedience.

In 1958, I moved from Flagstaff to Tucson. When Tony found out, he said, "I'm not going to stay here in Flagstaff. I'm coming with you." He insisted on moving to Tucson with me. Tony moved his wife and two kids without thinking twice about it. We became very close and we ended up making him down in Tucson.

One night, I left my house and went to downtown Tucson with one of my crew, Charlie Battaglia, to check on a crap game we were running. It was about two or two-thirty in the morning, and there was a problem. I told Charlie we better call Tony. When he answered the phone, he sounded like he'd been running. I asked him if he was okay, and he said yes. I told him I needed him right now. Tony lived out on East Speedway in Tucson, normally about a twenty-minute ride from us. He was downtown in fifteen minutes, and we showed the force we needed to solve the problem.

Later, we went to the old Flamingo Hotel for some coffee (in those days it was open all night) and I said to Tony, "When I called you, you sounded like you were running. Where the hell were you going at two-thirty in the morning? Were you outside?"

"No, I was getting laid," Tony said. "When the phone rang and you said 'I need you now,' I got up out of bed, said goodbye to my wife, and headed downtown."

Now, that's a silly story, but it tells you something about how a made member reacts with respect to his obligations and burdens. If he had questioned my order or said, "I can't come right now, I'm busy," he could never be part of our world. There's no such thing as a made member being un-available! One of the things you learn once you cross over the line into this other world, and you become part of this system, is that your life is not your own. Your *being* belongs to the group—not to any one person, not to yourself, your wife, or your children. That mentality, which lasted from 1930 until roughly 1968, was the glue that bound all of us together.

To live this way required rigorous discipline—a lesson instilled in me as a youngster.

With my father and my sister, Catherine, outside our home in Hempstead, Long Island, 1940.

For instance, one early and bright New York summer morning in mid-May, when I was about nine years old, my father came into my bedroom and announced that I was going with him into the city. He instructed me to dress in "visiting clothes." That was code for no play clothes.

It was at this point in my life that my lessons and the training started. Even at that young age, I could sense the command in his voice and knew better than to question why, when, or where. One thing you learn early in life is that you never question anything your father says; there would be plenty of time for questions, and probably answers, later in life.

A little before nine A.M., we heard a car pull into the driveway—a routine whenever my father went into the city. My "cousin Johnny" came in, and after the normal pleasantries, he sat down for a cup of coffee and some toast.

I called many of my father's associates "cousin" or "uncle": Cousin Johnny was Johnny Morales, my father's bodyguard and driver; Uncle Charles was Charlie "Lucky" Luciano; Uncle Albert was Albert Anastasia; Uncle Willie was Willie Moretti, who was also Frank Sinatra's godfather; Uncle Vincent was Vincent Mangano; and Uncle Tom was Tommaso

Gagliano. There were even a few real family members thrown in: Uncle Joe, Joseph Profaci, was my wife Rosalie's actual uncle, and Uncle Steve was Stefano Magaddino, my father's cousin and head of the Buffalo Family. Then again, to a young Sicilian boy from a large family—my mother was one of twelve siblings herself—having so many "uncles" seemed perfectly normal.

At breakfast that day, no one said a word about the trip into the city; the conversation centered on what my mother and sister were planning on doing that day and the neighbor, who was stopping by later to borrow our lawn mower. When we were done eating, the two men went into a small office off the kitchen and closed the door. That room had a churchlike presence; it was the only room in the house that was almost entirely off-limits to my sister and me. We were allowed in only for specific purposes, such as placing a coat in the closet or putting a package or some mail on the unpretentious desk at the far end of the room. Over the years, the mystery deepened whenever my father had visitors. They would confine themselves to that room sometimes for hours, coming out only to use the small bathroom in the hallway, or when my mother brought in a tray of espresso and biscotti. Sometimes my mother served lunch or dinner in the dining room, if the sessions were long.

After a while, Johnny and my dad came out and announced we were ready to leave. I got my jacket; I already had on my tie. When you went out with Dad, especially to the city, you never went anywhere without a tie, jacket, and long pants. In the 1930s and early 1940s, young men wore short pants or knickers

Johnny Morales, my father's bodyguard, driver, and number two.

*Our home, 61 Clermont Avenue,
Hempstead, Long Island.*

until they reached puberty, when they graduated to long pants like their fathers. Even at the age of nine, wearing long pants set me apart from others my age; to me, they felt like a sign that my manhood had begun.

After saying our goodbyes, we left the house. Our home in Hempstead, Long Island, was landscaped like a forest of Christmas trees. (In fact, each Christmas my father would cut down a tree, bring it inside the house to decorate, and plant a new one to replace it.)

When you got in the car, the seating arrangement was as much a ritual as where you sat at the dinner table. On the rare occasions when women were joining us, the men always opened the door for the women to enter first. That's just the way it was back then. When only the men were traveling, each man opened his own door, and each knew exactly where to sit. Johnny would get behind the wheel, Dad would get into the front passenger seat, and I always climbed into the rear passenger seat on the right side. As a youngster, I developed a serious mastoid condition in my left ear. My father assigned me the rear seat on the right side so that the cold coming in from the window wouldn't hit my left ear.

Aside from that, I always felt that sitting on the right side in the back was a privilege, as well as a position of trust. In the early years I didn't know why that was so. Later in my career, I learned the reason. Sitting in the right-rear seat gives you a clearer view of everything in front and to either side—while putting you in a better position to protect the people in front, should it become necessary to do so. And there was a strategic advantage to sitting in the back seat on the passenger side: As portrayed in *The Godfather*, if the person sitting in the front passenger seat had to be "taken for a ride," the right-side back seat was the strategic position for the person assigned to eliminate him.

Everything we did—and everything we saw or heard—had a purpose. We left nothing to chance. Whenever I went out with my father, I learned more about his old saying, "Courtesy is owed, respect is earned, and love is given." As I grew up, my subconscious replayed these lessons learned until my reactions became second nature. When women were present, we learned that, next to God, we are indebted to women—first for life itself, and then for making life worth living. When I was a youngster, women were always placed on a pedestal; our job was to separate the pedestal from the woman. We learned respect, which had nothing to do with affection or good manners. In addition, of course, we learned trust, loyalty, and obedience.

I always enjoyed the ride into the city. No matter how many times I made the trip, I usually saw something new. As I think back on that time, I realize now that we never took the same route twice on consecutive trips—another lesson. On this day, I thought the trip was to be just another "day out with the men." Little did I know that on that beautiful summer day, I would be tested, and taught a lesson that would stay with me for a lifetime.

We crossed the Williamsburg Bridge from Brooklyn to Manhattan and cruised our way to Elizabeth Street in Little Italy, where we stopped at a small coffee shop. A distinguished-looking man I knew as Uncle Frank got into the backseat of the car, sitting next to me on the driver's side. Uncle Frank was Frank Garofalo, whom I later learned was my Dad's *sotto capo* from 1930 until he retired to Sicily in late 1955.

Upon leaving Elizabeth Street, we traveled up Lafayette Street past Cooper Union and finally arrived at Times Square. In those days, Times Square was bustling with activity, clean, and frequented by the middle class and the rich. It was a Wednesday, and the area was swarming with people rushing to get to the theaters for the matinees. We stopped in front of a luncheonette/drugstore. My dad, in a matter-of-fact tone, instructed me to go into the luncheonette, get something to eat if I wanted, and wait for him or Johnny to come and get me. He made a point of instructing me not to leave or call anyone. After I got out of the car, he handed me some money, gave me the traditional Sicilian hug, and before I knew it I was alone

My father (far right) and Frank Garofalo,
sotto capo in the Bonanno Family, 1940s.

in Times Square—with money, newfound freedom, and time to myself.

It was a little after midday. I looked around and saw strangers scurrying around like ants searching for food or nesting material. In New York, people ignore each other unless your presence affects them. People have a tendency to mind their own business. Today was no different. I entered the luncheonette and sat at a table along the wall facing the door so I could see when someone came for me. A matronly woman (to a youngster like me, anyone over thirty seemed matronly) came over and asked if I wanted anything. I ordered a ham-and-cheese sandwich and a vanilla malted. Before placing the order, the waitress was New York–savvy enough to ask if I had any money. When I showed her the cash my father had given me, she smiled, turned on her heel, and said, "Coming right up!"

As the afternoon wore on, I started to get antsy. The attention span of any nine-year-old is short at best, but add to that the boredom of waiting and the strange surroundings, and you're adding anxiety to the equation. Soon it was approaching five o'clock. I had been in the luncheonette for almost four hours, and there was still no relief in sight. If this had been in any other city or at another time in history, the management would probably have called the police and reported that an abandoned youngster was in the establishment. But this was New York City in the early 1940s, before the United States had entered World War II, and life was much less complicated; people lived and let live. Fear and ill feeling had not yet fully entered the American psyche. Thank goodness, it was summertime. As afternoon ended and evening arrived, there was still daylight.

Only later did I learn that, from the moment I walked into the luncheonette, I was under constant observation by members of my dad's organization. From time to time, over the course of that afternoon, they walked in, bought something, hung around a little while, and then left. At no time was I ever actually alone. At one point it crossed my mind to go outside and look around, even to make a phone call. But then I remembered my dad's instructions, "Don't leave or call anyone!" So I just sat and waited.

Finally, at around six o'clock, almost five hours after I entered the luncheonette, Johnny and his brother Sal walked in, came over to the table, and asked if I was ready to go. They didn't have to ask twice. Without saying a word, we got back into the car and took off. A few short blocks later, we stopped in front of the Red Devil restaurant. Johnny parked the car and the three of us went into the restaurant. Seated at a table at the rear of the restaurant was my dad with a number of other men, engrossed in conversation and oblivious to our presence. Looking up, my dad invited us to sit and then returned to his conversation as if we weren't even there.

A rare photograph of the Red Devil Italian Restaurant on West 46th Street in New York City.

Later that night, on the way home to Long Island, the talk was mostly about the Yankees, the weather, and our plans to head out to see my mother's uncle in Jersey that weekend. No one mentioned anything about my afternoon's adventure, and I kept quiet. When we got home, I said goodnight to my dad and Johnny, kissed my mother, and went up to my room—all the while wondering what the hell today was all about. It wasn't until many years later that I realized the truth—that the whole day had been a test of my discipline and character. It was on that day that I started to learn, unknowingly, about the bonds of trust and obedience that held our people together. There would be many more days of lessons to follow.

After the Castellammarese War and the deaths of Masseria and Maranzano in 1931, our world went through a period of readjustment. The old-world Sicilians started assimilating into American society. There is an old Sicilian proverb that says, "In order to know a man you must know his father, and his father before him, and his father." In this country, it was getting to the point where nobody knew anything about the family history of some of these Sicilians, and this was starting to create a problem. The only way to resolve it was to stop making guys, because we didn't need anyone else, and we didn't want to risk weakening the Family network by admitting people whose background was unknown. After all, it was still unclear at this point whether the Commission would be able to keep the peace.

The thinking of the leadership was that quantity was not as important as quality. We could accomplish our goals just as easily with twenty-five hundred "good" men as we could with four thousand. So the Commission decided that, until further notice, no new members would be inducted into our world until the Commission gave its approval. You may have heard this described with the American shorthand expression "The books are closed." We Sicilians saw it as "closing the circle," until later on, when it would doubtless be "opened" once again.

Like everything else in life, there were exceptions to the rule. The ratification of the Commission in 1931 brought a new era of trust and responsibility, and it was understood that under certain circumstances a new member might be brought into the fraternity, even if the books were closed. When that occurred, the leader of the particular Family would pass around the name of the individual to each of the five New York Families. After reviewing the individual's background, any Family could object to admitting the person proposed. If there were no objections, the Family proposing the new member's admission would decide whether to induct him. The group leader, or sponsor, would take personal responsibility for that individual. It was important that the sponsor know everything about the member he was proposing; if the new initiate screwed up, the sponsor would suffer the consequences. This was as close as we came to having one big Family.

To my knowledge, only a handful of men were inducted into our world during the 1930s, 1940s, or the 1950s. It was this moratorium, and the Commission's tight control on admission into our world, that enabled the Families to live in relative peace and tranquillity from the early 1930s to 1951. With our world controlled by a common sense of responsibility, the Families no longer left a trail of bodies littering the streets.

This moratorium also served as a weeding-out process. For the first time, all new members brought in were known to all Families. The moratorium was primarily intended for the New York and Chicago Families; smaller Families such as Springfield, Illinois; San Jose, California; and Pueblo, Colorado, were given some leeway.

Many of the informal discussions about such things took place during the many times each week when the men in our world would meet, mostly at restaurants. In New York City, it happened at a series of Italian restaurants on West Forty-seventh Street between Fifth Avenue and Sixth Avenue or nearby.

In the 1950s, if you wanted to get a message to Albert Anastasia, you would go to the Red Devil restaurant. Albert would be sitting at the back table almost every day with his *sotto capo*, Tata Chiricho, or perhaps with group leader Tommy Rava. If you wanted to see Frank Costello, you would go over to the Vesuvius Restaurant, which he owned a piece of, on West Forty-seventh Street. People from the Mangano Family hung out at Patsy's restaurant on West Fifty-sixth Street.

If you wanted to meet my father, Joe Bonanno, you could go to La Scala on West Fifty-fourth Street at one o'clock in the afternoon on almost any day of the week, and he would be there. Everyone knew where everyone else was at all times. Even when the cops were nosing around, nobody gave it a second thought; they didn't bother us—because the cops in the area were all on our payroll!

There was a lot of protocol—which we called respect. If my father, or Albert or Frank, were sitting at their tables, the

At Canzoneri's apple orchard in upstate New York, 1938. My father (left) with Tony Canzoneri, who held World Boxing Championship titles in three divisions—featherweight, lightweight, and junior welterweight—who was also a Bonanno group leader.

Family's *sotto capo*, or a leader from another Family, or perhaps a group leader might join them. But a soldier would never sit down at a leader's table unless specifically invited. Without such an invitation, a soldier would simply sit at his own table with other soldiers.

Yet another myth concerns the qualifications for becoming a made member of our Family. Conventional wisdom has it that before we admitted a member into a Family, he had to "make his bones." This has taken on the meaning that he had to kill someone. Not true! Our Family included members from all occupations: lawyers, dentists, funeral directors, priests, firemen, mechanics, grocers, dockworkers, and other professionals.

We called upon them when we needed them. Once, when we were on the lam during the 1960s hostilities in the Bonanno Family, several of us were having dinner when group leader Joe Notaro had a heart attack. We couldn't very well take him to Columbia-Presbyterian Hospital, so we called a doctor in our Family, took him to that doctor's office, and his life was saved. Similarly, if one of our people was hit in a shoot-out, we would take him to one of our doctors.

We would never compromise any of our professionals, because if we did, they could never do us any good. These men weren't made in order to put them out on the street or to get them into Family businesses; they became part of our Family so that they could share their expertise with our Family without having to reserve anything while doing so. In our Family, at least, we never placed lawyers in a position where they would have to choose between their oath to the Family and their obligations as officers of the court.

Normally, when an inductee is initiated, the Administration of the Family is present. However, people from other Families may also be invited. When I was made, all five leaders of the New York Families were present, along with the leaders of the Boston and Philadelphia Families, and the complete Administration of the Bonanno Family.

Before the inductee is ushered into the room to appear before the members, the person conducting the initiation would "tie the circle" and explain the purpose of the meeting. Normally, no other business is transacted on such a special occasion, except for mundane announcements or some discussion with visiting Families if they happen to be present. The focus was on honoring the moment for the new members. The members are told the name of the person to be initiated; who he is; who his father is; who his grandfathers are; the name of the town where their family comes from in the old country; any information about jail time the person or his father or grandfathers have served; and the businesses or trades of his relatives. In other words, everything there is to know about the person and his family is revealed.

Then the floor is opened for discussion, and anyone is free to say anything he wishes about the candidate. In fact, the attendees are obliged to speak up—especially if what they know about someone might somehow put the Family in jeopardy or cast it in a bad light. Failing to say what one knows about an inductee, if it might jeopardize the Family, would expose one to the same punishment as the member himself would suffer after the damage was done.

This forthrightness is part of the concept of *omertà*—the requirement that we all must be loyal and completely open and honest with our own people. When you are completely open you are mentally naked, stripped of all pretense. An act of omission, in such circumstances, is the same as an act of commission. There was no guarantee that after everyone had said his peace, the person would be inducted. In fact, I attended one induction where the person was rejected after things were revealed about him in the open session. Of course, during this time the person proposed for membership was not in the room;

he was doubtless with the person sponsoring him, not even certain why he was there.

My uncle Frank told me the story of my grandfather Labruzzo's proposed induction into a Family in 1928. They took him to a place in Brooklyn where he was to be inducted. They were "in the circle" and the *consigliere* was explaining why they were there. As my grandfather looked around the room, he saw a man he didn't like. Addressing the *consigliere* in Sicilian, he said, "Can I ask a question?" (A potential inductee is generally given the opportunity to ask questions before the ceremony is complete.) The *consigliere* agreed.

Indicating one of the attendees, my grandfather asked, "Is he part of this group?"

The answer was yes.

"If he's part of it," my grandfather said, "then I don't want any part of this."

"Explain that?" the *consigliere* asked.

My grandfather explained that the man had caused him some offense—owed him money or something to that effect—and my grandfather didn't want to know him, didn't want to be his friend, and didn't want anything to do with him.

My grandfather was asked to step outside for a few minutes. Then the focus turned to the member, who admitted that he had wronged my grandfather—arguing that my grandfather was a nobody and he was a made guy. On this man's admission, they let my grandfather go; he was not inducted on that day, or any other day. This was unusual: Normally, if there was a problem, the person never left the room. After all, this was a secret society; once the inductee was in the room with the made members, he could identify each of them. If he did not become one of them at that point, it was more commonly because of some gross violation on the candidate's part—and it usually wasn't very good for his health.

There were many variations in the way these ceremonies were conducted, through the years and from Family to Family. The movie *Goodfellas* depicts Joe Pesci's character as knowing he was going to be made before he was brought to the house where the induction was to take place. In the Bonanno Family, we did not do it that way; proposed inductees usually had no idea that anyone else was even meeting in another room.

My own induction is a perfect example.

One day, around the end of June 1954, my uncle Frank called me. "I need your help. Later this afternoon you and I are going to take care of something." That's all I knew. He picked me up at around four o'clock in the afternoon. I didn't ask him where we were going or what we were going to do. I figured he would tell me what I needed to know when he was ready. As we drove off, he told me he had to make a stop to take care of a problem, and he wanted me there to protect his back—just in case. That started me thinking: if we were going to "see" someone, why didn't we have a piece on us? He answered my unspoken thought: "I just need to get some information here, and then we're going where we have to go."

We went into a warehouse with offices and walked into an empty room. He told me to wait there for him and left me alone. What I didn't know was that then, in another room, he met about twenty other men who were gathered there to discuss . . . me.

After about forty-five minutes, he returned. "Come in here with me," he said.

As we entered the room, I was greeted by a bunch of suits. I was startled; I had no idea what was going on. Then, as I scanned the room, I began to recognize some faces: those of Joe Profaci and Albert Anastasia, who were friends of ours from other Families. It was then that I realized that something special was about to happen. Uncle Frank and I were invited to join the circle, and it was tied again.

The procedure is generally the same for every initiation. After the *consigliere* (or another Administration member) explains what is going on, the floor is opened for questions. After questioning the inductee at length, some members still may not be satisfied. Several men, whom I sometimes referred to as the "interrogation squad," usually want to observe how the proposed member conducts himself when being confronted with questions, either friendly or hostile. They might observe his body language, his facial expressions, his voice; they watch for flashes of anger when the inductee is asked about personal or delicate matters concerning himself or his immediate family. I later learned that these members sometimes rehearse their questions in advance, in order to elicit specific reactions during the interrogation.

After the questioning, a revolver and a knife are placed on a table in front of the inductee. This symbolically demonstrates to the inductee that if we choose this life, it could lead to violence, and that we might have to use violence to protect ourselves.

Prior to the initiation ceremony, the outline of a saint, usually from a prayer card, is traced onto thin onionskin paper (like the second sheet under old-fashioned typewriter carbon paper). The paper tracing is then placed in the palms of the initiate. The inductee is asked to stand, and the initiation proceeds with the burning of the saint's image and the taking of the oath.

The religious significance of burning an image of a saint represents a higher level of obligation, in much the same way that a person places his hand on a bible while taking an oath in court, or the president of the United States does when taking the oath of office.

Then the initiate's finger is pricked with a needle to allow a drop or two of blood to drip onto the image. In the fifteen or so inductions I have attended, the leader asked, "Which finger do you use to pull the trigger?" and then pricked that finger.

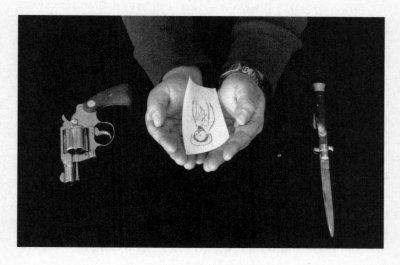

The beginning of the initiation ritual: the symbolic revolver, image of a saint, and knife.

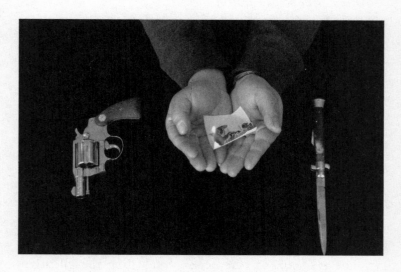

The revolver, the knife, and the burning saint.

Which finger was pricked was less important than the blood itself, which signified that he was taking the oath as a blood brother. Pricking the trigger finger was merely to reinforce an understanding of the dangers in our world and the bond among the members.

The paper image of the saint is then set on fire, and the oath is administered and repeated by the initiate.

The initiate doesn't hold the paper motionless while it's on fire, or it would burn his hands. Rather, he is instructed to toss the paper back and forth between the palms of both hands as he repeats the oath.

The oath, which is in Sicilian, is brief, and is not always said the same way each time; it can vary depending on the local traditions in the Sicilian town the person administering the oath came from. The actual words I used are:

> *Come si brucia questa Santa, cosi*
> *Gurio di bruciare le mie carne*
> *Per il Bene dei mie fratelli*
> *Per Defendere l'onore della nostra famiglia*
> *E per Proteggere la nostra constitucione.*

Roughly translated: "As this Saint burns, I swear to burn my being, for the good of my brothers to defend the honor of our Family and to protect our constitution."

After the oath, the remnants of the burned paper are reduced to shreds of black residue, and are balled up in the initiate's palm and then rubbed between his hands, shredding the ashy remnants further.

He then lifts his hands to his mouth, palms up, and blows the shreds into the air—symbolizing that if he violates the oath, his body will disintegrate in the same way.

The *consigliere*, or the person conducting the initiation, then asks the initiate if he understands the oath. If he does

Blowing the shredded remains.

not, it is repeated and explained to him. This complete under-standing is paramount; it could not be merely a rote recitation, as when a courtroom witness repeats "I do" after being sworn in by a bailiff. In our world, there was no room for ambiguity in interpreting the oath.

Your life—and the lives of your fellow members—depended upon it.

19

Rules and Punishment

Only a mad dog wants to hurt another human being . . .
without just cause.

Joe Bonanno

Those were words my father told me many times. The warning always left me curious, so one day I asked him: What did he mean by "without just cause"?

"That's for you to find out," he responded. "You have to make the determination of what's right."

In later conversations, he would explain that every man is responsible for his own actions. "When you take an oath or commit to something, you must do it. But you do it because of the commitment you made—never because you are forced or expected to do something. You must be in command of your actions, and take responsibility for everything you do."

The following story demonstrates what can go wrong when a member strays from such responsibility.

One time, a member caught his wife having an affair with another member. After putting himself on record with his group leader, he asked to see my father, the *rappresentante* of the Family. He complained to my father that others knew about her unfaithfulness, and it had become an embarrassment to him. Since the paramour was a member of the Family, however, he had come to ask permission from his *rappresentante*—to kill them both!

My father denied the request. If the member sincerely had such strong feelings about both the infidelity and the embarrassment, he said, he should have made his own decision, dispatched them both, and *then* presented himself to the Family Administration with the facts and let the Family decide his fate. In my father's judgment, either his feelings about the matter weren't strong enough, or he didn't trust the Administration enough, to put his faith in whatever decision they would make after the fact. By asking permission, the member was trying to make the Family responsible for his decision to act—"wiping his potentially bloody knife on the sleeves of others." This was not a manly thing to do, and the permission was denied.

The Rules That Governed Our World

From the beginning of time, every society has chosen a leader, or a group of leaders, to be responsible for establishing the rules or laws its people must follow, in order to ensure their coexistence in a civilized world. The simplest and most famous set of rules is the Ten Commandments, carried by Moses down from Mount Sinai.

In 2007, the *Los Angeles Times* printed an article claiming that a list dubbed the "Mafia Ten Commandments" had been discovered during the arrest of Salvatore Lo Piccolo, a top Mafia boss in Sicily. Lo Piccolo allegedly carried the list, described as a typewritten Mafia code of conduct, with him in a briefcase "at all times." The very idea of getting caught with a written list was ironic, as one Palermo-based journalist, Enrico Bellavia, correctly noted, because the *mafiosi* "all know the rules and for generations the Mafia has always avoided communicating other than by word of mouth." I never saw the Lo Piccolo document, although the type of conduct it reportedly describes would seem to resemble portions of the oral code of conduct of our world. But why would a Mafia leader have any written code of conduct in his possession? The very idea gives rise to skepticism about its authenticity, since it violates centuries of tradition.

As societies evolve, their rules tend to become more sophisticated—although they are not always fair, and can sometimes be brutal. The legal code written by Hammurabi, king of Babylon, consisted of an orderly arranged body of written laws so that all men would know what was required of them. The punishment for violation, "an eye for an eye and a tooth for a tooth," is still considered by some as the best justice for an aggrieved party.

As long as a society allows men and women to think independently, rules and laws will always be broken. Who is to say that those charged with the task of making the rules are always right? A perfect example is the enactment of the Eighteenth Amendment to the U.S. Constitution in 1919, which banned the "manufacture, sale, or transportation of intoxicating liquors" within or imported into, or exported from, the United States. The Amendment was repealed in 1933, much to the disappointment of those in our world. Nevertheless, civilization demands a system to control chaos. There must be a fair method to settle disputes or provide punishment when rules are broken.

In your world, a trial court is the tribunal where either a jury or a judge makes a factual determination as to who is right and who is wrong. If an individual believes there was legal error at the trial level resulting in an improper verdict for any reason (generally because the law was misapplied, or is claimed to be unconstitutional, or because the jury was given incorrect instructions), the legal system allows for an appeal to a higher court. The system does not provide swift resolution. In fact, it favors the alleged wrongdoer over the victim, in order to protect the innocent from wrongful punishment. Civil cases can take years to be decided and even longer to go through the appeal process. Meanwhile, the accused goes about his business, exhausting every avenue of defense—while the victim continues to suffer without having closure.

In our world, this never happens.

Distinguishing Right from Wrong

Especially in the decades from the 1930s through the 1960s, our world relied on a system of justice the roots of which were more than seven hundred years old. We followed certain rules, and had our own methods of settling disputes. While no well-ordered society tolerates indiscriminate and arbitrary violence, all societies use force at some level to enforce the rules of that society. Our world was no exception.

In considering the role of violence in our world, I do not expect you, as an outsider, to approve, condone, or even fully understand the rules we lived by, because you have never walked in our shoes. The old Sicilian tradition teaches a *personal sense of justice.* We define justice as a system of rules that gives each person his due. However, for this to work, everyone must understand what is right and what is wrong.

Our world is governed by the principle of strict accountability. Any action, especially of a violent nature, requires a member to be sure he is doing the right thing—because the penalty for guessing wrong can be severe. The appearance of impropriety, even if it turns out to be an innocent mistake or misunderstanding, can result in a beating or even death—with no potential for appeal, since by that time justice is served, it is usually too late.

The object of many of our rules is to help a man contain his emotions while striving to do the right thing for the Family, himself, his personal family, and his friends. Since nothing is ever in writing, interpretations of the rules can vary depending upon the facts of each case and the sense of personal justice involved. *But if the rules are open to interpretation,* you might ask, *how can a member know if he is violating them?*

The answer is that right and wrong are determined on a case-by-case basis. *Mafiosi* learn the distinction by listening, learning, and applying the traditional teachings of their elders. Punishment for violations also depends upon the facts of each case. As a result, it's incumbent on each member to be sure he is correct in his decision—lest it be his last. For decades, this served as a very effective deterrent to members acting without thinking, a considerable disincentive to members who otherwise might have acted precipitously. It encouraged our members to exhaust all avenues of resolution and accommodation before breaking the peace.

Respect vs. Equality

One of the hardest concepts to understand is the difference between respect and equality. Respect is a psychological principle involving interaction: it involves showing honor, esteem, and courteous regard for someone or something. Equality, on the other hand, means possessing substantially the same rights, privileges, responsibilities, and immunities as others in your society. Our tradition is based upon the principle of equality among all members.

In my day, members in our world were constantly balancing these two ideals—respect and equality—in order to maintain cohesive and smooth relationships with each other within the hierarchy of the Family and in their relationships with members of other Families. Confusion between respect and equality could affect one's behavior, and lead to unfortunate consequences.

After my father was orphaned, at the age of fifteen, he went to live with his mother's family. He developed a very close relationship with my uncle John Bonventre, his mother's younger brother, and a group leader in our Family.

Shortly before World War II, John visited Castellammare del Golfo, my father's hometown in Sicily. After he returned to the United States, he went to Buffalo to visit Stefano Magaddino, to bring regards and best wishes from family and friends in Sicily. Stefano, who was a cousin to both John and my father, was also one of the original five members of the Commission. After a dinner that night in honor of John's arrival, John and Stefano got into a discussion over some trivial matter involving a relative in Castellammare. In the heat of the moment, John took offense over something Stefano said, and spoke to Stefano in the guttural language of the Sicilian streets as they had done in their youth. Some of the others present were shocked at John's openly hostile tone. As in most such situations, by the end of the evening the two men had regained a certain strained cordiality. But the damage was done.

Within days of John's return to New York City from Buffalo, my father had been informed of the matter. Stefano was offended: Not only was he John's elder, but he was *rappresentante* of a Family, and he felt that John had demeaned him in front of others in his Family hierarchy. John should have restrained himself; if he had anything to say to Stefano, he should have told him in private. But John was one of the most forceful and convincing examples of manhood in both his per-

My father with John Bonventre, group leader, up-state New York, 1937.

sonal family and our Family, and to many, Stefano seemed the opposite, capable of immature, even childish, behavior.

One evening, shortly after his return, my father summoned John to a meeting. My father's leadership style was never accusatory. He asked John about his trip to Buffalo, and about the kinds of things relatives routinely ask each other. But John, one of our shrewdest group leaders, knew my father well, and he instinctively knew he had a problem. In keeping with our concept of *omertà*, where complete honesty and openness was the rule, John immediately gave his side of the story.

After listening to his explanation without interruption, my father told his uncle that he agreed that Stefano had acted in a boorish manner. "However," he added, "you are wrong." (Those of us who sat in on meetings with my father learned to dread that word, *However.* What followed could be very unpleasant.)

In our world, the master is our fraternity and we dogs all serve the master. To insult a dog is to insult the master. In this case, the insult to Stefano was disrespectful to his entire Family. "Further," my father added, "you confused respect and equality." Stefano was a leader of a Family, an elder in our world and an elder relative. John had committed a breach of our philosophy.

In keeping with our rule—that to every act there is a consequence—John was found to be in the wrong, and punishment was in order. But the matter was complicated by John's status as both a group leader in the Bonanno Family and a relative of both my father and the leader of the Buffalo Family, the very man he had wronged.

As far back as I can remember, my father had always preached that the closest relatives have the heaviest burdens. Other members had to be secure in the knowledge that we treated all members, relatives, or strangers, with the same respect and equality in the administration of our justice. And so it was that John Bonventre was removed as group leader in the Bonanno Family for a period of three years for his breach of the rules, for his breach of etiquette and respect, and because he should have recognized that his behavior would compromise his *rappresentante*. At the end of three years, his case would be reevaluated.

At an Administration meeting the following week, the members were informed of their leader's decision and were asked to ratify it. My father was never afraid to put his decisions before the Administration. In all the years I was a member of the Administration, I can remember only one time when my father's decision was not ratified—and that was in the early 1950s, when he announced that he was going to retire.

John Bonventre was replaced as a group leader by Michael Sabella, who served for four years, after which time John was reinstated and Sabella was given his own group as a reward for his faithful service. In 1958, after John retired to his native Sicily, his group was integrated with Sabella's.

Punishment

My father told me the following story:

Around 1931, before I was even born, a couple of group captains brought a member named Sal Amari, who ran the Family's numbers operation, up on charges for skimming money. Amari was brought into a room to face his accusers and the Administration of the Family. The *consigliere*, following custom and duty, served as counsel to the accused, to protect his rights.

"What you did was very dishonorable," my father told Amari, "not because of the money you stole, but because you stole from your own people." In keeping with his management and leadership style—and the traditional principle that financial infractions don't necessarily carry capital sentences—my father told Amari he was going to banish him from the Family.

Banishment is an old form of punishment, seldom used today. When it was decreed, however, it was an effective tool of discipline. Banishment meant that no made member in the United States—or Sicily, if appropriate—could have anything to do with you: no business contact, no social contact. The sponsor of the banished member would be appointed to supervise the banishment, thereby becoming the only made member with whom the fallen member was permitted to have contact. The sponsor would report to the *consigliere* on a monthly basis regarding the activities of the banished member.

Banishment was not always permanent. Depending upon the degree of animosity involved, or the seriousness of the offense, it could last two or three years. In Amari's case, however, word went out to all the other Families that Amari would be required to leave the country and go back to Sicily. If he did that, nobody would touch him. Amari packed his bags.

Four or five years later, someone told my father that Amari was back in town. My father was in no rush. He first sent word back to our friends in Sicily to verify what he was told, to confirm that Amari had not been sent back officially, through some arrangement with the Family in his hometown that had not been communicated to us. Sure enough, word came back that after three or four years in Sicily, Amari had gone to Rome; then he came back to Sicily and told everyone he was going back to New York. There was no arrangement with the Family in his Sicilian hometown, no permission to return to America.

Amari should have left well enough alone. It was natural for him to come back to the same neighborhood familiar to him, and we found him there immediately. In our world, there was no place to hide. Letting him get away would have been a signal of weakness to others: A member must never be allowed to think he's getting away with stealing from the Family. My father always tried to give everyone the benefit of the doubt, but in this case, Amari had no legitimate reason to return. That return trip to the United States cost him his life. They put his body in a coffin-size box, filled it with cement, and gave him an unceremonious sailor's burial in the East River.

When it came to the disposal of bodies, our "cemetery" was generally the swamps or the East River. The East River was dotted with cement chutes, which served as a type of spillway flowing directly into the river. Wood boxes, filled with a sufficient amount of cement to sink the box and the dead weight inside, made disposal convenient. And, since we controlled the warehouse district, detection wasn't a concern.

But that wasn't the only way we delivered our victims to their final resting places. There was also the "over and under" method, which was pretty foolproof. We had an interest in a funeral parlor, and when necessary they could supply caskets with a false bottom so two people could be buried together. Naturally, such caskets were twice as heavy. We made sure our people lifted the casket onto a gurney so the family of the person on top would never question the additional weight.

I'm not sure if this is how the idea of two-for-one sales originated, but it worked for us.

20

Omertà

A man has honor if he holds to an ideal of conduct even though it is inconvenient or dangerous.

Sicilian proverb

Silence is a remarkable element of life. It can conjure images of serene composure or of crippling fear. It is used to elicit conversation or to suppress information. Silence can have many names: In music, a moment of silence is called a rest. In the legal profession the principle protecting silence is the attorney/client privilege. In government, silence is often employed on the grounds of national security. In the confessional, we call it a sacred trust with God. In Italian, we use a word of our own for silence: *omertà*.

Sometimes, it's impossible to capture the true meaning of a Sicilian, Italian, Yiddish, or other foreign word or phrase when translating it into English. The result is usually a bastard definition, one warped by reductive thinking, misunderstanding, or just plain lack of knowledge. The word *omertà* comes from the Latin word for "humiliate," with connotations of humility or humbleness. In our Sicilian world, the concept of *omertà* came to refer to a system of double moral standards—with one set of rules for our world and another for outsiders. It is a principle of "us" against "you."

In the Sicilian dialect, however, *omertà* also draws on the meaning of the word *omu*, meaning "man," and on the word *onorevole*, meaning "to behave honorably." If you behave with honorability, you behave in a manly way—and if your behavior is manly, you are following the principle of *omertà*. A *mafioso* is a person who acts in a manly way—never saying anything that we know would put someone else in jeopardy, for instance, whether friend or enemy—even if it means death. We never wanted an enemy to go to prison. We wanted him on the streets . . . where we could get to him.

The supreme underlying meaning of *omertà* is subjugation—for the good of *il sistema*. In relationships among those in our world, tact, manners, courtesy, and persuasion by discussion—without compulsion—is required. Every transaction within our world requires complete openness—which can often involve humbleness or humility. To honor the principle of *omertà*, one had to behave honorably: to display a high degree of heroism and virtue, courage and cunning, in dealing with those who share his ideals. One's personal value was measured in terms of his adherence to these principles; the same could be said for one's family or even one's hometown (certain villages in Sicily were known for having stand-up men). It was reflected in the respect and esteem in which one was held.

To the outside world, however, the word *omertà* has taken on a far different meaning: Most take it to refer to a conspiracy of silence or code of silence—a misunderstanding and misrepresentation of the concept. This misunderstanding has been advanced, unfortunately, by the newer generations in our world, who have never been schooled in our traditions, and were prone to take shortcuts to explain things they really knew nothing about.

The problem grew worse after the 1970s, when most of the old-timers began to fade from daily involvement in our world, leaving no one to teach the newer generations. Until my time, there were old men in cafes, social clubs, or just sitting in the shared shade of the mulberry trees, who could recite the history of our ancestors for fifty generations. If one of these old men should stray even momentarily from the facts, others within hearing distance would immediately correct him. Today there are few, if any, who can correct these now-forgotten details.

Our concept of *omertà* did not apply to the outside world. When it came to the outside world, our concept of *omertà* could involve the opposite of complete openness. There, a kind of false *omertà* prevailed—a false courtesy, kindness, or condescension, which brings snares to unsuspecting troublemakers. To the outside world, silence was praised, giving rise to this double standard and the defiled version of *omertà* as a code of silence. In our world, that defiled concept of *omertà* did not exist. Therefore, when there were official meetings, whether they were Commission meetings, Family Administration meetings, or meetings with the crews and their group leaders, the principles of *omertà* prevailed. Within our world everyone knew that if all parties acted with total openness, kindness, and courtesy, few if any problems were unsolvable.

In order for *omertà* to work, of course, each person had to know the other completely. We could hold no secrets from one another. Since we knew one another's weaknesses, betrayal was unlikely—and when it occurred, all the parties involved recognized that the ultimate penalty was justified.

There are many real stories that illustrate this principle. But the story that may capture it best comes from the movie *The Godfather*. When Sal Tessio, Abe Vigoda's character, is found to have betrayed the Corleone Family, he asks the *consigliere*, Tom Hagen, to save him. "Tom," he says, "can you get me off the hook? For old times' sake? It wasn't personal, just business." Just as it would have been in real life, however, Tessio's plea was futile. Anyone in his shoes knew what to expect, and usually accepted the penalty without expecting an appeal.

This system only began to break down in the mid-1960s. We began to destroy ourselves through our own greed. We allowed a crack to develop within our world that no masking tape could repair. All the king's horses and all the king's men couldn't put Humpty Dumpty together again.

One of the best definitions of the values of a *mafioso* was expressed by Giuseppe Pitrè (1841–1916), a physician and scholar of Sicilian folklore, culture, and values, who wrote:

> The mafia is neither a sect nor an association, and has neither rules nor statutes. The *mafioso* is not a robber or a brigand. . . . The *mafioso* is simply a brave man who will put up with no provocation; and in that sense, every man needs to be, indeed has to be, a *mafioso*. The mafia is a certain consciousness of one's own being, an exaggerated notion of individual force and strength as "the one and only means of settling any conflict, any clash of interests or ideas"; which means that it is impossible to tolerate the superiority, or worse still, the dominance of others.

The modern understanding of the meaning of *omertà* pales in comparison with such insights. The idea of *omertà* popularized by the press and law enforcement is nothing more than a shortcut, designed to excuse the failures of law enforcement by demonizing the privacy of our world. And this remained true until the second half of the twentieth century, when the profile of Mafia members began to change. When the younger members of our world became swept up in the general greed of American society, a completely new avenue of attack was opened to law enforcement. That, together with the advent of new laws interpreted liberally by the courts—and with changes in our world from a conservative to a highly liberal leadership—prompted the erosion of the original principles of *omertà*.

21

The Family Business

The story of our world is the story of the accumulation of power and the dispensation of power.

Anthony Tarantola

Another common misconception shared by many outsiders concerns the Family business.

In the movie *The Godfather*, Michael Corleone famously tells his wife, Kay, "Never ask me about my business." In our world, however, this didn't refer simply to protection, numbers rackets, or other businesses considered illegitimate. It meant something much simpler and broader: *Don't ask me what I do when I go out the door in the morning.*

Our business included, but was not limited to, making book on horses, sporting events, and election returns. We were involved in hijackings of trucks carrying valuable goods, such as cigarettes or televisions (although on occasion the wrong truck was targeted, and we ended up with a load of Ping-Pong balls or collar stays).

But our real Family business involved managing relationships—solving problems and keeping peace within the Family. The individual members of the Family operated their businesses, legitimate or not. A member could run numbers within a designated four-block area of the neighborhood; only if someone else interfered by encroaching on his territory did it become our business. In New York, we had a Numbers Commission, which set rules governing how the winning numbers would be decided. The Brooklyn numbers and the New York City numbers were different. At a given racetrack—such as Aqueduct or Belmont—the Numbers Commission might designate the middle three numbers of the pari-mutuel handle of that day to be the winning numbers. If the handle was $1,962,321, the winning numbers would be 623. Everybody knew the number sequence in advance.

If a dispute arose in a neighborhood between two bookmakers, they would go to the group leader, who would be responsible for solving the problem. The group leader might receive an envelope of money in recognition of his work in keeping the peace—but it was not required. If the group leader couldn't solve a problem in his neighborhood, he could bring the matter "upstairs"—but a man who brought too many matters upstairs would lose respect in the eyes of the *rappresentante*.

Envelopes of money did find their way upstairs from the group leaders from time to time. Such "tribute," as it is sometimes called, is given out of respect, as a way to acknowledge appreciation for keeping the peace that allowed members to conduct their business without interference. Such tribute was never accepted during wartime, only in times of peace.

Once a matter was brought before a group leader, the parties involved were no longer responsible for its resolution; it was out of their hands. Once, the owner of the Eastside Social Club reached out to me for help in combating a bunch of kids in his neighborhood who were harassing the old men who socialized there. Once the owner approached me with the problem, it was my obligation to take the necessary steps to maintain the peace.

As I've mentioned, our made men were involved in legitimate business; they engaged in professional occupations as well as blue-collar work, and they paid taxes just like everyone else. We invested in real estate, insurance agencies, and wholesale food distribution serving restaurants, hotels, and even county jails. Our men owned liquor distributorships, banking and financing firms, garment- and coat-manufacturing businesses, vending machines, and investments in racetracks. One of the enterprises that *was* taboo in our world was counterfeiting, because we didn't want the Federal government meddling in any of our businesses.

The story of our world is the story of the accumulation of power and the dispensation of power. The key to success was knowing when to use that power to benefit those we could depend on. The following is an example of the proper dispensation of power.

The Chambermaids' Union in New York City was a small union, maybe three or four hundred strong, whose members were immigrants who cleaned hotel rooms and performed other menial tasks. At one point, the union was trying to exact a meager raise—five cents an hour—from the Waldorf-Astoria Hotel. The head of the union could get nowhere with the hotel management, who laughed the request off. Once they asked our Family to intercede, the problem became ours to resolve.

As a first step, we sent our contact from the labor council to visit the Waldorf management to make a second request. The second request was refused. Our response was simple. My father requested a meeting and explained that we understood management's position . . . and that it was "no problem." However, he also mentioned that, "effective tomorrow, you get no more garbage pickup, you get no more linen delivery, you get no more meat delivery, and you get no more liquor delivery." And we could keep that promise—because we controlled every one of those unions. Immediately, without another word being said, the chambermaids got their raise. I guess you could say he made the hotel's management an offer they couldn't refuse.

Along with everything else, we helped to preserve order in the vast network of businesses that enabled New York and other big cities to keep operating through much of the twentieth century. In exchange for a small payment, we ensured that fresh fish got delivered from the Fulton Fish Market to the restaurants and stores; we ensured that the garment industry, located in lower Midtown Manhattan, ran smoothly: every one of the trucks lined up on those city streets in the 1950s had its own assigned parking space, and if someone parked in a space assigned to someone else, the truck would be gone within a few hours.

In later years, Rudy Giuliani (first working in the U.S. Attorney's Office of the Southern District of New York and later being elected mayor of New York) called all of this "corruption"—and looking at it through a prosecutor's eyes, it's hard to dispute. Look at it through the eyes of the chambermaid, however, and you might feel otherwise.

As a cab driver once told me while driving me into the city from JFK Airport a few years ago: "At least when the mob ran this town, the town ran well. Everybody knew where they stood—and there weren't as many potholes!"

22

The Role of Social Clubs

True wealth comes from a good family and good friends.

Sicilian proverb

The Sicilian lives at the crossroads of time and space. The heart of the Sicilian is closer to heaven, and to hell, than you can imagine. Within him flows the blood of many races, and his culture is a combination of many cultures. His Christian religion incorporates, but does not displace, the paganism derived from his Greco-Roman traditions. Casting the "evil eye," using amulets for protection, using olive oil for healing—and, of course, the use of hand gestures to show power—continues to this day. In Italian we call this *stregheria* (witchcraft). A witch is called a *strega*; her male counterpart is a *stregone*.

The Italians and Sicilians are a very superstitious people. There was always an old Italian woman living in our neighborhood believed to have the ability to interpret dreams—a sort of sixth sense. If my father had a dream that bothered him, he might have a general conversation with one of these women, asking questions related to the dream in such a way as to prompt the old woman to explain what she thought was going on. For example: If the dream involved two men he knew walking in a dark alley and seeing a garbage can turned over and a man running down the alley, my father would ask the old woman what she thought about that. She might answer by warning my father to be on alert for danger. Armed with that information, he might pay special attention the next time the men in the dream appeared before him in real life.

My sister, Catherine Bonanno Genovese, recalls our mother's intense superstitions. If a door blew open in the house and no one was there, to her that was a sign that death was entering the house. Another sign of death was putting a man's hat on a bed, considered to be a bad omen. These beliefs even extended to dining out: A waiter should never pour wine with his left hand or hold the bottle with the back of his hand under the bottle pointing toward you. "Giving you the back of his hand" this way was a sure sign of disrespect; it was like telling someone he was going to die. Left-handed waiters had to learn how to pour with their right hand—or else!

Sicilians live by the "rule of three." Serious conversations are never held with three people at the table. Why? Because if anything leaks from a conversation among three people, you can never be sure which of the three leaked the information. Having two people speaking with each other eliminates the risk of blaming an innocent person. The rule of three applies in many aspects of life and death: Sicilians believe it takes three days for the soul to leave the body, which is why we hold wakes over a three-day period. We believe that it's unwise to name a third child with the same name as two others in the same family, lest something bad—such as death— befall the oldest.

Some of these superstitions were also just plain prudent. My father never sat with his back to a door or an open window, for instance; he always sat with his back against the wall, and no one was ever allowed to walk behind him. This may have been a superstition, but it was also a matter of safety, ensuring that no one walking behind his chair could get access to him without him seeing them.

Just as we cling to our superstitions for comfort and solace, as a people we have always created social enclaves where we could meet, socialize, and coexist peacefully among our compatriots. The Sicilian's homeland in the Mediterranean is a Garden of Eden from which he was cast out by the greed of foreign landlords. As a result he lives in a world of his own making, escaping the realities of society at large by replacing it with a tightly controlled circle of like-minded men.

Around 1905, a young man by the name of Angelo Caruso arrived in the United States from his native Italy. At first he settled in New Jersey, but soon he found that opportunity beckoned in the larger city of New York. Settling on the East Side, the young Angelo started mingling with other sons of Sicily, and before long he was accepted into the Cola Schiro Family. The Family's occupation of choice was taking advantage of the gift of Prohibition. During the Castellammarese War, Angelo rose to second-in-command under Maranzano; after Maranzano's death, he was selected as the leader of the Family.

A loyal and gentle man by personality, Angelo had endeared himself to the "boys of the first day," the men who stood by Maranzano during the Castellammarese War. After the war, the Families were reorganized. Angelo Caruso graciously stepped aside and became a group leader. It was then that my father, Joseph Bonanno, was selected as the new leader of what is still known today as the Bonanno Family.

Shortly after his retirement as leader, Angelo found a small storefront a short distance from his house on First Avenue on the Lower East Side of Manhattan. In his new capacity as group leader, with a crew of fifteen mostly non-Castellammarese members, Angelo needed a home. What would be better than a social club? In those days, you could

The Shoreview Social Club.

see the East River from First Avenue. Angelo found a new home there, on East Twelfth Street between First Avenue and Avenue A. One day, Angelo and some of his crew were standing in the club's doorway, trying to name the new club. One glance down toward the riverfront, and they decided to call it the Shoreview Social Club.

The story of the social club is as old as immigration and immigrants. The Irish in Boston, the Poles in Chicago, and the Germans in New York all formed such clubs within the larger ethnic enclaves where they congregated, societies where older members could play cards, eat pastries, and tell stories of their homeland.

During my time in New York in the early 1960s, the Shoreview was a routine stop on Mondays, Wednesdays, and Fridays. Tuesdays and Thursdays were reserved for forays into Brooklyn, where meetings were held at the Rex-Spinola

Democratic Club on Graham Avenue (a social club in spite of its prestigious name).

On occasion, for more sensitive discussions, we met at a smaller club on Central Avenue near Stanhope Street. I lived in East Meadow on Long Island, some twenty miles from our home turf of Brooklyn. Each morning I would drive to the city with one of my crew members. Whether we were going to Brooklyn or Manhattan, we arrived at our destination at roughly noon, ready for the day's discussions, and of course, the traditional cup of espresso.

Each club reflected the personality of its owner as well as its regulars. The Central Avenue club catered mostly to an elderly group of men, who had been involved in our world for years and were now able to reap the benefits of that association. The Shoreview, on the other hand, was a hub of activity, hosting members from both ours and other Families. The Rex-Spinola Club, with its more opulent decor, was usually reserved for more formal meetings or discussions.

The decor of the Shoreview was 1920s New York: heavy wooden tables and comfortable, mismatched upholstered chairs to accommodate the various rear ends that were planted on them for hours at a time. There were always three or four tables crowded with young men and old, sipping espresso, playing cards, or getting into some heated discussion. If it was raining, they'd pass the time betting on which raindrop would reach the bottom of the windowpane first. If there were overflow crowds, the men would open folding card tables and add more chairs at a moment's notice.

Angelo Caruso made a decent living catering to "the boys." Besides coffee and sandwiches from the grocery store on the corner, he would serve cannoli or Italian sweets from DeRoberti's on First Avenue. Occasionally, Angelo's wife would send over a pot of *pasta con sardi*, a Sicilian dish made with sardines, black currants, and fennel, treasured by everyone fortunate enough to be invited to partake. The only other items in the club were a small stove, a sink, and a cabinet to store some plates, silverware, and glasses. For all of us, it was a real home away from home.

But there was one lesson that captured the organizing principle of the club: No one stayed on his feet at the Shoreview, ever. It was a symbol that everyone there was on a level playing field. On one of my first visits after arriving on the New York scene, I was sitting at a table with three others when a guy we called Crazy Louie walked into the club. Louie came over to say hello and was introduced to the others seated next to me. When Louie waited a bit too long to make his choice—either sit or leave—he was *ordered* to do so.

23

Informers and FBI Intelligence Gathering

Songbirds have a predictable lifespan. The louder they sing, the shorter the life.

Albert Anastasia

Swedish physician Axel Munthe, in his 1929 book *The Story of San Michele*, describes an Italian practice from days gone by, in which songbirds had their eyes put out so that they could then be used as decoys for the capture of other birds. Some say that these were the original "stool pigeons." Another theory is that the term "stool pigeon" came from the technique of using pigeons to entice a hawk into a net, sometimes tying or nailing the pigeons to a stump or a stool. Whether we call a man a stool pigeon, a snitch, a stoolie, a backstabber, a coward, or a whistleblower, it all means the same thing to us: the mark of disloyalty.

In all cultures and in all languages, informers are despised. They are considered, even by the people to whom they spill their guts, as unsavory characters, scorned for betraying their friends to save themselves.

It is in this context that one must evaluate the story of Joe Valachi of the Lucchese Family. In the 1960s, after being given protection by the government, Valachi went before a Senate investigating committee—and national television cameras—to reveal his knowledge of the inner workings of the *cosa nostra*. He was such a low-level soldier that he never even understood that *cosa nostra* was the philosophy by which we lived, not an organization. Joe Valachi is often credited as the first "informer" to reveal long-sacred secrets of our world, and it's true that he gave those secrets international exposure that far surpassed any other stage in history. Yet, as every insider recognized at the time, what he testified to was old news to the authorities. Robert F. Kennedy, as U.S. Attorney General, had been looking for a new way to use the information, and it has long been suggested that, as an astute politician, he saw Valachi as the perfect vehicle to dispel rumors that the Kennedys were tied to "the mob." Valachi was coached for six or seven months before making his debut as the "star witness" before the McClellan Committee in 1963—a smart move given the fact that he couldn't say four words in a row without three of them being profane.

Informers like Valachi, Vincent Teresa of Boston, James Fratianno of Los Angeles, and Salvatore "Sammy the Bull" Gravano of New York all bargained for their lives or their creature comforts at the expense of friends, Family, and associates. But when a man betrays his Family or friends, he betrays himself. Forever after, he is destined to wander aimlessly in that purgatory of the subconscious and the soul, nevermore to find peace or contentment. Most end up scorned by Family and friends and forever marked with the label of informer.

To the best of my knowledge, there were no major informers among the true followers of our tradition in America. All of the major publicized informers were American-born. While some were involved with our world, they were products of the American mentality.

Some years ago, I was asked in an interview, "What is the one thing you would do to improve the conditions in New York

City?" I responded by saying, "After 1964, if I had the authority, I would have made all the streets one-way down to the D.A.'s office and the U.S. Attorney's office, to accommodate the rats rushing to be first in line to rat out their friends."

Certainly, not all information about our world was garnered through informers. In some cases—such as the FBI report on the 1957 Apalachin gathering—the agency was so far off-base it surprised me. In other cases, however, the FBI was extremely effective in its surveillance.

One example occurred during the so-called Banana War, the most difficult period in the history of our Family.

The conflict with Gaspar DiGregorio over control of the Family was a personally difficult time for me, since Gaspar also happened to be my godfather. Although my men and I all escaped from Gaspar's Troutman Street attack unscathed, the incident did real damage to our relationship. He had breached one of the traditional rules of our world by requesting a peace meeting to resolve differences—which, in our tradition, is a guarantee of safety for those attending—only to use the occasion to attempt to assassinate me and my crew.

To add to the web of deceit, I later found out that the setup had been arranged by Sorino Tartamella, the son of John Tartamella, my father's longtime *consigliere*—and my father's baptismal godson. Sorino, a made member of the Bonanno Family, went by the name "Bobby T" because he didn't like the name Sorino. After I discovered it was Sorino, I enlisted two of my crew, Carl Simari and Hank Perrone, and together we went to his house in Huntington, New York. We saw him through the window and were about to "send him on his way" when his wife, Frances, appeared. I called it off, because it would have violated our rules of engagement to put an innocent bystander in harm's way.

With the Bonanno Family suddenly in turmoil, the "puppet Commission"—the discredited former Commission members purporting to continue the traditional Commission after it was disbanded in 1961—tried to set up a meeting. Simone "Sam the Plumber" DeCavalcante, the leader of the New Jersey Family, contacted me on behalf of the puppet Commission and requested a meeting.

In the interest of peace, Carl Simari, Hank Perrone, Joe Notaro, and I drove to Sam's plumbing shop in Kenilworth, New Jersey, to hear him out. On the way, we picked up Joe Zicarelli, better known as "Bayonne Joe," one of our members who had strong contacts and business interests in the area. I was there in my capacity as one of the Bonanno leaders at the time, and the other guys were there because we were still in a shooting war.

Sam told us that the so-called "Commission" wanted to try to set up a larger meeting to discuss the resolution of the ongoing conflict. We spent a good forty-five minutes discussing how the meeting would be set up, with Sam stressing that everyone wanted my father to attend. I said I would try to reach out to him. After talking through all the logistics, we said our goodbyes and left. Out of four hundred people in the Bonanno Family, only five members knew of the meeting, its purpose, and the specifics of what was discussed. On Sam's side, only two people, Sam and one of his group leaders, knew firsthand what had transpired.

The next day, we were at the Shoreview Social Club when Crazy Louie came in and said, "Hey, Bill, there's a couple of agents across the street."

"You sure?" I said.

"They're there," Louie said. "You can spot 'em a mile away. They're there with their suits on, sitting in a car."

We were getting ready to leave the club anyway, so we walked outside. As was my habit, I looked both ways when I stepped out of the building. Twelfth Street is one-way going west and, just as Louie reported, the FBI agents' car was a little farther up the street. As soon as I stepped out, the two agents got out of their car and I recognized both of them. One was Dick Anderson, who at that time was responsible for monitoring the Bonanno Family. The other was Richard Wernersbach.

The two agents approached me and asked if they could talk to me for a minute. I had no problem with that. We had a friendly relationship with the Feds; they treated us with respect and we reciprocated.

"I understand you're going to have another meeting about the problem you guys got," Anderson said, referring to our friction with the questionable Commission over the Banana War.

"I understand you had a meeting with Sam the Plumber," Anderson continued, "and discussed the Commission's desire to get together with your father." There we were, me and two Federal agents standing on a corner of East Twelfth Street in New York City—just one day after our meeting with DeCavalcante in New Jersey—and it was clear that the agents knew not only who was present at the meeting, but what we'd talked about.

That hit me like a ton of bricks. Clearly, one of the six other people in that room had talked to the FBI. Otherwise, how did these two agents know where, why, and what we were talking about? All I could do was bluff. I looked at Anderson with a half-assed smile and said, "I don't know what you're talking about, but it sounds like you're throwing out guesses to get answers." That was the end of our conversation. The agents left quickly, without pressing the issue, making it clear that they'd just wanted to let me know that they all knew about what had taken place there. By then, Anderson knew me well enough to know I would be stewing over this. But what he really cared about was, what would I do about it? Would I start making phone calls? Arrange a hasty meeting? Or get in the car and go see someone about the problem?

I did no such thing. I just got in my car and left for the meeting I'd already scheduled, as if nothing happened.

Over dinner at La Scala that evening, Joe Notaro, Carl, Hank, and I talked through our situation. There we were, fighting a shooting war among our Family members, and suddenly someone was sharing the details of our most sensitive meetings with the Feds.

"Who's the mole in our group?" Joe asked.

It was a reasonable question. In our world, when you have a rat in your personal group, you have to act fast. The leader of such a group faces a challenge: He can't say openly that he smells a rat, because it could hamper his ability to ferret out the leak.

With just my closest inner circle, I had to decide how to find out the identity of the mole.

Throughout the next three days, we talked through the situation intensely. After a lot of soul-searching, Notaro, Morales, and I concluded that it wasn't any of our people. That meant there had to be another explanation. Maybe one of Sam's people was feeding the Feds information—though the chances were small, since only Sam and one other crew member had attended that meeting. Maybe someone had talked on a wiretapped phone. Or maybe it was some other FBI tactic we'd not yet discovered.

Only years later, when it was too late to do anything about it, did we find out what had happened. In the late 1960s, a grand jury in New Jersey indicted a whole bunch of guys, including Sam the Plumber. During one of the pre-trial discovery hearings, the judge ordered the U.S. Attorney's Office to supply the defense with all the material it had gathered during its investigation—without asking that the evidence remain under seal. He simply filed the information with the court and notified the press that he had complied with the judge's order. All of it instantly became public information.

As we soon learned, that discovery material included not just documents but tape recordings. And one of the tapes was of our meeting in Sam the Plumber's office. That explained why the government always seemed to be one step ahead of us: The FBI had installed a bug in Sam DeCavalcante's office.

Sam was the messenger between the puppet Commission and us—the *porto valigia*, we called him, a porter who carried the baggage back and forth between the groups. And apparently everything he said to anyone in his office was subject to FBI surveillance.

It wasn't that we never suspected the Feds of trying to bug us. In fact, Sam was constantly bragging that we could meet in his office without worry, because he had his phone checked for bugs all the time. Sam had a fancy pen set on his desk, which he tended to knock over when he gesticulated while talking, or when he was moving papers around his desk. Eventually, he had the pen set bolted to the desk. The FBI had broken into Sam's office and planted a bug in the fancy pen set . . . and there the bug would stay. As Sam sat there in his office talking to his group captains or talking on the phone, everything he said was recorded.

Most of the time, we gave the Feds a good run for their money. But sometimes they came out ahead—as they did with Sam the Plumber, who was convicted of extortion in 1969.

24

Can a Made Member Get Out?

Love is grand. Divorce is a hundred grand.

Anonymous

Another common misconception promoted by the media, as well as law enforcement, is that once you're a made man there is no way out. As usual, however, this is an oversimplification. It's important to distinguish between getting out of the life of criminal enterprise, and getting out of the ideology and philosophy of a *mafioso*. While the quotation above may be true—divorce in your world can come at a hefty price—divorce from the life of a *mafioso* can never truly be achieved until death.

Once you take the oath, your commitment to our world—to the *rappresentante* and the Family—remains binding for a lifetime. But there is such a thing as retirement from the active lifestyle. Retirement permits a made man to enjoy the benefits of a lifetime of loyalty and service to the Family. As we've mentioned, Al Capone assumed leadership of the Chicago Family after Johnny Torrio retired to Italy in the mid-1920s. Torrio eventually returned to the United States and settled in New York, living quietly and almost entirely under the radar until his death in 1957 of a heart attack while waiting for a haircut in a barbershop. The year before his death, he was one of the guests at my wedding at the Astor Hotel in New York.

During the era when our world was at the height of its power and influence, at least a dozen men successfully retired from the day-to-day activities of our world. Most of these men I knew personally, from *rappresentanti*, *consiglieri*, and *sotto capos* to *capodecini* and *soldate*. In 1953, Gaetano Gagliano, a *rappresentante* and an original Commission member, retired, replaced by Tommy Lucchese. Almost three years later, in late 1955, my father's *sotto capo* of seventeen years, Frank Garofalo, retired from active duty and moved to Italy. He returned to visit the United States on numerous occasions until his death in the 1960s. Anthony Accardo, the Chicago *rappresentante*, retired and lived out his days peacefully in Palm Springs, California, playing golf before returning to Chicago. He died of heart failure in 1992.

My father, Joseph Bonanno, stepped down from the leadership of our Family in 1968. He went on to live another thirty-four years in retirement in Tucson, Arizona. He passed his years in an adobe house in a historic area of Tucson, with a bodyguard living in a back apartment on the property. A female friend and caretaker, Teresa D'Antonio, the widow of a former Bonanno attorney, lived in the house when my father was in his late eighties. The house had a basement converted from a former bomb shelter, with a small secret room behind a false wall where he could hide if necessary. He died of heart failure in 2002 at the age of ninety-seven.

I also retired from the active lifestyle around 1968. I went on to write books, produce movies, film documentaries, and travel the talk-show circuit, explaining the history of our world and lifestyle.

Of course, Don Vito Corleone, the most famous *rappresentante* in Mafia "history" to retire from active duty, died while playing in his tomato garden with his grandson, in the movie *The Godfather*. All these men, real and mythical, spent their golden years in service to our tradition, using their wisdom and expertise to benefit all those in our world.

In recent years, others taking the retirement path have included Michael Franzese, a group leader and the son of Colombo Family captain Sonny Franzese. Michael won some fame as a writer and public speaker in his own right after his father went to prison. Mario Fracione, of Detroit, left the life to become a successful businessman in Michigan and public speaker for the Church of Latter Day Saints. Tony Thomas Gambino, Charles "Lucky" Luciano's grandson, has done the talk-show circuit.

But there's one story that, to me, captures the difference between "getting out" of the Mafia and retiring from active duty.

In January 2006, I was contacted by Charlie Carnesi, a respected New York lawyer representing John Gotti Jr. Carnesi was preparing for the retrial of a racketeering indictment pending against the younger Gotti and wanted to consult with me about practices in our world. Gotti's defense team was taking the position that John Jr. had "left the Mafia" around 1999, and therefore couldn't be guilty of the racketeering charges. In contrast, the prosecution offered the testimony of a number of "cooperating" witnesses, all of whom insisted that an individual cannot withdraw from the Mafia.

Carnesi saw me as the perfect example of a made member who had risen to the level of *consigliere*—and then got out. He hoped I might be able to offer some insight and testify on his client's behalf, refuting the cooperating witnesses by demonstrating that I'd been able to lead a productive, legitimate, and successful life outside the world of organized crime.

What Carnesi didn't realize, however, was that he was placing me in an impossible position. I lived in two worlds:

our world, which reinforced my obligation to help someone in our world if he reached out for help; and your world, where my testimony would certainly be attacked because of my prior felony convictions and my credibility would be on the line. A good prosecutor would force me to plead the Fifth Amendment, if he was smart enough to ask certain questions, and that would hurt John Jr. rather than help him. I didn't know Gotti or his father, but that didn't matter to me.

In a series of conversations, I explained the dilemma I was facing, and argued that my testimony would not be helpful to his case. I also tried to explain that the world I came from was much different than the world of organized crime today. But Carnesi, being a diligent lawyer, wouldn't take no for an answer and offered to fly to Arizona to meet me. I felt obliged to accommodate his request.

A week or two later, Carnesi flew to Phoenix. We met at the home of my friend Gary Abromovitz, a retired lawyer and as close to me as Tom Hagen was to Don Vito. After welcoming our guest with a customary Italian spread of meats, cheeses, and desserts, we spent the next five or six hours explaining why I couldn't give him the testimony he wanted.

In our world, at the time I was active, the *cosa nostra* was an ideology, not a group of men who considered themselves members of an organized crime group called the Mafia. I could never forswear the commitment I had made to the traditions I was taught to honor; nor would I want to. Carnesi thought in terms that just weren't applicable to the world I knew. I had retired from the active lifestyle of our world, but the idea of "getting out of the Mafia" belonged to a new generation, one I couldn't follow. Of course, if I'd been compelled to testify, I could have fielded the questions without much problem. But my testimony would have been subject to vigorous cross-examination, which would be detrimental to the defense—and possibly opening up a can of worms in my own life.

When the trial ended in March 2006, I was pleased to read that John Gotti Jr. had been acquitted of the charges against him—without the need of any testimony from me. Given the tenacity of his attorney, I wasn't surprised. I like to think my meeting with Charlie Carnesi helped him to understand our world as I'd known it.

I hope this book has done the same thing for you.

Epilogue

Gary Abromovitz

Early in the morning of January 1, 2008, an ambulance arrived at the Bonanno home in Tucson, Arizona. A few minutes later, it carried Bill Bonanno away to the Tucson Medical Center. Anthony Tarantola, Bill's right hand, called me at 8:30 A.M. Before he could say anything, I remember, I wished him a Happy New Year. But as soon as I heard the tentative tone in his voice, I knew something was wrong. Bill had had a massive heart attack. The emergency response team had shocked him five times with a defibrillator, but got only a slight electrical reading, failing to register a normal rhythm. "It didn't look good," he said. "Stand by."

Ten minutes later the phone rang again. I picked it up, barely able to say hello. "He didn't make it," Anthony said. The last of the Men of Honor ever to attend a Commission meeting was pronounced dead at 9:01 A.M. on New Year's Day. He was seventy-five years old.

I had met Bill twelve years before, under unusual and surprising circumstances. One morning in 1995 I was sit-

ting on the couch in the living room of my Phoenix home—
I had just been released after minor surgery—when I got a
call from a guy we called "Big Nick." Nick's kids and mine
were the same age; I knew him only because our kids played
on the same soccer team. But he knew I was a lawyer, and
he was calling me to ask for my help in getting someone released from the Maricopa County Jail in downtown Phoenix. (He didn't tell me the person's name.) I didn't practice
criminal law—and on that day I had trouble getting off the
couch—so I told him to call a friend of mine who was a
criminal attorney and to mention my name. That was the
end of the conversation, and of my involvement with Big
Nick's world—or so I thought.

About four months later, I got a call from Mickey Freiberg, a fraternity brother of mine at the University of Arizona.
After we graduated, I had gone on to law school; Mickey had
become a Hollywood agent. We hadn't spoken to each other
in thirty years.

After I got over the surprise of hearing from him, he told
me: "I'm walking down the street in New York City with
someone who would like to thank you. He comes from a different world and a different culture. I am his spokesman and
represent his family. I don't want to scare you, so I'm going to
tell you his name, and I'll make arrangements for you to meet
him." I had no idea what Mickey was talking about.

"His name is Bill Bonanno," Mickey said.

"What did I do to deserve his thanks?" I replied.

Mickey explained it all: Apparently the referral I'd given
Big Nick had worked out well. "Bill wants to thank you personally," Mickey continued. "He's inviting you to attend his
sixty-third birthday party in Tucson. It's in a few weeks."

"Thanks, but I don't think so," I said.

But Mickey told me to think about it and promised to call
me again in a few days.

Sure enough, he did. "You really don't want to say no to these people," he said. "You'll probably never meet people like this again. Bill would consider it a favor if you attended. And you can bring your wife!" I told him I'd think about it.

"Absolutely not," my wife said. "There could be FBI agents there, taking pictures. You're an attorney!" Most people, I realize, would have said the same thing. But I was tempted: It would be great to see Mickey again, and the trip would give me a chance to see Jerry Cartin, a Tucson lawyer who also was our fraternity brother and my roommate in law school. Besides, my curiosity had been piqued.

Mickey flew to Phoenix, and together we drove to Tucson to attend the party. As a joke, I bought a cassette tape of the soundtrack to *The Godfather* to play on the way there. Sensing my anxiety, Mickey filled me in on his history with Bill Bonanno and his father, Joseph Bonanno. The background music I'd chosen actually made me a little anxious, but Mickey did his best to assuage my fears. Mickey had built a strong relationship with these people. Neither of us ever imagined at the time that my relationship with Bill would last almost thirteen years and turn out the way it did—as best friends who shared an unwavering trust.

Bill had booked rooms at a nearby motel for all those attending the party, held at the historic Savoy Opera House and Trail Dust Town in Tucson. Mickey, Jerry Cartin, and I went to the restaurant next to the motel for lunch while waiting for our rooms to be ready. As we ate and reminisced, Mickey excused himself and told us to meet him at the motel because he had some business to discuss with Bill.

A short time later, we walked over to the motel. That was the first time I laid eyes on Bill Bonanno. He was walking toward us with two of his men and Mickey. He was a tall man, imposing, and the two men next to him looked like bodyguards. As I watched Mickey, I could tell that he'd developed a certain trust with Bill, allowing them to make jokes about Jews and Italians that an outsider would never attempt. Yet I also saw that Mickey knew just how far to go and stopped short of anything he believed might be taken the wrong way.

After Mickey introduced us, Bill invited us to sit around the pool with him. As if on cue, about twenty guys came out of the rooms around the pool and joined us.

For the next four hours, Bill told us stories about New York in the 1950s and '60s—about shooting and being shot at, about his years in prison and how the priests would smuggle in Italian food under their robes for him. I had no idea why he felt able to share these details with us, and admittedly the whole scene had me a little concerned. I wanted to ask questions, but I restrained my curiosity, recognizing that I was completely out of my element.

Time passed quickly. The party was due to begin at around six, and when Bill found out Jerry was my law-school roommate, he invited him to come along. As I later discovered, this was typical of Bill: there was always room for one more, and if he could do something for a friend he would do it, no questions asked. As he later told me, "You respect the dog because of his master"—meaning, if a friend asks you to help someone, you do it out of respect for the friend.

The Savoy Opera House has a long bar and a ballroom/banquet hall with seating for about three hundred and fifty people. When Jerry and I arrived, we were met at the door by one of Bill's men and taken to the bar. Bill immediately approached me and thanked me again for coming. He instructed the bartender to give us anything we wanted to drink. The bar area was filling up fast; we marveled at all the activity.

As I scanned the room, I noticed an elderly man sitting at a table, talking with a younger woman. A fedora was on the table next to his drink. When one of Bill's men saw me looking at the older man, he asked me, "Would you like to meet Mr. Bonanno Sr.?" Naturally, I said yes. The next thing I knew, Bill came over and ushered me over to meet his father and the woman, who turned out to be Bill's sister, Catherine.

When we approached the table, Bill spoke to his father in Sicilian. I caught only one of the words, *avvocato*, which I thought meant "lawyer" in Sicilian. Bill later told me he was explaining that I was the lawyer he'd mentioned. "He is a friend of mine," he added. At the time, I didn't understand the significance of the phrase. Later I learned the difference between saying "a friend of mine" and "a friend of ours." The phrase "a friend of ours" was reserved for "made guys," who were bound by the oath and whose loyalty was established. There was also what we termed the "inner circle," which could include others who were not made, not even Italian or Sicilian, but who were vouched for by a made guy and could be trusted. In my case, Bill placed a great deal of reliance on Mickey, and that was good enough for him to introduce me to his father, which showed the trust he had in Mickey. In the end, according to tradition, it was Bill who vouched for me and would have to answer, if things didn't work out.

Senior, as he was known, stood up and grasped my right hand in both of his hands. Looking straight into my eyes, he addressed me in a deep Sicilian accent: "Bill has told me about you and I wish to thank you for everything you have done for us. If there is anything we can do for you, please let us know." Again, I was dumbfounded; I had done nothing for them. I didn't know whether I was being sucked into something way over my head, or whether these people were genuinely reacting so strongly to a favor so small that nobody I knew would even think of giving it a second thought.

Soon it was time for dinner. The banquet room was full of exquisitely set round dinner tables, facing a head table about thirty-two feet long. The guests filed in, and Bill personally showed me, Mickey, and Jerry to one of the tables directly facing the head table. Later, during one of his toasts, Bill welcomed us as his "Jewish friends," making sure that everyone knew one of Bill's men was seated with us to "make sure we stayed in line." Everyone laughed. The only disruption I remember was the appearance of two priests, who arrived looking disheveled and complained of being "interrogated" when attempting to enter the opera house. Apparently, whoever they'd assigned to check out the guests before allowing them inside hadn't recognized the priests and was taking no chances. One of Bill's men quickly resolved the misunderstanding.

The seating arrangements at the head table were like a scene out of *The Godfather*. A priest sat at the far left; next to him was Joe Bonanno Sr. Next in line were Bill and his wife, Rosalie. Joey Bonanno, Bill's younger brother, and his wife, Karen, sat next to Rosalie, and Bill's sister Catherine sat at the end. Before dinner was served, Mr. Bonanno's grandchildren and great-grandchildren all marched up to the head table to kiss him goodnight. There must have been fifteen or twenty of them, from a baby held by Bill's daughter to kids nine or ten years old. Respect and discipline permeated the room. Singers from Las Vegas, courtesy of Big Nick, sang songs in Italian and Sicilian to the music of a live band. It was a fabulous night.

In the months that followed, Bill would call me from time to time, to say hello and perhaps ask me a few questions about civil or even criminal law. At first, I wasn't quite sure where this was going. I had heard stories of how "these guys" would lure you in and then start asking for money. With Bill, however, that never happened. Instead, what evolved was a friendship unlike any I had ever known. We respected each other's ability, and I loved hearing him recount the stories of his experiences during the heyday of his world. His past was like a different lifetime. We discussed Family and family, politics, and our own philosophies of life. Anyone who thinks the *cosa nostra* would be straightforward and easy to understand, I soon learned, would be wrong. Before I could understand what it was all about, I had to immerse myself in its history—with Bill Bonanno as my teacher.

From that point forward, Bill invited me to every party, baptism, wedding, funeral, or religious celebration the family held. Mickey would fly to Phoenix and together we would drive to Tucson. I noticed early on that nobody took pictures at most of these affairs—except for major events like Senior's ninety-fifth birthday party, a black-tie affair for which Bill hired a professional photographer.

Still, I wanted to capture my own memories of these events, and in the late 1990s—after I'd known Bill for about four years—I brought a camera to one of the parties. Leaving the camera in the car at first, I tracked Bill down and asked his permission before bringing it into the party. I was prepared for him to say no: After all, most public photographs of Joe Bonanno pictured him leaving a federal courthouse. Senior remained very secretive, cautious, and low-profile. Bill asked me to wait a minute. First he went over to speak with his number-two man, Anthony Tarantola; then he consulted Mickey Freiberg; and then he spoke with his father. He came back and granted me permission. From that point on, I became the unofficial photographer at these functions. Some of the photographs in this book are shots I took at these affairs.

With time, I became a kind of adviser to Bill; after we'd known each other awhile, he referred to me jokingly as "the Jewish *consigliere*." When he handed me a copy of *The Good Guys*, the book he'd written with former FBI special agent Joe Pistone, I opened it to find this inscription:

To Gary:

To the best Consigliere in the Business . . .
much better than Tom Hagen

> *Best Always,*
> *Bill*
> *2/07/05*

In 2000, Bill and I embarked on the adventure of writing a book of our own. I was intrigued with this place Bill referred to as "our world," and I thought there might be readers out there as eager as I was to learn what he knew: what really took place inside the meetings of the Family and the Commission, how the Families had functioned when *mafiosi* still practiced the old-world traditions. Over the next few years, we became best friends; we spoke by phone three times a week, and by the last two years of his life that increased to three to five times a day. He made the 120-mile drive to Phoenix at least three times a week, and seemed to think no more of driving back and forth in one day than he would of a trip to the market. Once, during one of those trips, he said, "Gary, if there is anything you ever need call me. I don't care what time it is. I'll drop what I'm doing and be there for you." He then asked, "Do you know why?" I let him answer the question himself. "Because I know you would do the same for me." That summed up the closeness of our relationship.

As we started work on the book, I suggested that we tape our conversations, and that we focus on the topics that always seemed to fascinate the American public, explaining them with the kinds of firsthand stories only he could share. After recording hours and hours of conversations, we wrote the three parts of this book: "The Birth of the Mafia," "The Commission," and "The Family." As we talked, I could tell that some of the subjects were very sensitive to Bill; when he became animated and his voice got louder, I could tell we were approaching sensitive ground. But he always answered my questions when he could, because he trusted our relationship. Only when we talked about someone being killed did he bite back. Once, when I asked, "Who did it?" he barked back, "It didn't matter who did it. We never talked about it. We just did it!" That was the end of that.

Now and then, I would ask him about apparent discrepancies between the account his father had given in his book *A Man of Honor* and Bill's own account. "My father had to be ambiguous in those days," he explained, "because people were still alive." More than once, he gave me a wise piece of advice: "Read between the lines!"

One day, he called from Tucson to tell me he'd agreed to appear on several TV shows to talk about his life in the Mafia, and before he did he wanted to drive to Phoenix and talk with me about something. We spent the afternoon discussing his concern about the questions he thought Oliver North or Gordon Liddy or some other interviewer might ask him. Finally, he revealed his biggest concern: "What if someone asks me if I ever killed anyone?"

That was the one question I had never asked him, and I specifically told him I never wanted to know the answer. This had nothing to do with my curiosity and everything to do with the knowledge that a capital offense had no statute of limitations. If the answer was yes, I didn't want the burden of that knowledge.

We came up with a solution. If he was asked the question, his response would be, "I have been asked that question many times, and I'm going to give you the answer . . . in my next book!" We figured that would close down any questioner—and it did!

This is that next book—and I can confirm that Bill always kept his promises. If you want to know the answer, I suggest you reread Book III, "The Family," and take the advice a very savvy man once gave me: "Read between the lines."

Acknowledgments

For twelve years, I heard many stories from Bill Bonanno about his life as a *mafioso*. Some stories were only revealed after the death of his father, Joseph Bonanno Sr., and after Bill was sure there were no contemporaries or relatives left who might be hurt by what was told. Bill was always concerned about possible reprisals; he wanted to protect his father, his family, and those people he referred to as being "in our world." Bill also wanted to tell the real account of how "this thing of ours" worked from a firsthand historical perspective—and the story of the Commission, which had never been discussed accurately by anyone in the know. I was not interested in aggrandizing the Bonanno Family, or offering any kind of rationalizion for why the Bonanno Family chose the life they led. Bill was fine with that.

It is only appropriate that my first acknowledgment goes to Bill, in gratitude for his honesty and willingness to tell us all about his world, and to set the record straight—at the risk of dispelling myths and revealing information that not so long ago could have incriminated him or even cost him his life. Bill's wish was to

The baptism of my grandson,
Grass Valley, California, 1996.

present a true historical record, to be used as a reference for historians interested in this world. Some critics may suggest that, in doing so, he violated *omertà*—but they should understand that the traditions and world he describes in this book no longer exist.

A great debt of gratitude also goes to Anthony Tarantola, Bill's second-in-command. In the 1980s, Anthony joined Bill in Tucson after the Bonannos moved there from New York. Anthony was schooled in the old tradition, first by his father and then through the years he spent learning directly from both Joe Bonanno Sr. and Bill. Anthony and Gary Cantalini, from the East Coast, spent five full days driving me around the boroughs of New York, showing me the settings of the events described in this book, from the 1920s through the 1960s. Their generosity, loyalty, and respect reflect the true conduct of a *mafioso* or, as we say in Yiddish, a real *mensch*.

Acknowledgments

To Catherine Bonanno Genovese, Bill's sister and the only living child of Joseph and Fay Bonanno, thank you for providing historical insight into the life of your father and your brother, and for spending so much time researching family pictures and sending them to me on a moment's notice anytime I made a request.

Thanks to Rosalie Bonanno, Bill's wife, for her generous support during the work on this book, when I kept Bill in Phoenix more than he was in Tucson in order to write and record his memories. Rosalie never hesitated to help in every way she could to complete this book.

There are many others who deserve thanks: Mickey Freiberg for being in my life, introducing me to Bill, and sharing good times together throughout this unexpected journey.

Frank Weimann, my agent at the Literary Group International, who was first contacted by Anthony, requested a copy of the initial draft of the manuscript, and insisted on sending it to Cal Morgan at HarperCollins.

Cal Morgan, my editor, deserves special recognition for his outstanding organizational skills, patience, diligence, and uncommon ability to explain and guide me through the process of publishing a book, from the first draft to the editing, copyediting, marketing, cover design, and so much more. His help in bringing the work together made it a book I know Bill would have been proud to call his own. I would also like to thank Carrie Kania, Brittany Hamblin, Dori Carlson, and Milan Bozic for their work in making this book happen.

Thanks go, of course, to my wife, Paula, for her enthusiasm while reading through draft after draft. And thanks also to my sister, Jeanne Milstein; my brother, Dr. Alan Abromovitz; and Dr. Maxine Turek for doing the same. Thanks to Mike Phillips, Herb Glickston, and Tom Ingram, who patiently listened to many of the stories during the writing of this book and for encouraging me to "make it happen," and to Bob Strander, who graciously provided his ranch and horses to Bill, Anthony, and me and joined us in out-of-the-way horseback rides in the pristine Arizona desert, where we could listen to Bill and Anthony recount the way things were in the old days in New York City. Also, to Hugh Milstein of Digital Fusion in Culver City, California, who artfully restored the rare photgraph of the Red Devil Italian Restaurant and donated his time and expertise attending and photographing many of the events in Tucson; David Lerner, for always being there for Bill and me when we needed to bounce ideas around and for providing copying equipment and technical support through United Imaging in Woodland Hills, California; and Steve Thoeny, my computer expert, who got me through all the times when technology changed during the last eight years when my computer needed urgent help and for his organizational skills.

A St. Joseph's Day Party in 1999. From left to right: attorney Jerry Cartin, Gary Abromovitz, Bill Bonanno, and Joe Bonanno (seated).

Acknowledgments

A special thanks to Jerry Cartin, one of my oldest and best friends, who traveled this journey with me and whom we all dearly miss.

A special thanks to my daughter, Jaime Abromovitz, whose proficiency in eight languages was critical in translating Joseph Bonanno Sr.'s notes from the original Sicilian, Italian, and French to English—and for acting as an interpreter in explaining the meaning of sayings and words that can only be understood by immersion in the culture of the people of Italy and Sicily.

I am forever grateful to my son, Mark, for his support and encouragement during the years I spent on this book, and for taking over and building *our* family business, which allowed me to concentrate on this book, and enjoy life even more.

Thank you to all those who overcame initial concerns of my involvement in a thirteen-year odyssey with these "men of honor"—which proved one of the most exciting times of my life.

Finally, thank you to Joseph Bonanno Sr. for the stories, discussions, dinners, parties, and fascinating times we spent together. I'm glad you were a friend—and not an enemy.

Glossary

Administration: The operating leadership of a Family, composed of *rappresentante* (the leader), *capodecini* (the group captains), and the *consigliere* (adviser to the *rappresentante*, and his liaison with other family members).

amazzalo: (*Sicilian slang*) "Kill him."

amici nostri: "Friends of ours."

ancora imparo: (*Italian*) "I am still learning."

banchistas: Bankers.

Beati Paoli: "The Blessed Pauls," a secret confraternity whose lair is hidden under the Piazza Beati Paoli, in the Capo district of Palermo, Sicily's capital city. Some consider this secret society the beginning of the modern Mafia.

Black Hand: A group originating in Spain made up of non-Sicilians using extortion tactics to prey on immigrant Italians. Also known as Mano Negro.

boss: One of several popular names for the head of a Family.

"boys of the first day": Maranzano's war cabinet at the start of the Castellammarese War, consisting of Joseph Bonanno, Gaspar DiGregorio, Joe Stabile, Buster Domingo, Vincent Danna, Martin Bruno, and Charlie DiBenedetto.

campieri: (*gabellotti*) Private armies hired by estate managers in western Sicily to protect large agricultural estates around the time of the unification of Italy in 1861; the first security patrols and protection rackets.

Camillo Benso di Cavour: Founder of the Italian newspaper *Il Risorgimento*, and one of the three principal leaders of the revolution for the unification of Italy.

Camorra: A group from southern Italy (non-Sicilian) that evolved into highwaymen and extortionists in the early 1900s; the group preyed on Italian immigrants.

capo: (pl. *capi,* but *capos* in American usage) A captain in a Family's organizational structure.

capodecina: (lit., "a leader of ten") The head of a crew that may vary in size from a few to more than twenty.

capo di tutti capi: A title meaning "boss of all bosses"—a position that no longer existed in our world after 1931.

carabiniere: Federal police.

Castellemmare del Golfo: A village and township in western Sicily, an area where peasants and their leaders emerged to establish *il sistema.*

Castellammarese: Sicilians from Castellammare del Golfo.

Castellammarese War: A war that took place from 1929 to 1931 between the Masseria group (primarily from Palermo and Naples) and the Maranzano group (from Castellammare del Golfo). During this conflict the Luciano/Lansky group, sometimes called "the Combine," originally sided with Masseria, but Luciano eventually had both his rivals, Masseria and Maranzano, killed.

chiazza: A dialect variant of *piazza,* a town square.

The Commission: An organization established by the leaders of the American Mafia Families in 1931, designed to mediate among the Families and thus allow them to coexist safely.

Committee of Peace: The Commission's original name.

compare: (*Italian*) A baptisimal godfather—considered closer than blood in the Sicilian culture.

confraternity: An association of men, established to provide religious education.

consigliere: A spokesman elected by members of a Family to represent their interests by interacting with the *rappresentante* on their behalf.

cosa nostra: (lit., "this thing of ours") A way of life, not an organization.

crew: A group of soldiers (*soldate*) of varying numbers, reporting to a Family's *capo*.

dispatched: Killed (or ordered to be killed).

Don: A term of respect for a person of a higher station, equivalent to "Sir"; used in conjunction with the person's first name (e.g., Don Vito, not Don Corleone). Lowercase when used as a noun: a Mafia don.

Family: The most accurate term for an organized group of Sicilian and Italian men in our world sharing an ideology. (Always with an upper-case *F*; "family" with a lower-case *f* always refers to the immediate family, not the men of our world.)

Fasci Siciliani: Short for Fasci Siciliani dei Lavoratori (Sicilian Workers Leagues), one of the first socialist movements of southern Italian rebels (1891–94), whose aim was the collective organization of farmers, workers, and miners.

forestieri: Foreigners.

gabelloto: (pl. *gaballoti*) The overseer(s) of the large Italian estates.

La Giovine Italia: (lit., "Young Italy") A secret organization determined to overthrow the Bourbon dynasty.

Giuseppe Garibaldi: A nineteenth-century military and nationalist leader; one of the three principal leaders of the unification of Italy.

Giuseppe Mazzini: A visionary nineteenth-century patriot; one of the three principal leaders of the unification of Italy.

Godfather: A name adopted by the U.S. government, the movies, the media, and the public to describe the leader of a Family;

popularized by the 1969 novel *The Godfather* by Mario Puzo and its 1972 film adaptation directed by Francis Ford Coppola.

group leader: The leader of a crew. (See also *capo* and *capo-decina*.)

inviolable: Too sacred to be violated, such as the oath taken by members of the early secret society called *La Mano Fraterna*, or the Brotherly Hand.

King Bomba: King Ferdinand II (1810–1859), the Bourbon king of the Two Sicilies, who received this nickname after ordering the bombing of Messina during the Sicilian Revolt of 1848.

made: American term for the selection of a new member of a Mafia Family (e.g., "to be made").

Mafia: A name used by government authorities for criminal organizations.

mafioso: (pl. *mafiosi*) A person practicing an ideology or state of mind based on the old Sicilian traditions; someone who acts in a manly way.

La Mano Fraterna: (lit., "the brotherly hand") A seventeenth-century secret society of *mafiosi*.

Mano Negro: See *Black Hand*.

mensch: (*Yiddish*) A person of integrity and honor.

Mezzogiorno: The area south of Rome. The word *mezzogiorno,* which literally means "midday," also refers to the modern Italian regions of Abruzzi, Campania, Molise, Puglia, Basilicata,

Calabria, and the islands of Sicily and Sardinia, named because of the intensity of the sun at midday. Italians often refer to southern Italy as *il meridione* ("the South").

Mustache Pete: An American pejorative term for Sicilian immigrants who followed the traditions and ways of the old country.

notary: In Italy, a position of respect, achieved after lengthy training in aspects of business; in America, this position was exploited by immigrant opportunists to prey on other Italian immigrants.

novitiate: A period of instruction used by the secret society *La Mano Fraterna*, or the Brotherly Hand, required for any new member.

omertà: A policy of loyalty and complete openness and honesty in dealing with people in our world, but not with people in the outside world. Commonly misunderstood as merely a "code of silence."

our world: The *mafiosi* way of life, based on the ideology of *il sistema* or *Cosa Nostra*.

padre di famiglia: (or simply *padre*) Father of the Family.

paesano: (pl. *paesani*) Countryman (-men); sometimes spelled *paisano* (in southern Italian dialect).

la parentesi fascista: The oppressive Fascist regime of Benito Mussolini (1922–45).

persona d'onore: A person of honor.

picciotti: (lit., "the young ones") Originally, insurgent groups of peasant boys, field workers who retreated to the hills in the region outside Palermo.

prominenti: Distinguished Italians who helped immigrants in America to better themselves.

rappresentante: (pl. *rappresentanti*) Leader of a Family; the actual term used for what popular culture considers a "Godfather."

Risorgimento: A series of nineteenth-century revolutionary insurrections designed to bring about the unification of Italy. Led by Giuseppe Mazzini, a dedicated visionary for revolution; Giuseppe Garibaldi, a military leader and man of action; and Camillo Benso Cavour, founder of *Il Risorgimento*, a newspaper that became the official voice for the Italian national movement.

savva brucharno la carne: (lit., "The meat must burn") A warning to shoot close enough to burn the skin in order to ensure a kill.

Sicilian Vespers (*Vespri Siciliani*): A thirteenth-century Italian secret society; also, an uprising in 1282 by the people of Palermo against the French in reaction to the attack and rape of a young Sicilian girl.

il sistema: (lit., "the system of life") Sicilian term for the *mafiosi* way of life (interchangeable with *cosa nostra*); also called *il sistema del potere* ("the system of power").

soldato: (pl. *soldati*) Soldier, the lowest rank of made men. (See *made.*)

sotto capo: The "underboss," he acts as the "alter ego" of the godfather under certain circumstances. In some Families, he may be considered the second in command.

Stoppaglier: The group that established *il sistema* in Sicily. In the vocabulary of the *picciotti*, the word referred to saboteurs.

strega: (*old Italian*) A female witch.

stregheria: (*old Italian*) Witchcraft.

stregone: (*old Italian*) A male witch.

tagliare carne e osso: (lit., "cutting through the meat and bone") Getting to the heart of the matter.

Tammany Hall: The political machine that controlled the Democratic Party in New York through much of the nineteenth and early twentieth centuries. Tammany expanded its political constituency by enlisting the immigrant community, extending them help in finding work and gaining citizenship in exchange for loyalty toward Tammany candidates in city and state elections.

tradition: A shared understanding of honor, principles, and way of life, based on centuries of teachings passed down by our ancestors.

"tying the circle": A ritual, conducted at the start of each Family meeting, in which members clasp hands with one another, forming a symbolic bond.

veddani: The plural of *viddanu*, a dialect slang term for *contadinu*; literally, a person who owns a small piece of land and perhaps a house and a mule; in common use, a person of low social status.

Vendicatori: Probably the first secret society adhering to a *mafiosi* philosophy; formed in the twelfth century to avenge popular wrongs and abuses of power in Sicily.

Index

Index

Index